Ethel
Osterhird
1989

SIMON AND SCHUSTER'S

Guide to

BIRDS OF THE WORLD

by Gianfranco Bologna

Edited by

JOHN BULL

Simon and Schuster

New York

Originally published in Italy under the title *Uccelli* in 1978 by Arnoldo
Mondadori Editore S.p.A., Milano

SIMON AND SCHUSTER and colophon are registered trademarks of
Simon & Schuster, Inc.

Manufactured by Officine Grafiche di Arnoldo Mondadori Editore, Verona
Printed in Italy

10   9   8   7   6   5   4   3   2   Pbk.

Library of Congress Cataloging in Publication Data

Bologna, Gianfranco.
    Simon and Schuster's guide to birds of the world.

    Translation of Uccelli.
    Bibliography: p.
    Includes index.
    1. Birds.   2. Birds—Identification.   I. Bull,
John L.   II. Title.   III. Title: Guide to birds of
the world.
QL673.B6213   598   80-39507

ISBN 0-671-42235-9

CONTENTS

EXPLANATION OF SYMBOLS

HABITATS FREQUENTED

 tropical forest

 maquis (scrub), woodland, temperate forest

 desert, arid regions

 rocky regions, ruins, mountains

 marsh, sandy coasts, lagoons, coastal waters

 sea

 lakes, inland waters

 cliffs, sea coasts

 grasslands, countryside, savanna, undergrowth, steppe, tundra

 coniferous forest, deciduous forest

MIGRATORY HABITS

 migratory

HABITS

 daytime

 partly migratory

nocturnal

nonmigratory

crepuscular

Right: Mourning Doves (*Zenaida macroura*), drawing by John James Audubon (1785–1851) from his work *Birds of America*, first published between 1827 and 1838.

The Wonder of Flight

There is no doubt that more books have been written about birds than about any other class of animal. It is their ability to fly that has intrigued man most of all. If we are to choose just a few examples of the importance that birds have had in popular folklore, literature and the arts, we have only to think of the Egyptian paintings, ceramics and reliefs representing Horus, the falcon-god, or Nekhebet, the vulture-goddess, who supervised births in Egyptian religions; the Greek myths of Prometheus and Tityos, who were torn to pieces by eagles and vultures for having offended the gods; the Etruscan "augurs" who predicted the future by interpreting the flight of birds; the famous geese of the Capitol, which saved Rome during the Gallic raids; of eagles, the symbol of Rome and its power, fluttering on the standards of those invincible legions, and the symbol of the Austro-Hungarian empire; of the Thunderbird, or Voc bird, in the pre-Columbian mythology of Central America and the Caribbean; of the owl, symbol of Athens and sacred to the goddess Minerva; of the dove, symbol of peace in Christendom; of Garuda, the favorite bird of Vishnu; down to the marvelous paintings by ornithologists John Gould and John James Audubon in the nineteenth century (the four hundred beautiful illustrations in Audubon's work *Birds of America* were called by Cuvier "the most splendid monument ever erected by man to nature") and, to mention just two names, the paintings and drawings of Chagall and Braque in the twentieth century. But this is just a handful of examples, chosen somewhat at random, to show something of the wide interest aroused in man by the fascinating world of birds.

We shall now briefly describe the main features of birds. In the context of the scientific classification of the animal kingdom, they form a class in the phylum Chordata. They are vertebrates (animals with vertebrae) and Amniota (i.e., vertebrates with an amnion, which is an embryonic membrane forming a cavity filled with a fluid that envelops the embryo). They can fly (although some species are flightless, despite the fact that all birds are descended from flying forms), since their front limbs have been transformed into wings, and only their hind legs are used for walking or running on the ground. They are homoiothermic, or warm-blooded (i.e., they have a constant body temperature), although some species have revealed cases of marked temperature drop and even a sort of winter lethargy or hibernation. A bird's heart is divided into two parts, each consisting of two cavities, and there is total separation of arterial blood and venous blood. Birds have a beak, or bill, consisting of modified jawbones and sheathed with a horny covering called the rhamphotheca. Finally, birds lay eggs, which are hatched.

During the last century, the evolutionist Thomas Huxley defined birds as "glorified reptiles" because, in the slow evolutionary process that has led from a world showing the first

Imprint of the skeleton of *Archaeopteryx lithographica*, the oldest known bird, found in the Jurassic stratum in Solnhofen (Bavaria). This specimen is in the British Museum, London.

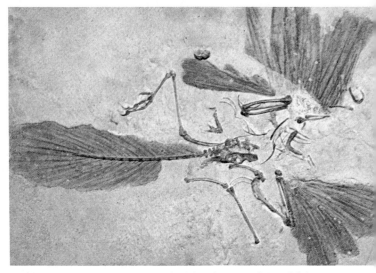

signs of life to a planet peopled with a huge variety of living things, birds probably did originate from reptiles. Far back in time there were flying reptiles (the famous pterodactyls), and the two classes of animals have many features in common. Palaeontological documentation about the transition from reptile to bird is thin, but we have been lucky enough to find fossil remains that, in all probability, show us the missing link in the evolutionary chain that connects these two forms: these remains are of the famous *Archaeopteryx lithographica*.

The ornithologist Colin Harrison, an expert in the palaeontology of birds, dates the start of the gradual evolutionary process that created birds from reptiles between about 225 and 180 million years ago, in the period that geologists call the Triassic. As we have already said, this derivation can still be detected today from certain reptilian-type features shown by birds. We need merely mention the legs and toes, which are covered with horny scales like those of reptiles; the very similar nails; the articulation of the cranium with the backbone by means of a single occipital condyle (in mammals there are two condyles, which restrict the head movements); the air sacs that form an extension of the lungs and are present in certain reptiles such as the Chelonia and Chamaeleontidae; the laying of eggs, which is common in many reptiles; in the newborn young, the small "tooth" at the tip of the mouth or beak, used to break out of the egg; the structure of the so-called pecten, or comb, present in the anatomy of the eye in both classes; and the similarities existing between the red corpuscles and the hemoglobin in the blood.

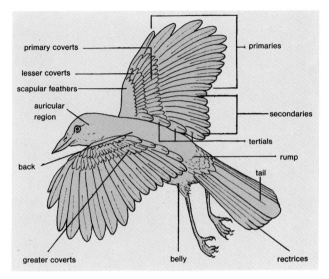

primary coverts — primaries

lesser coverts —

scapular feathers—

auricular region

secondaries

tertials

rump

back

tail

greater coverts

belly

rectrices

The Plumage

One of the most remarkable features of the class of birds is their plumage, which, among other things, is vital for flying. Birds' ability to fly results from various factors having to do with economy of weight, strength and endurance, and the lightness of the various structures. The cutaneous apparatus in vertebrate groups consists of the skin, or cutis, which covers the entire surface of the body and is made up of two quite different layers: the uppermost epidermis and the lower dermis. The skin gives rise to the glands, scales, squamae, nails, horns and feathers—in fact, all those structures that are present in vertebrates. The skin of birds is very thin and has no glands; the only exception is the uropygial, or preen, gland, which is situated near the tail and secretes an oily substance used by the bird to smear over its feathers with its beak, thus making them waterproof. This gland is particularly developed in waterfowl, but does not exist at all in ostriches, cassowaries, bustards, various Columbiformes (pigeons and doves) and parrots.

In the case of birds the skin structures are, therefore, the feathers, which form the plumage, and weigh on average about 6 percent of the total weight (3 or 4 percent in penguins and about 12 percent in tits). The plumage is extremely important because (1) the feathers can trap a considerable quantity of air, thus protecting the bird from heat dispersion and keeping the body temperature high; (2) it is often brightly colored, thus meeting the needs of these animals' social life; (3) as already mentioned, it forms a vital surface that guarantees flight, and it

13

In birds the feathers occur only in certain parts of the skin, called *pterylae*. The featherless areas are called *apteria* and are protected by the feathers in adjacent areas. Left: the pterylae and apteria on the back (left) and (right) of a bird. On the right, a typical feather and detail of the rachis with the parallel series of barbs and barbules.

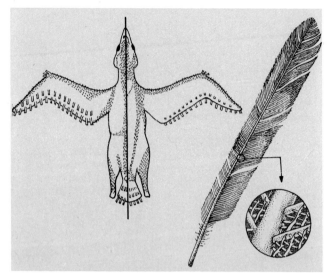

is designed to meet the requirements of lightness, softness and endurance; (4) although it derives from the papillae of the dermis, the plumage is a biologically dead structure that does not need vascularization.

In the plumage of a bird we can usually distinguish different types of feathers: contour feathers, or plumes; down feathers; semiplumes; and filoplumes. The contour feathers form the bulk of the external structure of the bird, giving it its shape and coloring, and in effect its contour (in addition, the feathers which are mainly used for flying, the remiges——wing quills—— and rectrices, are also contour feathers). The down feathers are situated beneath the contour feathers. The semiplumes are in effect halfway between the contour feathers and the down feathers. The filoplumes can in some cases be bristly and like hairs.

The feathers originate as horny formations from a thickening of the dermis, connected and nourished by a dermic papilla which gradually lengthens and slopes rearward. When the feather has grown its various parts, the dermic papilla retracts, leaving it empty and devitalized.

Birds lose their feathers for natural reasons (annual molting phenomenon) or because of accidents; in both cases the cells forming the dermic papilla are stimulated to reproduce a new feather. The feather has two distinct parts: the first, called the calamus, extends from the point of attachment to the skin (where there is a hole called the inferior umbilicus) to an upper hole (called the superior umbilicus); the second, called the rachis, extends from the superior umbilicus to the tip of the feather. The rachis has two lateral series of barbs, each of which is in turn equipped with two series of barbules, one turned toward the tip of the feather and the other turned sideways. The texture of the feather, called the vexillum, or vane, is always perfect, because of the large number of hamuli, or hooks, which hold the series of barbules together. At the level of the superior umbilicus there is a tuft of barbs and in some species (birds of prey, some Passeriformes, Anatidae, Ardeidae, cassowaries and emus) there may also be a smaller structure that has a miniature rachis, with miniature barbs and barbules, called the hyporachis, or aftershaft.

The beak gently sorts out any damage that a branch or any other solid object might cause to a feather. The plumage does not grow over all the skin of a bird (except for penguins and ratites, where it is uniform) but only in certain areas called pterylae, where the feathers are evenly distributed; the featherless areas are called apteria. Special plumage structures include the vibrissae, which are hairlike and are often present at the base of the beak in certain species of birds of prey, and the so-called pulverulent down in the Ardeidae (herons, bitterns, etc.), which is continually breaking up and forming a sort of fatty powder used to clean and preen the plumage. Birds pay a great deal of attention to their plumage; it is preened with the beak or scratched with a foot, which, depending on the species, is raised either above or below the wing to reach the head. In herons the foot has a special combed nail. In addition, birds wash regularly; some species actually "sunbathe" or take "sand baths"; others catch ants with their beak, or let ants run through their plumage, thus using the formic acid with its insecticidal action.

The most important feathers for flying are those that grow from the front limbs: (1) three or four pollical remiges that are attached to the pollex and form the so-called alula, an important flight structure because it moderates vortices and helps to channel small air currents, thus increasing, with the tail open, the breaking surface for landing; (2) the primary remiges, nine to twelve in number, growing from the bones of the manus and the middle digit; (3) the secondary remiges, ranging in number from nine (in small Passeriformes) to forty (in albatrosses); (4) the tertiary remiges, growing from the humerus. Other feathers include the coverts, which protect the regimes both above and below.

In cross section, a bird's wing has a convex upper surface and a concave lower surface. In the words of the ornithologist Wesley Lanyon (1973), "A bird's wing has two functions: it works like an airplane's wing, and like a propeller. The airplane and the bird use the same physical laws. Air moves more quickly over the large curve of the upper surface of the wing, causing a greater pressure below the wing and the necessary lift to remain airborne."

There are various types of flight: flapping flight, dynamic gliding, and soaring. In flapping flight the wing is moved downward and then raised. This movement, which is obviously repeated fairly rapidly, enables the bird to remain airborne and move forward in the air. There is a flight posture in which certain species, and not necessarily only large ones, remain static in the air, beating their wings at great speed; in this way they pro-

Top: An example of flapping flight in the European Robin (*Erithacus rubecula*).
Bottom: An example of gliding in a Black-browed Albatross (*Diomedea melan-ophrys*).

Top: An example of soaring in a Griffon Vulture (*Gyps fulvus*). Bottom: an example of hovering flight in a nectar-feeding bird.

duce not a forward thrust but merely a thrust working against the force of gravity. This is known as the "Holy Ghost" posture and is used by many birds of prey, shrikes, terns, kingfishers, and so on.

Dynamic gliding is used in particular by large sea birds that have long slender wings, such as the Procellariformes (petrels and albatrosses) and some gulls. During this type of flight the bird makes long gliding flights with the wind or diagonally to it, losing height. Over water the lower air layers are slower-moving than the upper levels, because they are affected by friction with the water mass; when a bird stops its gliding flight, by changing direction and heading into the wind, it gains height by using the force of inertia and the increasing strength of the wind in the upper air layers. Soaring is used by various birds, particularly the large species with long, broad wings (such as vultures, eagles, storks, pelicans, and so on); in order to gain height, these species use rising hot-air currents, which form mainly in open regions where the sun makes them rise by increasing the temperature of the air above them, as a result of a reduction in the density. Soaring birds use hot-air currents to fly upward to a certain height, and then they glide or soar to reach a different height.

A specific type of flight is the vibration, or hovering, flight used by hummingbirds, which can remain in the air in the same spot and even fly backward. They can do this because of the special shape of the skeleton of their front limbs.

Plumage Coloring

The coloring of the feathers can be the product of various factors. The presence of pigments, such as melanin and carotin, is due to assimilation via food and causes the red, yellow and orange coloring of birds and the intermediate shades down to dark-brown and black. The particular structure of the barbs, combined with a pigment that absorbs rays with a longer wavelength, determines blues and white (but not the white of albino birds). Chromatic aberrations include (1) *albinism,* due to an inability to synthesize pigments; this can be total in cases where the bird is completely white with a red iris, or partial, which is more common; (2) *isabellism,* with pale colorations tending to isabella-reddish or *café-au-lait;* (3) *acyanism,* or *flavism,* with yellowish colorations, sometimes accompanied by albinism. An interesting pigment is the one called *turacin,* which can fade or turn pale directly on a living bird without damaging the plumage. Turacin is present in the dark-red marking on the wings of a group of birds found in tropical Africa; these are members of the touraco family belonging to the order Cuculiformes, family Musophagidae. If you were to hold a touraco in your hand, your skin would be tinged with red, but this would not affect the bird. The remainder of the green colorings of touracos is due to another pigment called turacoverdin. Birds on the whole can also have additional colorings or modifications to the plumage caused by the plumage itself becoming worn, by dirt, by pollution, and by the use of the uropygial gland, the secretion from which, in some species, is colored with iron oxide, which darkens the plumage (this is the case with the rust-colored belly of the Bearded Vulture).

Rock Ptarmigan (*Lagopus mutus*) in its summer (top) and winter (bottom) plumage.

Molting

At birth the various species of birds can be divided into two broad categories, Nidifugae and Nidicolae (further and more precise distinctions will be analyzed under the heading "Reproduction"), depending on whether they can move away from the nest or have to stay in the nest for a certain time before becoming independent. Nidifugous birds are born with their down feathers, whereas nidicolous birds or born virtually naked and only start to develop feathers while spending the postnatal period in the nest. Birds are then liable to periodic molting of the plumage, during which the feathers drop out and are gradually replaced. On the whole, in most species, birds molt twice a year, once before and once after reproduction. The prenuptial, or winter, molting is not a complete one and does not affect the wing and tail quills, which are vital for flying. In some species the postnuptial, or autumnal, molt may be total and almost simultaneous, as in the case of ducks for example, leaving them unable to fly for the duration.

The molting period varies from species to species. In the case of albatrosses, pelicans, gannets and birds of prey it is usually fairly long. Because of the molting phenomenon, many species present different-colored plumages in the spring-summer phase and the autumn-winter phase; what is more, for identification in the field, ornithologists have to bear in mind the different coloring in immature, young and adult individuals, and in many species these are very conspicuous. The adult coloring of the plumage may not be assumed for several years (as in the case of certain large gulls, gannets, birds of prey, and so on),

Skeleton of a bird.

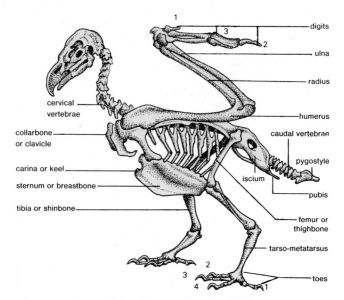

cervical vertebrae

collarbone or clavicle

carina or keel

sternum or breastbone

tibia or shinbone

digits

ulna

radius

humerus

caudal vertebrae

pygostyle

iscium

pubis

femur or thighbone

tarso-metatarsus

toes

or it may appear within a few months after birth.

Molting occurs in birds for a variety of reasons having to do mainly with the endocrine system (an important function in the occurrence of molting is that of the thyroid gland and the front part of the hypophysis) and, obviously, the environmental situation, such as more daylight. Today close studies are being made of the patterns of molting, a task made easier by the careful analysis of birds caught for ringing.

The Skeleton and Muscles

The skeleton of a bird can be described broadly as follows: (1) the cranium, with an appendage formed from the cutaneous apparatus, the beak, or rhamphotheca (the horny sheath covering the jaw arches); (2) the vertebrae, which vary in number from thirty-nine (in certain Passeriformes) to sixty-three (in swans), the neck vertebrae, contrary to the case of mammals where there are always seven, vary in number from eleven (in certain parrots) to twenty-five (in swans); (3) the front limbs which have been transformed into wings and consist of the humerus, the radius, the ulna and a series of mainly merged bones that form the equivalent of the mammal's manus or forefoot, the "fingers" present in birds are the index and, in more rudimentary form, the thumb and middle finger, the others being missing; (4) the rib cage, with the number of ribs varying from three to nine and with a sternum, or breastbone, that, in the flying species, has a wide carina, to which the pectoral muscles are attached; (5) the pelvic girdle, which develops from the synsacrum (where the lumbar and caudal vertebrae are usually completely fused) and consists of three interlocking bones—ilium, ischium and pubes; (6) the lower limbs, consisting of a femur, a tibia with a small fibula, the tarsal-metatarsal bones (the bony segment that, in the case of birds, is usually called the ''leg'') and the digits (not more than four in number). In a bird's bone the medulla, or marrow, is either slight or absent. The air sacs, which are linked to the bronchial tubes, penetrate the hollow bones.

The muscular apparatus is strong: it envelops the skeleton, making the silhouette of the bird's body nimble and streamlined. In the wing, some muscles enable the bird to lower the limb (such as the pectoralis major muscle), while others enable it to raise it (such as the supracoracoid muscle). In the feet there are powerful flexor muscles which close the digits and extend the limb. They also help the bird to perch on a branch or other support: in this way the bird can even go to sleep without falling off because the digits take a tight hold of the branch, thanks to the remarkable strength of the flexor muscles.

The Senses

The nervous system consists of: (1) a central nervous system made up of the encephalon (inside the cranium) and the spinal cord (contained in the vertebral canal), which is protected by the three membranes called meninges, known as the *pia mater,* the arachnoid membrane and the *dura mater;* (2) a peripheral nervous system consisting of nerves and ganglions; (3) an autonomous nervous system consisting of the so-called sympathetic and parasympathetic systems, with nerves and ganglions that govern the bird's vegetative life and fan out in the glands, intestines, blood vessels, et cetera; (4) the sensory organs.

The encephalon consists of the forebrain (known as the *prosencephalon,* which is divided into two hemispheres made up of an outer layer of gray matter and an inner layer of white matter); the midbrain (*mesencephalon*); and the hindbrain (*rhombencephalon,* which contains the coordination center of the bird's movements and muscular contractions—that is, the cerebellum).

Sight

Most birds have their eyes in a lateral position, with an angle formed by the optic axes which may be as great as 120 degrees in some Passeriformes and 145 degrees in pigeons. Bird of prey—the nocturnal species in particular—have their eyes in a frontal position, with an angle of up to 90 degrees. This is also because, for predators, binocular vision is preferable. The birds with the most restricted binocular vision—between 6 degrees and 10 degrees—are parrots, whereas penguins have monocular vision, with each eye virtually independent. The remarkable mobility of the neck makes up for the virtual immobility of their eyes in their sockets (except for certain cases wherein the eyes are mobile in their sockets).

The anatomical structure of birds' eyes is like that of other vertebrates, with the sclera, cornea, iris, retina and crystalline lens. In addition, the bird's eye has a structure known as the pecten, which is found also in reptiles, but not in mammals. The retina, however, has a larger number of cones (the cells which make it possible to see colors) and, in the case of birds with twilight or nocturnal habits, rods (cells which are sensitive to minimal amounts of light). In birds there are two areas of maximum visual acuteness, the so-called *foveae;* man has just one. Three membranes provide external protection for the eye—an upper membrane, a lower membrane and an intermediate membrane called the nictitating membrane, which, in waterfowl, protects the eyes under water.

The Other Senses

After sight, hearing is the most developed sense in birds, and it is linked structurally to their sense of equilibrium. The ear has no external structures. Internally, after the tract that leads from the outer aperture to the tympanum, or middle ear, it consists of a middle ear that leads from the tympanum to the outer bony wall of the inner ear, or labyrinth. This latter in turn consists of the cochlea (that is, the organ of hearing) and three semicircular canals, attached to the organ of balance. Nocturnal birds of prey have an asymmetrical arrangement in their ears. Close studies of barn owls have shown that, even when there is no light, their hearing can accurately detect the prey, because the prey produces slight noises as it moves. Some species of birds—such as the Oilbird (*Steatornis caripensis*), a caprimulgiform (nightjar, or goatsucker) found in caves in South America; and salanganes (*Collocalia esculenta*), which are Old World swifts—use a sort of "sonar" device to move in the dark (this device enables them to detect obstacles with their sense of hearing).

The sense of smell in birds does not appear to be very highly developed, even though recent studies have shown that certain American vultures detect carcasses with their sense of smell (especially carcasses in wooded areas, where the rich vegetation makes it hard to see things). The team working with ethologist Floriano Papi has also shown that the sense of smell might be important for homing pigeons—in fact, it would appear to help them find their way back to the pigeon loft.

Taste does not appear to be a very highly developed sense either.

As for the sense of touch, it should be mentioned that various species of birds have certain types of tactile receptors (the beaks of certain waterfowl have a large number of tactile corpuscles).

Temperature and Thermoregulation

Birds have a circulatory system with dual circulation (venous and arterial) like mammals; and the heart is divided into four cavities (two auricles and two ventricles). Like mammals, birds are homoiothermic (warm-blooded) creatures—that is, they have an internal temperature that does not change with variations in the outside temperature. This is the converse of poikilothermic (cold-blooded) animals, whose internal temperature varies according to the temperature outside.

The energetic equilibrium in every living thing is maintained by the production of energy (which may be produced, for exam-

Detail of the eye of an Oilbird, or Guacharo (*Steatornis caripensis*).

ple, by the assimilation of food) and the dispersion and loss of energy. In birds, this assimilation is used to maintain the homoiothermic level, and thus the animals' equilibrium by thermolysis (loss of heat) and thermogenesis (production of heat). The body temperature in birds varies from 39 degrees C (102° F) to 42 degrees C (107.6° F), and even reaches 44 degrees C (111° F) in some Passeriformes.

Some species of birds can withstand a temporary drop of their internal temperature (temporary hyothermia). This happens, for example, in certain hummingbirds (*Calypte annae, Selasphorus sasin, Oreotrochilus estella*) during cold desert nights, in certain goatsuckers (*Caprimulgus europaeus, Phalaenoptilus nuttalii*) and in the swift (*Apus apus*). The ability to regulate the body temperature is not acquired immediately at birth, but after a certain period of time; because of this, the parents often cover their young with their bodies to protect them from cold or intense heat.

The respiratory apparatus consists principally of the lungs and air sacs, which have various ramifications in much of the body. As a rule there are nine of these sacs: two cervical sacs situated in the neck beside the backbone, an interclavicular sac in front of the trachea (windpipe), two front and two rear thoracic sacs, and two abdominal sacs, which are the most developed of all.

The Vocal Organ and Acoustic Displays

In vertebrates sounds are produced by the larynx. But in birds the organ of phonation is the *syrinx*, which is situated at the

Structure of the vocal apparatus of a songbird, showing the syrinx.

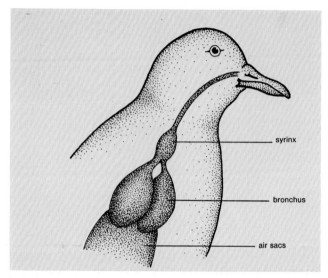

fork that leads from the trachea to the two bronchial tubes; its structure varies from species to species. Not all species of birds have the same sound-producing abilities: various species of waterfowl and seabirds have very rudimentary vocal expressions. On the contrary, there are very elaborate and diversified vocal expressions in certain Passeriformes——for example, in the species belonging to the *Oscines* (Passeres) or Acromiodae, where the syrinx is equipped with five to nine pairs of muscles attached exclusively to the bronchial rings. (These muscles regulate and control the vocal sounds made by the birds in question.) In addition there are three membranes that form the vibratory organ, while the trachea, interclavicular air sac and the mouth act as sound modifiers. The power of the sound produced by some species such as the Common, or Gray, Crane (*Grus grus*), whose cry can carry for a mile and a quarter (2 km.), is caused by the numerous circumvolutions of the trachea, which in this species may be up to 5 feet (1.5 m.) long.

The study of bird song is an important field of ornithology. Nowadays ornithologists have access to acoustical equipment and tape recordings that can accurately analyze the frequencies, intensity, volume and pitch of vocal sounds. The song of a bird is analyzed graphically on sonograms, where the line of the abscissae marks the times and the line of the ordinates marks the frequencies. Birds produce sounds with higher frequencies than those produced by the human voice. The vocal sounds produced by birds can be divided into (1) attractive cries and calls, which can have different meanings (sexual if

Top to bottom: Sonograms of a Cardinal (*Cardinalis cardinalis*), Robin (*Erithacus rubecula*), Mockingbird (*Mimus polyglottos*) and Screech Owl (*Otus asio*).

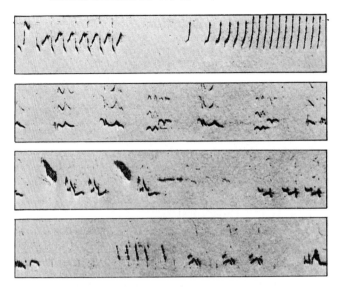

they occur during nuptial displays; contactual if they indicate the location of the bird making the call, or enable pairs, groups or colonies to remain in touch with one another, or serve as alarm signals; and so on); (2) actual bird song, which is characterized by the duration of the song and by the wealth and variety of the notes used, which, in turn, relates specifically to relations beteen the two sexes and to territorial behavior; (3) juvenile or subsong, which is an elementary form that needs polishing.

As various studies have shown, the ability of young birds to learn songs varies from species to species. In some we find a remarkable imitative ability——for example, the Mockingbird (*Mimus polyglottos*)——which extends to copying the human voice (as in various species of parrots, and in the mynas).

Bird song has fairly accentuated variability, even in different populations of the same species, to the extent that we can talk in terms of bird "dialects."

The acoustic displays of birds depend on various internal and external factors that influence the period, duration, and start of the song, et cetera. External factors include environmental conditions, such as light and temperature; internally, bird song is governed by the sex hormones.

After the study published in 1920 by H. E. Howard about the territoriality of birds, the full song of the Passeriformes came to be considered as an expression of territorial ownership. Further research, including the work done by R. A. Minde, F. S. Tompa and N. Tinbergen, has shown that in some cases, this

Structure of a bird's digestive apparatus.

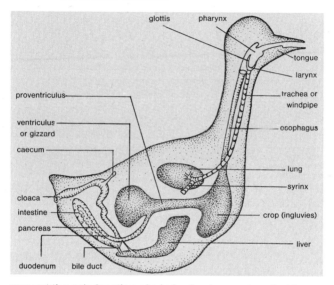

was not the only function of a behavioral procedure that is very complex and uses a great deal of energy.

The ornithologist C. K. Catchepole has shown, for example, that the song of certain marsh warblers—the Reed Warbler (*Acrocephalus scirpaceus*) and the Sedge Warbler (*A. schoenobaenus*)—which ceases almost completely after the formation of pairs, must have a function that is more sexual than territorial.

In the case of another marsh warbler, the Great Reed Warbler (*A. arundinaceus*), singing continues during migration and in winter. This has been confirmed by various ornithologists. The song, therefore, cannot have just a sexual and territorial significance. In this respect the ornithologists I. C. T. Nisbet and L. Medway have suggested a correlation between the emission of the song and competition for the most favorable sites in the wintering area, especially in relation to younger birds; as a result, this procedure builds up relations of dominance and subordination.

WHERE AND WHAT BIRDS EAT
The Digestive System

In the digestive system of birds we find (1) the beak, or bill, and the mouth, in which there is no mastication and food is swallowed whole; (2) the esophagus, through which the food passes after swallowing and in various species has an extension that temporarily stores food (in certain species this extended section takes on the form of a large pouch, the *crop*; this occurs in pigeons, parrots and gamebirds); (3) the stom-

ach, which consists of a glandular stomach, also called the proventriculus, and controls the chemical action produced by the gastric or peptic juices needed to attack the alimentary proteins; and a muscular stomach—the ventriculus, or gizzard—which performs the mechanical action of grinding up the food; (4) the intestine, which does not have the clearly distinctive features that it does in mammals—although we find a middle intestine that, in the initial section, contains the duodenal loop to which the pancreatic and liver ducts are connected; a small intestine, where the process of assimilating substances useful to the organism is most conspicuous; and a terminal intestine that, in some species (especially those with a vegetarian diet) branches off from two caeca and terminates at the rectum. The rectum opens into the cloaca, which is where the renal excretory ducts and the ducts of the sex organs also open.

Features of Alimentary Adaptation
The constant use of the beak inevitably causes wear and tear, but this is made up for by its continual growth process. The salivary glands are very developed, particularly in woodpeckers, where they make the long, extendable tongue especially sticky, and in jays, swallows and swifts. In swifts, during the breeding season, they increase in size, because saliva is used as mortar in building their nests made of mud and pieces of vegetable matter. (In swifts belonging to the genus *Collocalia,* one finds nests built entirely of hardened saliva—these are the famous "bird's nest" dishes in Chinese cuisine.)

27

Carmine Bee-eaters (*Merops nubicus*) feeding in a group.

Among birds there is a great variety of alimentary adaptation. It is most evident in the form of the beak and feet and legs: we find strong, hooked beaks in birds of prey; long, pointed beaks in herons; short, tough, conical beaks in granivorous species, more slender beaks in insectivorous birds, and so on. Specific beak shapes indicate more specialized eating habits, as in the Shoebill (*Balaeniceps rex*) or Boat-billed Heron (*Cochlearius cochlearius*). We also find even more curious cases, such as that of *Anarhynchus frontalis*, the Wrybill, a New Zealand shorebird whose beak is angled to the right, or that of the Scissorbill or Skimmer, whose upper mandible is shorter than the lower.

The diversity of alimentary adaptations offers an assorted sampling in the world of birds. Let us take a look at just a few examples——shrikes belonging to the order Passeriformes make food stores by impaling their prey (usually large insects and lizards, but also small rodents) on thorns, spines and the tips of branches; other Passeriformes, the nutcrackers, which are "good-natured" Corvidae, hide nuts and the seeds of conifers for the winter under the ground wrapped in mosses and lichens: they manage to relocate nearly all their "larders" with amazing ease in the first days of spring, when the ground is still snow-covered, and use them to feed their nestlings. In the case of the Bearded Reedling (*Panurus biarmicus*), the diet is insectivorous, but becomes granivorous in winter; the ornithologist G. Spitzer has studied how this is possible: the bird effects a strengthening of the musculature and horny plates of the stomach and takes in numerous small stones.

The granivorous diet is eased by the presence of a very strong beak, palate and cranium; these features enable the bird to crack open grains and seeds; alternatively, with a combined movement of the jaw and mandible, or by pressing the seed against the palate (which has special ridges), the same end is achieved. Birds with a vegetarian diet (granivorous, frugivorous, etc.) have an important role as seed scatterers; when expelled with the bird's excrement, the seeds retain their germinative power.

Apart from granivorous and frugivorous species of vegetarian birds, we should also mention the nectar-eating species. These include the species belonging to the family Trochilidae (i.e., the hummingbirds), the Coerebidae (honeycreepers), the Meliphagidae (honeyeaters), the Nectariniidae (sunbirds), the Drepanididae (Hawaiian honeycreepers) and some species of Old World parrots (the lorikeets); as well as feeding on nectar, all these species also eat insects that they come upon in flowers.

As for the carnivorous diet, food includes mammals, birds, reptiles, amphibians, fishes and carcasses, as well as spiders, worms, insects, mollusks, et cetera. In many species, especially among the Passeriformes, a granivorous diet is adopted in autumn and winter; this is complemented and often replaced by an insectivorous diet in spring and summer, when the young are reared.

The high metabolism of many species necessitates a fairly constant eating process. For this reason various insectivorous species contribute considerably to containing the populations of various species of insects.

Birds may feed either on their own or in groups, depending on the species.

As regards the species that feed in flocks, some ornithologists, such as R. K. Murton, A. J. Isaacson and N. J. Westwood for the Wood Pigeon (*Columba palumbus*), J. R. Krebs for the Great Blue Heron (*Ardea herodias*), and C. J. Feare, G. Dunnet and J. I. Patterson for the Rook (*Corvus frugilegus*), have shown that members of large flocks feed better and more plentifully than isolated individuals of the same species. This happens both because the search for food by the members of a group is a constant process—since it is unlikely, given the number of birds, that they will be taken by surprise by a predator, whereas the isolated feeder has to be constantly on the watch for the arrival of a predator—and because a flock feeding will flush out a larger number of potential prey than will an isolated individual. Ornithologists W. A. Thompson and I. Vertinsky have suggested with mathematical models that the large number of individuals in a group feeding increases the possibility of the various members of the group detecting a polymorphic prey (i.e., a prey that has different "forms" in a given population). This occurs because the predator usually has an image of the prey that, in the case of group feeding, can be replaced by a less plentiful form of a polymorphic species, once a previous form becomes scarce.

In flocks which feed in groups one can observe all the various forms of interaction between the members of it. As a rule, by observing threatening or aggressive attitudes, one can deduce

The male urogenital system (left), and the female urogenital system (right).

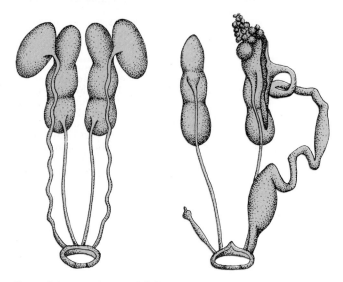

the existence of a social hierarchy in groups belonging to these species. Within the social hierarchy, individual ranks are established and can be recognized by specific threatening postures. In species belonging to the family Corvidae, for example, there is a marked social hierarchy in the groups, even though in the case of the Red-billed Chough (*Pyrrhocorax pyrrhocorax*) ornithologists D. Holyoak and S. Lovari have noted a low incidence of threatening or aggressive interactions between members of feeding groups.

THE NEST: A JEWEL OF NATURE
The Reproductive System
In the abdominal cavity of male birds, above the kidneys, we find the testicles, or testes (which mammals have in an external scrotum); these increase in size during the breeding period and move downward where the local temperature helps the production of spermatozoa. Before making their way to the cloaca, the spermatozoa pass through the epididymus and the vas deferens. They do not pass through a penis, because this is absent in birds (except for ratites (ostriches, etc.), ducks and curassows, where there is a primitive structure that is erectile and can be evaginated).

Copulation is swift and is repeated many times; during this act the cloaca of male and female birds is juxtaposed and the male fertilizes the female. The female has only one functioning ovary, the left one, which increases in size during reproduction, while the right ovary (apart from certain Falconiformes, where it simply does not work) is atrophied.

30

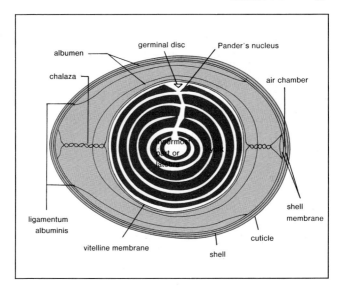

Once released from the ovary and fertilized, the eggs pass into the oviduct, where first the albumen and then the shell enclosing the egg are formed, then into the uterus, the vagina, and the cloaca; and then they are laid.

The egg is formed in the oviduct; in the tract called the *magnum* it is encased by the albumen; in the following section, the *isthmus,* the membranes of the calcareous shell are formed. In itself the egg is an amazing, self-sufficient structure, consisting basically of the shell (made up of up to 97 percent calcium carbonate), the albumen, also known as white of egg (the chemical composition of which is usually fixed in the various species, and enables scientists to make important electrophoretic analyses for the study of evolutionary affinities), the vitelline membrane, the yolk and the germinal disc. The sex hormones affect the seasonal variations in the plumage, displays connected with reproduction (singing, the territorial instinct, nuptial displays, the formation of fleshy and colorful appendages, etc.) and aggression. The phenomena occurring in the reproductive cycle are therefore influenced both by the action of the sex hormones and by the action of external environmental factors such as the daily photoperiod, the quantity of food available in the habitat, et cetera.

Territory

Generally speaking, territory is defined as any area defended by a bird at any moment during its life. It can be deduced from this that any area in which a bird is present, but which is not being defended by it, cannot be called a territory. Ornithologist

Little Egrets (*Egretta garzetta*) mating.

Margaret Morse Nice has proposed a classification of various types of territory: the first type, an area with a variable surface (depending on the species occupying it) where reproductive behavioral procedures (mating, nuptial displays, etc.), nesting and the rearing of young take place, and where the occupiers of the area can find sufficient food (this type of territory is found particularly among the Passeriformes and Piciformes); the second type, an area where all reproductive procedures, nesting and the rearing of young take place, but where there is no provision for the food search, which takes place outside this territory in hunting areas or by collective gathering by several pairs of birds (we thus have territories for reproduction and neutral feeding areas, which may sometimes be defended collectively against possible intrusion by creatures alien to the group using them); the third type, an area for courtship displays (called a *lek*), which has a restricted reproductive significance, because it has to do only with displays by males, whose purpose is to procure females (the nest is then built elsewhere), and no alimentary significance (this type of territory occurs with the Tetraonidae, Cotingidae, garden birds, etc.); the fourth type, which resembles the second, but differs in that the territory defended includes only the nest and the area in its immediate vicinity (the type of territory found among colonial birds, particularly seabirds nesting in large colonies—penguins, albatrosses, gannets, gulls, cormorants, etc.), while outside the nest birds with this type of territory use common feeding areas; the fifth type, which is divided into two parts—one for nesting and the other for feeding; and the sixth type,

Long-eared Owl (*Asio otus*) in threatening posture.

which is occupied not only during the breeding season but also throughout the winter. We can also add a seventh type of territory, which has to do with sheltering and resting places for birds outside the breeding season (these are smallish areas and, as a rule, have only a behavioral significance). It must be mentioned that various species of birds defend a certain territory by chasing away intruders who approach the edge of it either to rest or to hunt.

The concept of territory is very important in ornithology and plays an essential role in the life of birds. By arranging themselves in territories, which may vary in type and size, birds have the possibility of making optimal use of the natural resources, as regards nesting sites and feeding areas.

The patterns used by birds to install themselves in a territory vary from case to case. At the beginning of the breeding season males belonging to both migratory and nonmigratory species begin to establish themselves in an area of their favorite habitat, which still has only vague limits, and signal their occupation of their territory with visual and vocal signs. The other birds, on arriving, settle among the birds already there, and in this way the existing territories are more clearly defined. There are cases of areas where territories are close together or where the territories of different species overlap; but there are other areas where there appear to be unoccupied neutral zones. The delimitation of a territory may be in various forms: often features already present in the area are used, such as fence posts in the country. In any event, the limits depend on various factors and vary from zone to zone (on the basis of the geographical formation of the place, the availability of food,

33

Diagram showing the territories of various pairs of birds. The outermost lines mark the *family* areas, which might overlap slightly; the innermost lines mark the *nesting territory* and the actual *nest* (the darkest point). Territorial defense involves the greatest degree of aggression nearest the nest.

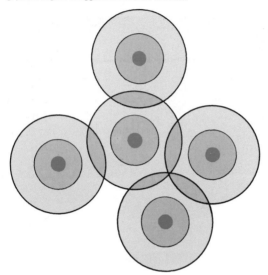

sites suitable for nest building, and so on). In these territories the male usually attracts the female and mates with her—although frequently, a previously formed pair chooses the territory together—and in some cases, as in the case of hummingbirds, it is the female who displays a conspicuous territorial behavior. The surface area of the territory varies depending on the species and on the seasonal and local environmental situation.

In some cases—as we have learned from studies of migrations—it has been possible to perceive a loyalty to the same territory, or at least to the same area, chosen for nesting by the same bird the year before.

Territory is marked out by means of visual and vocal displays (flights designed to indicate territorial defense, singing, threatening postures against possible intruders, etc.). In defending their territory, birds usually express their aggressiveness with threatening postures that have the effect of warding off intruders. Among individuals belonging to the same species we find ritualized behavioral patterns that enable birds to establish a relationship of dominator and dominated without shedding any blood—an important phenomenon that obviously contributes to the preservation of the species.

Ornithologist R. E. Ricklefs writes (1976):

"Solitary birds often establish territories in areas where they spend the winter; and we have seen how migratory species, such as shorebirds, sometimes establish around them transitory territories in which to procure food. These territories may be occupied for a few minutes or several hours. A territory situated below the high-water mark can only exist for as

Pair of Black Grouse (*Lyrurus tetrix*).

long as the area is uncovered by the ebb tide. A bird might leave such a territory for a few minutes, while it looks for food elsewhere, but it can quickly re-occupy it."

Courtship

In his book *The Social Behavior of Animals,* ethologist and ornithologist Nikolas Tinbergen attributes several functions to the courtship procedures: the synchronization, coordination and orientation of the behavior of the two sexes in time and space; the maintenance of reproductive isolation (which, by means of precopulative or postcopulative isolating mechanisms, avoids the birth or survival of hybrids between different species); and the suppression of behavioral displays other than sexual ones (such as, for example, aggressive instincts). The ornithologist G. F. Makkink has described the ceremony that precedes mating between a pair of Pied Avocets (*Recurvirostra avosetta*): First of all, both birds briskly preen their feathers; then, after a while, the female lowers herself, thereby indicating to the male that she is ready to mate, whereupon mating takes place almost at once. In Herring Gulls (*Larus argentatus*), as Tinbergen again observes, both sexes raise their heads time and again, and emit a cry with each such movement; after a while the male takes the initiative, approaches the female, and mating occurs.

Three specific attitudes, which generally take place near an old abandoned nest or near branches where a nest might be built, characterize the courtship of the Grey Heron (*Ardea cinerea*: a loud warning cry, an attitude in which the neck is

Male and female Satin Bowerbird (*Ptilonorhynchus violaceus*) by a typical nest.

stretched backwards, and a bowing movement.

J. Huxley and K. E. L. Simmons have described the curious nuptial display of the Great Crested Grebe (*Podiceps cristatus*): The two birds parade with a series of attitudes that culminate in each one seizing a clump of waterweed in its beak, and taking an upright, breast-to-breast position in the water. In the case of the extraordinary bowerbirds belonging to the family Ptilonorhynchidae, found in New Guinea and Australia, the males of some species even built small "bowers" of twigs, stalks, grass, leaves, et cetera, specifically for their courtship. In the case of the Satin Bowerbird (*Ptilonorhynchus violaceus*), the bower is even blue in color. This is achieved by using a small piece of bark as if it were a brush, and as the dye, charcoal and bits of fruit mixed with the bird's saliva.

In some species, courtship takes place in specific zones called *leks,* or *arenas,* where several males parade to procure females. Detailed studies of group courtship have been made by A. J. Hogan-Warburg about the Ruff (*Philomachus pugnax*), by E. T. Gilliard about the Guianan Cock of the Rock (*Rupicola rupicola*), and by D. W. Snow about the White-bearded Manakin (*Manacus manacus*). Leks have various functions: they promote encounters between the sexes and ensure the fertilization of females by dominant males who have the highest status in the social order.

Nuptial displays demand a high expenditure of energy, especially because of the marked state of excitation that goes with them. But they are extremely important precisely because they coordinate and synchronize the sexual cycle, an essential ele-

Two male Ruffs "dueling" (*Philomachus pugnax*).

ment for successful reproduction. In various species we find polygamy, which is generally associated with habitats in which the distribution of resources is most varied.

The existence of a difference in quality between different territories makes it more convenient for a female to choose an already paired male in a territory that is better than the choice made by an unpaired male in a less suitable territory. G. Orians (in D. S. Farner and J. R. King, eds., *Avian Biology*, New York, Academic Press, 1971) underlines the importance of the suitable habitat in polygamy, and hence the availability of the food requirements of the young while they are being reared. Out of 354 supervised Great Reed Warbler (*Acrocephalus arundinaceus*) nests, ornithologist A. Dircz has reported that at least 12 percent belong to polygamous (mainly bigamous) males and are situated in areas particularly rich in foodstuff. There is an average of 2.2 young leaving each nest. In the oriental subspecies of the Great Reed Warbler (*A. a orientalis*) ornithologist T. Saitou has observed 16 percent of males to be polygamous, and 12 percent unpaired, these latter being the last to arrive. The average number of young leaving each nest is 3.2.

In some species we find polyandry (the union of one female with several males); this occurs in three-toed quails, jacanas, painted snipes, phalaropes, et cetera; in these species the females are more brightly colored and take the initiative in courtship rituals.

The Nest

The nest is the structure that protects the eggs and the new-

Top: Nest of a Hammerhead Stork (*Scopus umbretta*).
Bottom: Nest of a European Roller (*Coracias garrulus*) with young.

born young (especially in the case of nidicolous nestlings). The variety of nests in the world of birds is fascinating. Numerous species build elaborate structures. The Dark-necked Tailorbird (*Orthotomus atrogularis*) builds its nest out of vegetable matter inside two leaves sewn together or in a single large leaf that is also sewn up with a thin length of thread; weaverbirds, and in particular the Sociable Weaverbirds (*Philetarius socius*), build large collective nests—ornithologists E. C. and N. E. Collias observed an old colony made up of four communal nests, the largest of which was 15.7 feet (4.80 m.) long, 11.8 feet (3.60 m.) wide, and had 125 openings; the Penduline Tit (*Remiz pendulinus*) builds a distinctive suspended bag-shaped nest; birds of prey, which use the same nest year after year, increase its size each year as more material is added; certain Australian moundbirds (Megapodidae) build huge nests of earth and vegetable matter, using the heat produced as it decomposes to incubate the eggs. Many species build rudimentary nests, others lay their eggs on the ground, in sand and among pebbles.

The Emperor Penguin (*Aptenodytes forsteri*) covers the single egg laid with a fold of its abdomen, and virtually carries it around with it, supported by its webbed feet.

The anis (belonging to the genus *Crotophaga*) build nests with several other pairs. In some species it can happen that two females lay their eggs in the same nest (as, for example, in the case of the Stone Curlew (*Burhinus oedicnemus*) in Kent, England.)

The nest is a structure used almost exclusively for reproduc-

tive purposes (in some cases it is used as a resting place). The influences of the hormonal system combined with the physiological changes that take place in the bird's body in the reproductive period determine the construction of the nest. The choice of the site, the materials used and the time taken to build it, and the activity of the male or female in the construction, all vary from species to species.

Laying the Eggs and Rearing the Young

In birds, reproduction usually takes place once a year; in some species it may occur two or three times (or even four). In other species, such as the Wandering Albatross (*Diomedea exulans*), reproduction occurs every two years. In some species, in special cases linked with specific environmental conditions (such as, for example, a shortage of prey) nesting may not occur at all; this happens, for example, in Arctic regions with the Snowy Owl (*Nyctea scandiaca*)——in years in which there are plenty of natural prey (such as the rodents called lemmings, whose populations are subject to conspicuous fluctuations) it lays up to seven, eight or even twelve eggs, but in years when lemmings are few in number it may not nest at all and may, instead, move south in search of food.

A unique case is a population of the Sooty Tern (*Sterna fuscata*) found on Ascension Island in the South Atlantic, which nests about every nine months.

The interval and duration of the reproductive cycle vary with the latitude in question, and with the various species. As a rule, reproduction coincides with an optimum situation of the species in its proper habitat (in fact, the hatching of the eggs and the rearing of the young generally correspond with the greatest availability of food in the habitat). But consideration must always be given to the possibility of adverse climatic situations in which entire broods might be destroyed. However, many species produce a substitute clutch if the first one is destroyed by adverse weather conditions or predators. The equatorial regions do not have clearly defined reproductive periods because of the specific environmental conditions that prevail in them. Although some species of birds in these regions maintain a rhythm of one to three broods a year, they do not have very fixed hatching periods; these occur on the whole all year round.

The eggs that are laid vary in shape (pear-shaped, oval, elliptical, etc.), size, color and quantity, depending on the species. The period when eggs are laid also varies, depending on the species and the environmental conditions.

Incubation takes place in various species when the first egg is laid, in others when the last is laid. In the first case, when the young are born their ages will differ by several days (in some species, such as birds of prey, there are cases of cannibalism which affects the last young to be born). When incubating, the bird covers the eggs with its belly, which, during the breeding season, fills with blood vessels and loses its feathers; these ventral sections are called brood patches, or incubation plates, and transmit heat to the eggs.

In the newly laid egg the first phases of the development of the embryo contained in it take place; these then stop and start once again some days later, in certain cases, as soon as the parents start to sit on the eggs. For its development the embryo needs heat produced during the brooding period and feeds on the yolk until the chick is completely formed. While being sat on, the eggs of some species may even be abandoned for several days——up to a week in the Manx Shearwater (*Procellaria puffinus*).

When the incubation period is over, the nestling breaks through the shell of the egg with the help of a sort of growth on the jaw, called the "egg-tooth," which disappears as the chick starts to grow.

Ornithologist Margaret M. Nice has classified newborn birds based on the degree of independence they show when they hatch from the egg. We thus have the following groups:

(1) precocious, or nidifugous, with the eyes open, covered with down, leaving the nest on the first or second day, subdivided into the following groups: (a) young independent of their parents (Megapodiidae, moundbirds); (b) young that follow their parents but find food on their own (ducks, geese, swans, sandpipers, avocets, stilts, phalaropes, stone curlews, etc.); and (c) young that follow their parents and are fed by them (grebes, divers (loons), cranes, rails, etc.); (2) semiprecocious, with the eyes open, covered with down, but remaining in the nest until they learn to walk on their own, and fed by the parents (flamingos, gulls, terns, skuas, alcids, nightjars, etc.); (3) semihelpless, covered with down, unable to leave the nest, and fed by the parents, divided into: (a) those with the eyes open (storm petrels, storks, ibises, herons, falcons, etc.); and (b) those with the eyes unopened (nocturnal birds of prey); (4) helpless, or nidicolous, with the eyes closed, naked or with very little down, incapable of flying, fed by the parents (pelicans, gannets, cormorants, parrots, pigeons, cuckoos, swifts, kingfishers, hoopoes, woodpeckers, jays and many Passeriformes).

The prompting of the adult, by both nidicolous and nidifugous nestlings, provides a series of stimuli——in fact, in many Passeriformes the bright coloring of the mouth inside stimulates the adult to deposit food in it. The frequency of feeding varies from species to species. The period in which the young are reared is also variable, depending on the species——in some Passeriformes it lasts thirteen to twenty days, whereas in albatrosses it can last for eight and a half months.

In various species of birds we find a form of parasitism in which the eggs are laid in the nests of other species, which then rear the uninvited young as their own. These include the numerous species of cuckoos, certain species belonging to the families Indicatoridae (honeyguides), Icteridae (American orioles) and Ploceidae (weaverbirds), plus one species of duck, the Blackheaded duck (*Heteronetta atricapilla*).

Top: Mute Swan (*Cygnus olor*), example of a bird with precocious (nidifugous) young. Bottom: Greater Flamingo (*Phoenicopterus ruber*), with semiprecocious young.

Top: Scops Owl (*Otus scops*) with semihelpless young.
Bottom: Eurasian Bullfinch (*Pyrrhula pyrrhula*) with helpless (nidicolous) young.

THE RIDDLE OF MIGRATION

One of the most intriguing aspects of the bird kingdom is the phenomenon of migration. As we are told by ornithologist Jean Dorst (1970), the origin of migration can be traced back to the Tertiary era, during which the alternation of the seasons must have given rise to movements similar to those observed today. In the Quaternary period these movements became more clearly delineated, particularly in glaciation periods. In fact, in these periods the species with a northern distribution were in all probability forced to move to more southerly regions because of the advancing cold, and then returned north during the interglacial periods when the climate was less harsh. Thus, a combination of environmental and climatic conditions and internal physiological conditions gave rise to the phenomenon of migration.

As a rule, after nesting, birds leave their breeding areas, although some species remain in close contact with them and make up the so-called nonmigratory, or sedentary, species. In some species there are movements that apparently have no precise direction; these are known as erratism, or nomadism. Migration proper entails an outward flight from the nesting area to the wintering area, a flight that is also called the postnuptial flight, or flight of passage, and a return flight from the resting area to the nesting area, which is called the prenuptial or return journey. In migratory terminology, we also have *winter visitors,* a term that refers to species present in a given area during the winter, and *summer visitors,* found in a given area during the summer.

Migration is studied in various ways. Direct observation of migrations, particularly in areas where there is a concentration of migratory birds, is a much-used method—observers analyze the quality and quantity of the species that pass over or rest, the direction of their movements and their behavior in relation to climatic conditions, et cetera. Some ornithologists have used telescopes directed at the moon, or have used radar, or have even followed migrating flocks in airplanes.

One of the most common ways of studying migrations is ringing (banding). This was used on an empirical basis by various ornithologists in the past, but on a scientific basis only since 1899. In that year the Danish ornithologist H. C. C. Mortensen ringed (banded) 164 Common Starlings (*Sturnus vulgaris*) with zinc rings that showed the year and place of ringing. From then on this method has spread throughout the scientific world, using light aluminum-base rings. Each ring attached to a bird carries a serial number and the abbreviated and internationally recognized name of the institution involved. The serial number refers to registers in which, for each bird ringed, the date and place of ringing are entered, together with the developmental stage in which it was ringed (nestling, immature or adult), sex, state of health, molting, size, weight, et cetera. If and when ringed birds are recaught they supply extremely interesting data about the age of the bird, the movements it has made and so on. Ringing is a serious and scientific operation, and it must be carried out by students who are qualified to collect all the vital data about the birds caught.

Bird migrations take place in different forms depending on the species and the climatic conditions. For this reason we find localized migratory movements that follow very precise routes, such as, for example, the Bosphorus, the Straits of Gibraltar and the Sicilian Channel for the migration from Europe to Africa and vice versa; and migratory movements that follow a variety of routes. Many species prefer to migrate by day; others by night. When they migrate, birds usually make use of passes, valleys, watercourses and so on, even though it is hard to lay down precise behavioral patterns in their movements (for example, the meteorological developments in an area will often determine the route taken and the pauses during migration).

Migratory flights have become legendary for the distances covered. Take for example the Lesser Golden Plover (*Pluvialis dominica*), which flies from Alaska to the Hawaiian Islands covering a distance of 2,175 miles (3,500 km.) apparently without stopping, and the Arctic Tern (*Sterna paradisaea*), which sets out from its nesting areas along the northern coastlines of the Northern Hemisphere and spends the winter in the southern regions of the Pacific, Indian and Atlantic oceans.

By studying the comings and goings of various species in a given region it is possible to delineate the precise seasonal periods within which, broadly speaking, the various migratory species are present, taking into account at all times any possible climatic variations. For the Rhone delta (in the Camargue) Jacques Blondel has drawn up the following seasonal periods (which are used by ornithologist E. A. di Carlo for a wetland area near Rome): (1) the prespring season (from mid-February to the first ten days in March); (2) the spring season (from the second ten days in March to April or May; (3) the summer season (May 15 through June to July 30); (4) the autumn season (August 1 to September 30); (5) the prewinter season (October 1 to November 30); (6) the winter season (December–January–February).

In the migratory species molting usually takes place before the migratory journey, to enable migrating birds to be in top form as far as their plumage is concerned. There are also molting migrations that take birds to suitable areas, where they then change their feathers (this happens above all with species that molt completely and all at once, as in waterfowl—the Anatidae). Various ornithologists have observed migrations of this type for various species of ducks, for the Eurasian Shelduck (*Tadorna tadorna*), the Wood Sandpiper (*Tringa glareola*), et cetera. The migratory impulse is determined by a series of attendant circumstances such as the environmental situation and the internal physiological state of the bird (the daily photoperiod would, seem, for example, to influence the development of the sex glands, according to William Rowan's studies). In order to prepare for its migration, the bird stores up energy reserves. Orientation on migratory flights has been the object of in-depth studies by various ornithologists. It has been possible to detect probable indicators that have brought to light the im-

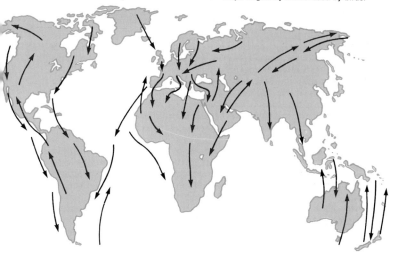

Major migratory routes used by birds.

portance of the position of the sun and its movements in day-time migrations (plus the geographical position of mountain ranges and river systems, and wind direction when the sky is overcast), the position of the moon and the stars on nocturnal flights, the possible use of the earth's magnetic field, and so on. On migratory flights some species reach remarkable altitudes and speeds.

WHERE AND HOW BIRDS LIVE
Environment and Adaptation
Life on earth is made possible by the sun's rays reaching its surface. The intensity and duration of these rays either directly or indirectly condition the climatic situation, which in turn affects the type of vegetation present in the various regions of the world. The sun's energy is partly used by plants that, by means of the photosynthetic process, construct energy-rich organic substances using inorganic compounds (water, mineral salts, carbon dioxide). Animals eat plants, assimilating and consuming the energy needed for their survival. Life on earth is thus the result of far-reaching interactions between living organisms and the nonliving environment; these two are closely linked to each other. The ecological system is the environmental framework that embraces all organisms and the environment of a given area with clear-cut features. The following elements in an ecosystem can be listed: (1) the inorganic substances that take part in the recycling of matter; (2) the organic compounds (proteins, carbohydrates, lipids, humus) that link the biotic with the abiotic; (3) the climatic

order (temperature and other factors); (4) the productive elements (especially green plants), organisms that can produce food from simple inorganic substances; (5) the macroconsumers, mainly animals that feed on other organisms or on particular organic matter; (6) the microconsumers, mainly bacteria or fungi, that decompose the complex substances of dead organisms, absorbing some of the decomposed products and releasing inorganic nutritive substances that can be used by the productive elements.

We can apply the first two laws of thermodynamics as basic to the system of life: (1) the law of the conservation of energy—energy can be transformed but not destroyed; (2) the law of the "cost" of energy—every transformation of energy is accompanied by losses of heat energy, which is dispersed in the atmosphere.

In ecosystems the energy flow acts as a "vital motor," forming series of food chains made up, in effect, of productive elements, macroconsumers and microconsumers or decomposing elements. Every living organism in its environment interacts with all the elements in it, living and nonliving, and thus has its own place and its own function in the environmental balance. The physical space, the role played and the position of the organism in relation to the living conditions form the so-called "ecological niche" of the organism itself. E. P. Odum (1973) has, in one sentence, summarized the concepts of habitat and ecological niche by saying that the habitat is the "address" of an organism, while the niche is its "biological profession." The concept of the niche then introduces that of competition between organisms. This competition exists whenever the niches of two species coincide.

Among the abiotic elements that we can single out in an ecosystem there are light, temperature, atmosphere, water, soil, pressure, and climate. By climate, as a general rule, we mean the average state of the atmosphere determined by the daily and seasonal conditions and variations in a series of factors—temperature, humidity, the amount and nature of precipitation, the amount of sunlight, cloud, wind direction and speed, and other atmospheric factors such as fog, frost and storms. In addition we have, in the ecosystem, such other important elements as environmental resistance, which can be defined as the whole range of unfavorable factors that condition the size of a living population (potentially, populations could expand exponentially) and the limiting or conditioning factors—that is, those elements that are present and important in the formation of the organic substance of all living organisms, both animal and vegetable (oxygen, carbon, hydrogen, nitrogen, phosphorus, sulphur, calcium, magnesium, potassium, iron, manganese, copper, zinc, etc.).

The presence of an organism is thus conditioned by the maximum- and minimum tolerance levels of the various abiotic elements present in the ecosystem which it can support. Some species show a wide range of tolerance in different environmental conditions, while others are closely associated with precise environmental conditions, the absence of which can seriously endanger the very survival of the species. The term *euryoeic* is used to define the species that cope well with different environmental conditions, and *stenoecic* for those species more strictly reliant on one or more environmental factors; the more eclectic species, with no specific requirements, are called *ubiquitous*.

Populations

The ecologist Odum (1971) has drawn up the following levels of vital organization, the last four of which are of the greatest ecological interest: (1) protoplasm; (2) cells; (3) tissues; (4) organs; (5) organisms; (6) populations; (7) communities; (8) ecosystems; (9) the biosphere. The term *population* means a group of organisms of the same species found in a given area and having various characteristics typical of the group and not of single individuals. The population is the basic unit of evolution, and its dynamic aspect includes the following factors: birth, death, migration and immigration. If it did not come up against limits, the growth of a population would be exponential and virtually unlimited. But in nature there are numerous factors that help to regulate the growth of a population—disease, adverse climatic conditions, predation, competition for food, environmental suitability, accidental causes, et cetera. These are all factors that restrict the capacity of a population to expand.

Population growth is, therefore, not exponential; it follows, in graph form, a logistic curve that shows us how it grows until it reaches a limit equivalent to the effective tolerance level of the environment in which the population is living. This limit is defined by ecologists as the "carrying capacity of the environment." From this we can deduce that the dynamics of a population depend not only on the elements mentioned above but also on the reproductive potential of the species and on the carrying capacity of the host environment. Ornithologist A. M. Laskey, for example, has observed the three successive hatches in one breeding season of the Eastern Bluebird (*Siala sialis*) in a park in Nashville, Tennessee. For the first brood 34 nests were observed, and they produced 170 eggs and 123 young; the second brood involved 35 nests, 163 eggs and 90 young; and the third brood brought 33 nests, 122 eggs and 52 chicks. On average, each brood of the common bluebird has 5 eggs; so, theoretically the first brood would produce $34 \times 5 = 170$ eggs, the second $35 \times 5 = 175$ eggs, and the third $33 \times 5 = 165$ eggs. In practice various environmental and physiological factors are at work in the production of eggs and hatching of young; they affect the different broods in different ways, and Laskey extracts the following values in percentages: first brood, percentage of eggs produced 100, percentage of young born 72; second brood 93 and 51; third brood 74 and 32.

The logistic growth of the population includes a point at which the population in its proper environment has a maximum expansion. By keeping this fact in mind and studying closely the demography of the population, man can also affect its growth (by hunting and fishing). The demography of the population means that in the case of such intervention man must carefully analyze the fertility tables (i.e., the average number of young that a female produces at each different age) and the survival

Colony of Common Murres (*Uria aalge*).

tables (i.e., the number of individuals living at each different age, and the number that die at each different age, and the average time lived by the remaining individuals of each different age.)

We must also consider the net rate of reproduction or substitution (i.e., the average number of females that a female produces in her lifetime) and the reproductive value (i.e., the number of children passed on by an individual to the next generation). Hunting is nowadays a superfluous activity that contributes, sadly, to the indiscriminate destruction of many birds whose populations are already seriously threatened by pollution and environmental alterations in general.

Ornithologist O. S. Pettingill (1970) has described the composition of bird populations in midseasonal periods. This composition reveals the following groups of individuals, depending on the season: (A) midsummer population: (1) summer residents (nesting adults aged one year or more, nonnesting adults of one year or more, young born that year, nonnesting immature individuals of one year or more); (2) nonmigratory residents (same categories as in point 1);

(B) midwinter population: (1) winter visitors; (2) nonmigratory residents;

(C) midspring and midautumn population: (1) birds of passage; (2) nonmigratory residents; (3) summer residents.

We have already mentioned some factors that limit the level of a population, such as adverse climatic conditions, environmental suitability, and so on. But there are also various factors that, conversely, contribute to population increases—the number, consistency and variations of broods, the age at which sexual maturity is reached, the longevity of the birds in question, and so on. The age at which sexual maturity is reached varies from three months in certain Passeriformes, such as the weaverbirds *Taeniopygia castanotis, Lagonosticta senegala* and *Lonchura striata,* to three to five years in certain birds of prey, to eight to eleven years in certain albatrosses. It is hard to say how long birds live in the wild; ornithologists J. Dorst (1973) and J. Fisher and J. Flegg (1974) have drawn up the ages reached by various species. Here are some, although they obviously cannot claim to be absolute figures: Old World White Pelican, 52 years; Andean Condor, 52 years; Bateleur Eagle, 55 years; Fulmar, 22 years; Red Knot, 13 years; White Stork, 19 years; Barn Owl, 10 years; Eurasian Swift, 21 years; European Blackbird 11 years; Great Tit, 7 years; House Sparrow, 23 years; European Robin, 8 years and 4 months.

Any study of populations and their dynamic aspect must also mention the cyclic fluctuations occurring in some species and the major movements (often nothing less than invasions) that some species make when the particular food they require becomes scarce and they are forced to move to other areas, sometimes far away, in search of food—e.g., crossbills, nutcrackers, Bohemian Waxwings, et cetera. For various reasons, which often have to do with climatic changes, some species are modifying their areas of distribution; one such is the Cattle Egret (*Ardeola ibis*) which has been expanding in America since about 1930, when a small group of individuals spread out from British Guiana; another is the Collared Dove (*Streptopelia decaocto*) which has spread from Asia Minor throughout most of Europe, gaining more and more territory each year; and another is the Fieldfare (*Turdus pilaris*), which, since a migrating flock in 1937 veered from its usual route and ended up in Greenland, has become partly nonmigratory in that area.

The Zoogeographic Regions and Environments
The complex events and considerable changes that the earth has undergone through the various geological periods have contributed to the present-day distribution of living species. Changes in the features of terra firma, climate and environment, the formation of barriers such as mountains, seas and deserts, glacial periods with interglacial periods, earthquakes and volcanic eruptions are all events that have made their contribution to the presence and distribution of life on earth. In analyzing present-day and past distributions of fauna and flora, naturalists have felt the need to divide up the earth's surface into regions, thus making a classification of the world's different zones. We thus have the following regions: (1) the palaearctic region including Europe, North Africa and northern Asia; (2) the nearctic region including North America (some experts combine the palaearctic and nearctic regions under the term holarctic); (3) the Ethiopian region including Africa south of the Sahara (in which we have the Malagasy subregion embracing Madagascar); (4) the Oriental region including tropical Asia and western Indonesia; (5) the Australasian region

including eastern Indonesia, Australia, Polynesia and New Zealand (the latter is often placed in a specific New Zealand subregion); (6) the neotropical region, including the West Indies and Central and South America, with the Antarctic subregion often taken as a separate region altogether).

Various types of environment can be drawn up in the different regions, based on geological conditions, the conditions of the soil, vegetation and climate. The following is a broad division into environmental zones with specific climate, vegetation and fauna: (1) polar regions (ice floes and tundra); (2) coniferous forests (taiga); (3) temperate forests; (4) prairies; (5) deserts; (6) tropical forests; (7) mountains; (8) oceanic islands; (9) inland waters; (10) the sea.

HOW BIRDS ARE CLASSIFIED
Systematics

In natural scientific circles the need has always been felt to arrange and classify the large variety of existing and extinct species in suitable groups. Although various attempts had been made in the past, it was an eighteenth-century Swedish naturalist, Carl von Linné (or Carolus Linnaeus) (1707–1778), who proposed and developed a system that is universally used today: binomial nomenclature, in which each species is specified by a first name starting with a capital letter, which indicates the genus it belongs to, and a second name, in small letters, which indicates the species (a third can be added where necessary to denote a subspecies).

The animal kingdom is generally divided into numerous groups, the principal ones being, in descending order: kingdom, phyla, type, subtype, class, subclass, order, suborder, family, subfamily, genus, species, subspecies.

In the past, and until the appearance of Linnaeus, species were separated one from the other mainly on the basis of morphological and visible differences. Evolutionistic ideas, particularly with the work of Darwin and Wallace, began to demonstrate the great importance of the natural process of change, mutation and evolution. Helped by the great advances in the study of evolution as a principle uniting the various phenomena of the natural world, and as a result of progress in the fields of genetics, ecology and demographic dynamics, modern scholars have elaborated a biological and dynamic concept of species: the species is a group of natural populations either effectively or potentially capable of producing themselves by interbreeding. A species is thus a complex of natural populations that reproduce among themselves, that have their own hereditary store in common, and that have acquired a state of reproductive isolation in respect to other species. The mechanisms of natural evolution do not act on the single individual, but on the hereditary store of these populations.

The methods of investigation used by systematic research to

The zoogeographical regions.

Palaearctic region

Nearctic region

Oriental region

Ethiopian region

Neotropical region

Australasian region

ORDER	FAMILY	ORDER	FAMILY
Sphenisciformes	Spheniscidae (Penguins)	Columbiformes	Pteroclidae (Sandgrouse)
Struthioniformes	Struthionidae (Ostriches)		Columbidae (Pigeons)
Casuariiformes	Casuariidae (Cassowaries)	Psittaciformes	Psittacidae (Parrots)
	Dromaiidae (Emus)	Cuculiformes	Musophagidae (Touracos)
Rheiformes	Rheidae (Rheas)		Cuculidae (Cuckoos)
Apterygiformes	Apterygidae (Kiwis)	Strigiformes	Strigidae (Owls)
Tinamiformes	Tinamidae (Tinamous)	Caprimulgiformes	Steatornithidae (Oilbirds)
Gaviiformes	Gaviidae (Divers or Loons)		Podargidae (Frogmouths)
Podicipediformes	Podicipedidae (Grebes)		Nyctibiidae (Potoos)
Procellariiformes	Procellariidae (Petrels)		Aegothelidae (Owlet-frogmouths)
	Diomedeidae (Albatrosses)		
	Hydrobatidae (Storm Petrels)		Caprimulgidae (Nightjars)
	Pelecanoididae (Diving Petrels)	Apodiformes	Apodidae (Swifts)
			Hemiprocnidae (Tree Swifts)
Pelecaniformes	Phaethontidae (Tropicbirds)		Trochilidae (Hummingbirds)
	Fregatidae (Frigatebirds)	Coliiformes	Coliidae (Mousebirds)
	Pelecanidae (Pelicans)	Trogoniformes	Trogonidae (Trogons)
	Sulidae (Boobies)	Coraciiformes	Alcedinidae (Kingfishers)
	Phalacrocoracidae (Cormorants)		Todidae (Todies)
	Anhingidae (Darters)		Momotidae (Motmots)
Ciconiiformes	Ardeidae (Herons)		Meropidae (Bee-eaters)
	Balaenicipitidae (Shoebills)		Leptosomatidae (Cuckoo-rollers)
	Scopidae (Hammerheads)		
	Threskiornithidae (Ibises, Spoonbills)		Coraciidae (Rollers)
			Upupidae (Hoopoes)
	Ciconiidae (Storks)		Phoeniculidae (Wood-hoopoes)
Phoenicopteriformes	Phoenicopteridae (Flamingos)		Bucerotidae (Hornbills)
Anseriformes	Anhimidae (Screamers)	Piciformes	Galbulidae (Jacamars)
	Anatidae (Swans, Geese, Ducks)		Bucconidae (Puffbirds)
			Capitonidae (Barbets)
Falconiformes	Cathartidae (American Vultures)		Indicatoridae (Honeyguides)
			Ramphastidae (Toucans)
	Pandionidae (Ospreys)		Picidae (Woodpeckers)
	Accipitridae (Harriers, Kites, Eagles, Hawks)	Passeriformes	Eurylaimidae (Broadbills)
			Dendrocolaptidae (Woodcreepers)
	Falconidae (Falcons, Caracaras)		Furnariidae (Ovenbirds)
			Formicariidae (Antbirds)
	Sagittariidae (Secretarybirds)		Conopophagidae (Antpipits)
Galliformes	Megapodiidae (Megapodes)		Rhynocryptidae (Tapaculos)
			Pittidae (Pittas)
	Cracidae (Currassow/Guans)		Philepittidae (Asities)
			Xenicidae (New Zealand Wrens)
	Tetraonidae (Grouse)		
	Phasianidae (Pheasants)		Tyrannidae (Tyrant Flycatchers)
	Numididae (Gruineafowls)		
	Meleagrididae (Turkeys)		Pipridae (Manakins)
	Opisthocomidae (Hoatzins)		Cotingidae (Cotingas)
Gruiformes	Mesitornithidae (Mesites)		Phytotomidae (Plantcutters)
	Gruidae (Cranes)		Menuridae (Lyrebirds)
	Aramidae (Limpkins)		Atricornithidae (Scrub-birds)
	Psophiidae (Trumpeters)		
	Otididae (Bustards)		Alaudidae (Larks)
	Rallidae (Rails)		Hirundinidae (Swallows)
	Turnicidae (Hemipodes)		Motacillidae (Wagtails, Pipits)
	Heliornithidae (Finfeet)		
	Rhynchochetidae (Kagus)		Campephagidae (Cuckoo-shrikes)
	Eurypygidae (Sunbitterns)		
	Cariamidae (Seriemas)		Pycnonotidae (Bulbuls)
Charadriiformes	Jacanidae (Jacanas)		Irenidae (Leafbirds)
	Rostratulidae (Painted Snipes)		Laniidae (Shrikes)
			Vangidae (Vangas)
	Haematopodidae (Oystercatchers)		Bombycillidae (Waxwings)
			Dulidae (Palmchats)
	Charadriidae (Plovers)		Cinclidae (Dippers)
	Scolopacidae (Sandpipers)		Troglodytidae (Wrens)
	Recurvirostridae (Avocets, Stilts)		Mimidae (Mockingbirds, Thrashers)
	Phalaropodidae (Phalaropes)		
	Dromadidae (Crab Plovers)		Prunellidae (Accentors)
	Burhinidae (Thick-knees)		Turdidae (Thrushes)
	Glareolidae (Coursers, Pratincoles)		Timaliidae (Babblers)
			Sylviidae (Warblers, Old World)
	Thinocoridae (Seedsnipes)		
	Chionididae (Sheathbills)		Muscicapidae (Flycatchers, Old World)
	Stercorariidae (Skua, Jaegers)		
	Laridae (Gulls, Terns)		
	Rynchopidae (Skimmers)		
	Alcidae (Alcids)		

ORDER	FAMILY	ORDER	FAMILY
Passeriformes (Cont.)	Paridae (Tits)	**Passeriformes** (Cont.)	Fringillidae (Finches)
	Sittidae (Nuthatches)		Ploceidae (Weavers)
	Certhiidae (Treecreepers)		Sturnidae (Starlings)
	Dicaeidae (Flowerpeckers)		Estrildidae (Weavers)
	Nectariniidae (Sunbirds)		Oriolidae (Orioles)
	Zosteropidae (White-eyes)		Dicruridae (Drongos)
	Meliphagidae (Honeyeaters)		Callaeidae (Wattlebirds)
	Emberizidae (Buntings)		Grallinidae (Magpie-larks)
	Coerebidae (Honeycreepers)		Artamidae (Woodswallows)
	Thraupidae (Tanagers)		Cracticidae (Bellmagpies)
	Parulidae (Warblers, Wood)		Ptilonorhynchidae (Bowerbirds)
	Drepanididae (Honeycreepers, Hawaiian)		Paradiseidae (Birds-of-Paradise)
	Vireonidae (Vireos)		Corvidae (Crows, Jays)
	Icteridae (Orioles, Blackbirds)		

analyze the evolutionary affinities of the various groups use all the various fields of modern zoological research: palaeontology, biochemistry, physiology, ethology and ecology. Specific studies of the immunological properties of the red corpuscles, the protein composition of the albumen of eggs, and the morphological differences in early stages of life have shed considerable light on the biological affinities of different species.

The Classification of Birds
In the class of Birds some ornithologists make a distinction between two subclasses: Palaeornithes (or ancient birds) and Neornithes (or recent birds).

The first group includes all the extinct species, whereas the second is subdivided into three superorders: Odontognathae (extinct species), Palaeognathae (ostriches, rheas, cassowaries, emus, kiwis and tinamous), and Neognathae (all other birds). Fisher and Peterson, in *The World of Birds,* suggest three subclasses: Saururae (extinct birds), Odontolcae (extinct, toothed birds) and Ornithurae (including certain extinct birds and all living birds).

In this book we have followed the latest classification of the class of Birds, as elaborated by various ornithologists, the first and foremost by Alexander Wetmore, and modified by the monumental work by J. L. Peters and his successors, the *Check-list of the Birds of the World* (see pages 56–57).

LET'S STUDY AND PROTECT BIRDS
Bird Watching
Careful and considerate bird watching is the basis of data gathering for ornithology as a discipline. In addition, it is a highly rewarding naturalistic hobby that is extremely popular in many of the world's countries.

The important thing—and this applies to all fields of research—is to be serious about your own hobby; gather your data in a thorough way, using where possible methods that have become internationally standardized and are thus similar and comparable; note down only what you are sure of, and make your observations carefully, patiently and accurately. In order to make your hobby a useful one, you must obviously learn to identify the various species of birds, and you must not forget to learn the basic concepts of biology as they apply to these wonderful vertebrates. In addition, it is best not to remain isolated, but to subscribe to ornithological magazines and journals and join serious and scientific organizations and clubs. Studying birds means having books, and this text is aimed at being an introduction to the study and protection of birds. Since 1934, when the famous ornithologist Roger Tory Peterson published his *Field Guide to the Birds of the Eastern United States,* a vast number of guides have been published to help people identify birds in the wild in almost every corner of the globe. For bird watching you will also need a basic minimum of equipment. And at all times you must respect the natural surroundings in which you find yourself.

Essential equipment includes a good pair of binoculars (there are countless types on the market), a notebook and writing implements for making on-the-spot notes and sketches of species that you cannot at first sight identify. You must also note down the essential features regarding the shape, coloring, flight pattern, behavior, song and habitat in which the bird was seen, and when. For binoculars we would recommend 8 x 30, 8 x 40, 10 x 40 or 10 x 50 types (a good binocular guide, including telescopes and cameras recommended for bird watching, has been published by the ornithologist Jim Flegg, of the British Trust for Ornithology). When quoting the above numbers for binoculars, the first number indicates the magnification obtained, and the second indicates the diameter of the lens in millimeters and also denotes the brightness of the binoculars. Other data for each model of binoculars denote the image clarity perceived by the human eye and the performance in poor lighting conditions, in particular in twilight.

An optional item of equipment that can be most useful is a good telescope mounted on a tripod. Another useful device is to have records of the song and other sounds made by the various species, to make it easy to identify them in the wild. The Société d'Etudes Ornithologiques has been publishing a series of sound tracks in collaboration with the Ornithological Laboratory at Cornell University, New York.

Data gathering is of vital importance in bird watching. It is essential to follow serious and scientific methodologies that have been internationally standardized. Attempts have been made for some time now to achieve this standardization; in particular the British Trust for Ornithology, in Europe, has been moving in this direction, and in 1971 it organized—in collaboration with the Vogelwarte Radolfzell of Schloss Moggingen—a convention on the standardization of European Ornithology. A study group was then set up for the ''Standardization in European Ornithology,'' and there have been, in each of several countries, various conventions dealing with census-taking methods and atlas projects aimed at compiling maps of the species nesting.

Here is a standard form for reporting sightings of birds:

1. Name of bird watcher.
2. Name of any bird watcher with you on the sortie.
3. Site or location of observations (refer to standard Ordnance Survey maps).
4. Date of observation (mention times at which observations were made and the percentage of the total area covered during the sortie).

5. Data gathered: type of vegetation, weather conditions (cloud cover, wind, temperature, rain, visibility, etc.); environmental features (type of terrain—rock, stony, gravel or scree, coarse sand, fine sand, mud or ooze, clay, humus, peat, etc.; sloping or otherwise, presence of surface water, expanses of water at hand, manmade buildings nearby, etc.).

6. List of species observed (for each species indicate the number of different sightings made—you can use terms like "a lot" and "various," but you must give some idea of the amount implicit in them; for example, 'various' may mean anything from one to ten sightings; if possible, make notes of the sex of the individuals sighted, the sighting with the largest number of individuals observed together and the approximate, presumed number of individuals of that species present in the area; all the various observations about behavior and other features that you consider worth mentioning).

Although it is extremely important to gather data about nests, it is even more important not to disturb them and menace the future of the young in them. Limit your visits to nests to just one or two, and try to be content with observing them from a distance, being careful not to damage the surrounding vegetation so that you will not alter the protection provided for the nest by the natural environment. If in doubt, consult an expert ornithologist. Nesting data are very important. For many years now the

Footprints of birds: (1) pheasant; (2) grouse; (3) gull; (4) loon; (5) heron; (6) coot; (7) stork.

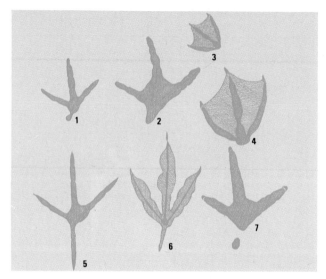

British Trust for Ornithology has been gathering data about nests and nesting on standardized forms and cards issued by the Nest Record Scheme, and has also elaborated special forms for data gathering concerning colonial species (Colony Nest Record Card). We can use this B.T.O. model for suggesting a standard card for gathering nesting data:

1.   Name of bird watcher.
2.   Site of bird watching (detailed map reference).
3.   Year.
4.   Species.
5.   Position of nest (where it is situated——in a tree, in rocks, on the ground, etc.——and at what height and in what type of environment, etc.).
6.   Measurements (taken when nesting is over——length, depth, materials used for construction, etc.).
7.   Conditions in which found——(a) under construction, (b) at brooding time, (c) with young.
8.   Visits made (indicate for each visit the date, the exact time, the number of eggs or young present and any other notes you consider to be of interest——if there is an adult bird present, if it is sitting on the eggs, feeding the young, etc.).

All the notes you jot down in your notebooks during your various outings can be copied out into special exercise books, grouped according to species, place, chronological order of outings, et cetera.
Bird watching can entail many areas of study and research:

Analysis of the contents of the droppings, or excreta, of a
Long-eared Owl (*Asio otus*).

keeping a check on a specific area for several years to analyze
the comings and goings of migrations depending on the meteorological conditions and the environmental changes of the
area itself; checking the nesting patterns; studying the behavior of the various species; gathering and classifying feathers,
plume feathers, bones, skulls, et cetera; analyzing the contents of excreta or droppings (pellets that contain the indigest-
ible remains of the prey of certain species like herons, birds of
prey, bee-eaters, etc.) in order to obtain data about the diets of
those species.

Another important factor in ornithology is all the data that can
be collected on dead individuals or individuals captured alive
for ringing. Useful measurements include the over-all length
(measured with the specimen fully extended, from the tip of the
beak to the tip of the tail), the length of the wings (which is
taken with the wing folded, not extended), the length of the
beak or bill (measured from the point where the jaw joins the
cranium), the length of the tail (from the base of the central
rectrices to the tip), the tarsus (taken from the bend of the tibia
to the start of the toes) and sometimes the claw on the hind toe
(all measurements are taken in millimeters). Another important
element, which is often essential for the identification of some
birds, is the wing formula—i.e., the shape and relative mea-
surement of the primary remiges. The ''European'' numbering
of the remiges starts from the outer part of the wing. As mentioned by the ornithologist S. Frugis in his *Enciclopedia degli
uccelli d'Europe,* in some species it is possible to establish a
bird's approximate age by analyzing the terminal outline of the

Right: Colony of King Penguins (*Aptenodytes patagonica*) photographed from the air.

remiges, which are generally more rounded in adults and more pointed in young specimens.

Bird Population Census Taking

In modern zoological field research it is extremely important to make not only a qualitative analysis of animal populations, but also an in-depth quantitative analysis of them. These studies are very useful for obtaining a clear idea of the general conditions existing in a given habitat or environment, for analyzing the situation of the various species in consecutive years and hence for investigating the possible causes of fluctuation and variation.

In recent years bird population census taking has become very important in ornithology, and various techniques for that activity have been thoroughly studied. In order to take a census of a bird population the following two conditions are paramount: (1) the theoretical possibility of recording, one by one, single individuals, either visibly or orally or by some other feature that is evidence of their presence; (2) the stability of the population in question in the chosen area for a period in which you can bring the census itself to completion. The methods used for taking a bird population census vary depending on the group of birds to be considered. Species that nest in colonies (particularly seabirds that nest in rocky parts) are easy to count by direct observation and aerial photography. And migratory species that gather in large flocks in specific areas in winter, such as marshlands, are also easy to count. In fact the International Waterfowl Research Bureau (IWRB) organizes annually, in about mid-January, a simultaneous counting of ducks and coots in the major marshland zones in the western palaearctic region, often using aircraft to facilitate better observation; here verbal descriptions are used, with the help of a portable tape recorder, to give the number of different species present, and observers often back these up with photographic evidence. We can thus make a distinction between complete censuses, with which it is possible to count up all the living individuals of a species, and sample censuses—i.e., those carried out in limited areas, and taken as a representative sample.

Further than this, censuses can be defined as absolute, when they enable us to know the total number of individuals present in a given area, or relative, when they are expressed with a proportional figure in relation to the real density that remains unknown. In-depth studies have been made to work out census-taking methods that can be used with species of birds living in closed habitats, like woods (Passeriformes, Piciformes, and certain Columbiformes).

The area that is preselected for a census must be as representative as possible of the entire environment under study and must be described in detail. The mapping method consists of making a series of visits in the reproductive season to the preselected zone, marking on a map the points where there has

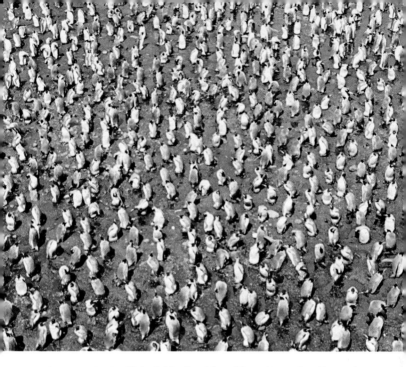

been contact with individuals of the different species (the male singing, alarm calls, direct observations, etc.). By analyzing the results, recurrent contact with individuals of the same species in the same place can provide fairly conclusive evidence of the existence of a territory occupied by a pair. The surface area of the zone chosen for the census taking may vary from twenty-five to seventy-five acres (10–30 hectares), and even extend to 250 acres (100 hectares) if you are taking the census of larger species such as woodpeckers). In this area you must mark out a series of paths running perpendicular to one another and situated about 150 feet (50 meters) apart——(up to 300–700 feet (100–200 meters) in the case of woodpeckers. You must then make several dozen copies of the detailed map of the area (scale, 1:2,000), which will be used on all outings; these must be made at times when the birds are particularly active and in good atmospheric conditions. Record all contacts by means of a series of standardized symbols.

After a certain number of outings or visits (say ten or fifteen), you can gather the data for each species on a separate map. When analyzing the data, there will obviously be several problems, while the results of the census can be obtained by applying validity tests to the data gathered, as well as efficiency tests, although this is not the place to go into these in any detail. A population of small territorial Passeriformes, for example, during the reproductive season is made up of: (1) males that control a territory, form a pair and mate; (2) males that, with two or more distinct territories, mate and breed, possibly in both territories; (3) females who, in the territory, are paired with these two categories of males; (4) unpaired males with territories; (5) migrating males and females, or birds that are erratic or in postnuptial dispersion; (6) young in the nest and, after the nest has been abandoned, vagrant young.

All these categories must be recorded when taking a census. In England the British Trust for Ornithology organizes the Common Bird Census every year; during this, various ornithologists supervise a series of sample areas, making several visits to it (at least eight) in the reproductive period to map out, quantitatively, the pairs of nesting species. In so doing they also keep a check on any variations, year in, year out, and look for the possible causes of them. A census-taking method was worked out by ornithologist C. Ferry; to carry it out, you must select from the area under observation a more or less straight slice——between 1,500 and 3,500 feet (500 to 1,000 meters) long——and work your way slowly through it in good atmospheric conditions, noting all the individuals observed or heard, and any other sign that might indicate their presence. The highest figures then recorded for each pair are used; the number of the pairs recorded is divided by the length of the "slice," which gives the numbers that correspond to Ferry's index of each species and which are proportionate with the density of the same.

Ornithological Clubs, Organizations and Journals
As already mentioned, it is truly very important for anyone interested in ornithology, at any level, not to remain isolated. To coordinate and encourage all scientific bird-watching activities embraced by ornithology, every country has its own ornithological associations, which ensure an ever more efficient development of ornithological studies and publish data and studies made in appropriate reviews and journals, at the same time carrying out the basic task of getting enthusiasts together.

The Protection of Birds
The life of a given species in a given environment is the amazing result of a delicate combination of individual, environment, evolution and adaptation. Ornithologist Robert E. Ricklefs writes (1975):

The adaptation of organisms corresponds to the environmental characteristics, and natural selection acts simply by translating the environmental characteristics into adaptation. The habitat of each species embraces many characteristics. One is given by the physical and chemical factors of the environment to which the species is exposed. Another is represented by the other species——predatory, parasitic, and other——which an individual will interact with. A third pattern of action is the contact with individuals of the same species by means of sexual behaviour, family bonds and social interaction. All these environmental features help to mould the adaptation of an organism.

Each species that lives in a habitat today is part of the environmental balance governed by the laws of nature and has, over thousands of years of evolution, adaptation, improvement, and so on, supplied the place and the role that that species fills. In this progressive evolutionary process various species have become extinct, while others have given rise to new species.

The awareness that each natural element is part of a strictly balanced whole—just as the parts of a mosaic make a perfect picture—has escaped *Homo sapiens* for too long, and as a result man has indiscriminately meddled with the environment, preying upon it and plundering it without ever aligning his actions to those of nature, of which he is a part, and on which he depends. The egocentric attitude of industrialized and technological man, setting himself arrogantly at the center of the universe with nature at his beck and call, has led to the irrational running-down of natural resources in the interests of making an immediate profit, which benefits only a small and powerful elite, and is reaching a critical point. Our present-day society has made a status symbol out of the material acquisition of superfluous goods, with not a thought for the price we have paid and the higher and higher price that we shall pay in the future in terms of the quality of our lives, on an individual and collective level.

The remedies for the irrational consumer onslaught of our consumer society do exist, even though they require a profound reversal of social tendencies together with a cultural revolution. We need to totally reevaluate the qualitative values of our existence. We must eliminate destructive speculation and selfish private interests behind the deterioration that we are now witnessing, in order to promote a life that is in perfect harmony with nature, that uses nature in a rational way by means of organized planning of any activity that will affect the environment. We must contain the rate of growth of the world's human population, eliminate all superfluous goods and products and stop the serious squandering of energy resources caused by consumerism.

Throughout the world, the major environmental crisis now facing us has triggered studies and research aimed at finding an alternative program to propose to governments, politicians, industries and scientists. The work of Barry Commoner, of the Center for the Biology of Natural Systems at Washington University in St. Louis, is dedicated to a fierce criticism of the consumer society, in which technology itself is not brought to trial, but rather the use of it, which serves a few but is fatal for the rest of us; the investigations carried out at the instigation of the Club of Rome by various institutes and scholars; and the *Blueprint for Survival* brought out by the review *The Ecologist*. In this area, most particularly in Europe, recent years have seen the emergence of full-fledged political movements under the umbrella of ecology.

The destructive activities of man have obviously had remarkable repercussions on the lives of many animal species, some of which have been wiped off the face of the earth forever. Indirect actions such as the progressive alteration of natural environments and pollution in general, together with direct activities such as indiscriminate hunting, have reduced the numbers of many species and destroyed some for all time. To see which are the most threatened, we should take into account each species' present situation, starting with the following seven criteria laid down by ornithologist Paul Geroudet (in S. Frugis,

65

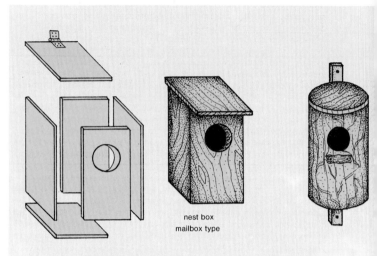

nest box
mailbox type

ed., *Enciclopedia degli uccelli d'Europa*, 1971–72):

1. Extension of the nesting area and relative changes in the last decade.
2. Actual number of the population and the general trend of its evolution.
3. Ecological and ethological sensitivity (especially the dependence on a specific biological habitat or on a specific type of food, the need for social life and safety, the adaptive capacities).
4. Viability (particularly the rate of reproduction and natural mortality).
5. Direct dangers (hunting or other such activities, the encroachment of pesticides, etc.).
6. Indirect dangers (the alteration or destruction of biological habitats and food resources).
7. Possibility of organizing effective protective measures and improving the general situation.

Here are some examples taken from a long and saddening list of species threatened with extinction:
On the island of Bermuda an interesting procellariiform used to build its nest; it is mentioned in the log of a sixteenth-century Spanish captain called Diego Ramirez and was called the Cahow (*Pterodroma cahow*) by the local natives because of the song sung by adults of the species at night during the reproductive period. An English colony that was set up on the island in 1609 brought with it the black rat. The rats preyed on

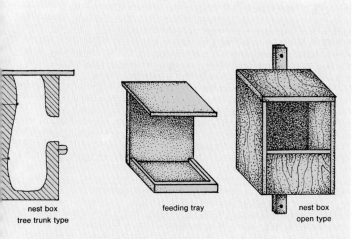

nest box
tree trunk type

feeding tray

nest box
open type

the Cahow nestlings, and the settlers caught the young birds for the table, to such an extent that for three centuries the species was considered to be extinct. A nesting colony of Cahows was detected in 1945. In 1951 ornithologists R. Cushman Murphy and F. Mowbray discovered seven nests of this species, but today it is again threatened by the natural competition posed by another seabird, the White-tailed Tropic-bird (*Phaethon lepturus*), which takes over the Cahow's burrow nests, as well as by the accumulation, via the food chain, of strong concentrations of DDT and other insecticides, which have contaminated the marine fauna in the Cahow's feeding areas.

September 1914: in the Cincinnati Zoo, the last Passenger Pigeon (*Ectopistes migratorius*) died; this species had been extremely abundant in the past, but had been mercilessly hunted and literally wiped out. In past centuries this columbiform had been very common and widespread; people even tell of airborne flocks obscuring the sun. But both the nesting colonies and the migrating flocks were the objects of systematic destruction by every conceivable means, to the point where, toward the end of the nineteenth century, the species had become rarer and rarer. Protective measures were taken far too late, and today, because of man, the species has disappeared forever.

In New Zealand there was a sturdy indigenous rail, the Takahe (*Notornis mantelli*) which was for a long time considered extinct, since there had been no information about it for about fifty years. In 1948 a sighting of it was made, however. At one

67

time this species was well distributed in the North and South islands of New Zealand: at the present time it has a population of about 2,000 pairs confined to an area of about 250 square miles (650 sq. km.) in the Fiordland National Park, including the Murchison Mountains and a small adjacent area.

Examples of species already extinct or doomed to extinction would make a long list. Among the extinct species are the Great Auk (*Pinguinis impennis*), a flightless seabird, common in North Atlantic islands and coastal regions, particularly in Iceland, where it was mercilessly hunted for many years and died out completely in 1844, on Eldey Island; the Dodo (*Raphus cucullatus*)—a columbiform common on Mauritius in the Indian Ocean, and likewise ruthlessly hunted, as well as being threatened by all the domestic animals imported by settlers—which finally disappeared for good in 1681. Among the numerous threatened species, are the Mauritius Kestrel (*Falco punctatus*), possibly the rarest bird in the world, only 13 found in Mauritius; the California Condor (*Gymnogyps californianus*), found in the coastal region of California with 50 or 60 examples; the Whooping Crane (*Grus americana*), which nests in the Wood Buffalo National Park in central Canada, and winters in the Aransas National Wildlife Refuge in southern Texas, totalling about 80 individuals.

Protecting nature certainly does not mean ''mummifying'' it; rather, it means managing it rationally and in a scientific way, in harmony with the laws of nature and for the well-being of the community as a whole. It is evident that any international plan for the conservation of our natural resources, as we have already seen, must have a general program to control man's meddling with the earth's surface, be it in the form of building, industry or agriculture. Today, luckily, it seems that the conservation ethic can hold its own as an accepted philosophy of life. It is nevertheless undeniable that the revolutionary implications of a different emphasis in the relationship between man and nature, based no longer on the unchecked squandering of the environment but on a harmonious equilibrium, is widely opposed by the influential economic interests that exist in the world today. For this reason the act of protection has also become urgent and widespread, to be embarked upon before it is too late and wherever it is possible.

Considerable effort to coordinate this line of action has been made at an international level, in order to establish a worldwide plan. To this end, 1922 saw the creation of the International Council for the Protection of Birds, 1948 the creation of the International Union for Nature Conservation and Natural Resources, and 1961 the World Wildlife Fund, operating at the international level and at a national level in many countries throughout the world.

Among the immediate and tangible measures concerning the protection of birds that can be instantly put into action, let us mention: (1) studies and research concerning the biology, requirements and status of the most threatened species—an essential basis for any effective protective action; (2) the creation of parks, refuges and reserves to preserve specific habitats; (3) strictly enforced legislation to do with hunting; (4) direct actions to promote environmental recuperation (among steps to be taken, where the environmental balance has been meddled with, we can mention the establishment of artificial nests; and among steps aimed at "recovering" habitats we can mention the reintroduction of birds); (5) nesting in captivity for the rarest species.

There are many examples of such actions being taken across the globe; all the threatened species are the objects of in-depth research, and in various places there are now major projects aimed at the reproduction of rare species in captivity. Deserving special mention are the program that has been carried on for years at the Cornell University Ornithology Laboratory, for the reproduction in captivity of birds of prey (this program also includes the release of subjects born in captivity to the wild), and the program embracing ducks and geese from all over the world in the hands of the Slimbridge Wildfowl Trust in England, which, among other successes, has stopped the extinction of the rare Nene, or Hawaiian Goose (*Branta sandvicensis*). Numbers of natural areas of major importance have been turned into parks, reserves and refuges and have enabled numerous species to survive in the wild state.

When it comes to reintroducing species, it is necessary to carry out in-depth studies aimed at taking into account the ecological and behavioral characteristics and needs of the species to be reintroduced, as well as the features of the site into which they are to be released. It is also necessary to make careful preparations with the animals to be reintroduced (studying the subspecies, relations between the sexes, etc.) and to study the method of release. Obviously, subjects reintroduced must be carefully followed and watched.

Reintroduction can be embarked upon only when all the causes previously responsible for extinction have been removed from the habitat into which the subjects are to be released. Reintroduction projects have been planned and, in large part, undertaken in Europe, for the Griffon Vulture in the Massif Central in France, for the Bearded Vulture in the western Alps (Haute Savoie), for the Eagle Owl in Sweden and Germany, and for the White-tailed Eagle and Great Bustard in England. Another active measure concerning protection is the use of artificial nests. These devices increase the possibility of finding suitable nesting sites for various species.

For some time now, in order to safeguard the small and seriously threatened populations of vultures still present in Europe, artificial nesting sites have been organized with carcasses provided on an *ad hoc* basis; the purpose of this is to make it easier to find food for those useful species. This system has been organized for the remaining nuclei of vultures in Sardinia, in the form of a World Wildlife Fund project headed by ornithologist Helmar Schenk. All these efforts, plus simpler tricks of planting vegetable fibers used for nesting and for feeding wild young, have already borne fruit in many instances. But it is still important for us to realize that we have to do a great deal to alter the present-day critical situation, using the example of our own existence, by disseminating ideas about animal protection and the rational management of nature, and by belonging to groups that are struggling to live by those ideas.

1 ACANTHIS FLAMMEA
Common Redpoll

Classification   Order Passeriformes, Family Fringillidae.
Characteristics   About 12.5 cm long (5″). The upper parts have a grayish-brown coloring streaked with black; the throat and upper part of the breast are pink in the male; the sides are yellowish pink with black streaks; the belly is whitish; the forehead and top of the head are red or crimson, and on the head itself there is a brighter red marking. There are black markings above and beneath the beak.
Habitat   Northern forests, especially birch, conifers (or with alder, willows and junipers); mountainous regions, tundra
Distribution   Northern Europe, northern Asia and North America. Sometimes moves farther southward.
Life and habits   Generally nests in conifers, birch, alder or willows. The nest is cup-shaped, made of brushwood, twigs, roots, lichens and down. Female lays 3–7 eggs (usually 4 or 5), and hatches them herself for 10–13 days. The nidicolous nestlings are fed by both parents and leave the nest after 11–14 days. The Redpoll lays 1 or 2 clutches each year. It feeds principally on seeds (especially birch and alder), but is also insectivorous.

---

2 ACCIPITER GENTILIS
Northern Goshawk

Classification   Order Falconiformes, Family Accipitridae.
Characteristics   About 48–58 cm. long (19–23″), resembling a large Sparrow Hawk. The male is smaller than the female. The adults have a dark ash-brown coloring in the upper parts, while the lower parts are whitish and closely barred with dark markings. The upper parts of the young are paler, tending to reddish, and the lower parts are tawny, with large dark brown markings.
Habitat   Lowland and mountain forests and woods, interspersed with open spaces.
Distribution   Europe, palaearctic Asia, North America.
Life and habits   Nests in trees. Lays 1–5 eggs (more commonly 2 or 3) at intervals of 3 days. Incubation falls largely to the female, who is fed by the male during this period, and lasts 36–41 days. The nestlings develop their feathers within 18–38 days after being born. At about 40 days they leave the nest and at about 45 days will make their first flight, becoming fairly independent at about 70 days. The Goshawk is a fearsome woodland hunter, pursuing its prey through trees, and often flying very low and swiftly, showing great agility. It hunts birds, particularly crows, pigeons, thrushes, pheasants and partridges, and members of the Tetraonidae, as well as mammals (hares and mice), lizards and insects. It eats its prey on the ground.

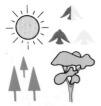

3 ACCIPITER NISUS
Eurasian Sparrow Hawk

Classification Order Falconiformes, Family Accipitridae.
Characteristics About 27–37 cm long (11–15″). The female, which is larger than the male, has dark-colored upper parts and whitish lower parts finely barred with dark brown markings. The male is dark (blackboard- or slate-gray) in the upper parts and barred reddish lower parts. In the young the upper parts are brown with reddish-edged feathers, and the lower parts have broader bars.
Habitat Lowland and mountain woods and forests interspersed with open spaces.
Distribution Europe, palaearctic Asia, northwest Africa.

Life and habits Lays just one clutch of 4 or 5 eggs (sometimes 2, 6 or 7), in a nest made of brushwood, branches, vegetable matter, et cetera, and built in trees, preferably coniferous woods. The eggs are laid at intervals of 2–4 days. The incubation, which is the task of the female alone, starts when the second or third egg is laid and lasts 35–42 days. The male feeds the female during the incubation period. The young develop their feathers within 13–28 days and are ready for their first flight after 32 days, but continue to depend on their parents for a further 27 days, approximately. The Sparrow Hawk hunts by flying low along the edge of woodland above the undergrowth, catching mainly birds and their nestlings, as well as small mammals and insects.

4 ACROCEPHALUS ARUNDINACEUS
Great Reed Warbler

Classification Order Passeriformes, Family Sylviidae.
Characteristics About 19.5 cm. long (7″) the largest of the European marsh or reed warblers. The beak is longer and broader than in other species of European warbler, and there is a conspicuous eyebrow. The plumage is dark chestnut brown in the upper parts and paler in the lower.
Habitat Marshlands, canebrakes, by rivers and lakes.
Distribution Europe, Africa and Asia.

Life and habits Nests among reeds, building a nest made of interwoven vegetable matter and supported by the reeds themselves. There is a single clutch, usually of 4–6 eggs (rarely 3), which are incubated for a period of 14–15 days by both parents. The nestlings are reared by both parents and remain for about 12 days in the nest. The Great Reed Warbler emits a song that ornithologist G. Mountfort defines as "harsh and prolonged"—a wide range of notes that sound like *karrakarra, krik-krik, gurk-gurk-gurk*. It feeds mainly on various insects and invertebrates. A pair has been observed in Hungary feeding its young with small fish.

5 ACROCEPHALUS SCHOENOBAENUS
Sedge Warbler

Classification   Order Passeriformes, Family Sylviidae.
Characteristics   About 12.5 cm. long (5″), with striking cream-colored eyebrows. The coloring is dark brownish, with several bars in the upper parts; the rump is tawny, and the lower parts are paler. Young individuals have a more yellowish coloring with a few markings at the top of the breast and on the throat.
Habitat   Wetlands, canebrakes, low vegetation with scrub.
Distribution   Europe, Asia and Africa.
Life and habits   Nests among reeds or in low vegetation. Lays a single clutch consisting of 3–8 eggs (usually 5 or 6). Incubation is the responsibility largely of the female, for 13 or 14 days. The nidicolous nestlings are reared by both parents and remain in the nest for 10–12 days. The Sedge Warbler feeds mainly on insects and other invertebrates.

6 AEGITHALOS CAUDATUS
Long-tailed Tit

Classification   Order Passeriformes, Family Paridae.
Characteristics   About 14 cm. long (6″). The adults have a white head, neck and lower parts (of the numerous subspecies *A. c. caudatus* has a completely white head, whereas *A. c. rosaceus* has a broad black eyebrow). The back is usually grayish black, the rump reddish, and the tail long and tapering. In young individuals the sides of the head and nape of the neck are brownish, and the back is brown. Flight is undulating and irregular.
Habitat   Woodlands, parks and gardens.
Distribution   Europe and Asia.
Life and habits   It builds a nest typically in the fork of a tree or in bushes. Both the male and female help to build it. The resulting nest is oval shaped, made of mosses, lichens and vegetable matter, with an opening in the upper part. The pair may take up to three weeks to build it. In it 5–16 eggs (usually 8–12) are laid and incubated mainly by the female, who is fed by the male, for 12–14 days. The nidicolous nestlings leave the nest after 14–18 days; the Long-tailed Tit makes erratic movements, sometimes in groups of fifty-or-so individuals. It feeds on insects, larvae, spiders and other invertebrates.

7 AEGYPIUS MONACHUS
Cinereous Vulture

Classification Order Falconiformes, Family Accipitridae.
Characteristics About 105 cm. long (40"), it has a uniform dark coloring tending to dark brown. The head and neck have bluish-gray naked skin with blackish down on the head and a collar of feathers round the neck. Immature birds have the head covered with thick black down. In flight it looks impressively large, with a slightly wedge-shaped tail.
Habitat Lowlands and wooded mountainous areas.
Distribution This vulture is becoming increasingly rare. It is found in central Asia from Turkey to Afghanistan, Mongolia and the Urals. The Cinereous Vulture reproduces in considerable numbers in southwestern Spain and on Majorca; there are smaller populations in Yugoslavia, Greece and the Crimea, while odd pairs or individuals have been observed in Cyprus, Crete and Sardinia.
Life and habits Generally nests in trees, building a large and rather crude nest which is used year after year. In it it lays a single egg. Incubation, for which both parents are responsible, lasts 52–55 days. The nestling is fed by its parents with regurgitated food, and develops its plumage in 30–60 days. The first flight takes place after about a hundred days. The young bird remains in the nest for a further six weeks. The Cinereous Vulture feeds almost exclusively on carrion, very rarely on small injured animals or very slow-moving animals like tortoises.

8 AGAPORNIS FISCHERI
Fischer's Lovebird

Classification Order Psittaciformes, Family Psittacidae.
Characteristics Lovebirds reach a length of 13–17 cm. (5–7"), with a short round tail and mainly green plumage. According to various ornithologists there are 6 to 9 species of lovebirds. The name "lovebird" (*Agapornis* means "bird of love") suggests the very close bond that unites each pair of this species. Fischer's Lovebird has dark greenish plumage uppermost, with greenish-brown breast and head except for the front part, which is slightly reddish; there is a white ring round the eye.
Habitat Wooded steppes and forests.
Distribution Eastern Africa.
Life and habits Often found in tight groups where food, consisting mainly of seeds, is readily available. The nest is made in hollows in trees, and while some species of lovebirds carry the building materials to the nest site with their beak, others transport it by wedging it in the plumage on their back or rump. Five or six eggs are usually laid, and they are incubated by the female for about 21 days. The nidicolous nestlings leave the nest after about 40 days, but remain with their parents for a further fortnight or so.

9 AGELAIUS PHOENICEUS
Red-winged Blackbird

Classification   Order Passeriformes, Family Icteridae.
Characteristics   One of the commonest species in the family, this bird is 20–25 cm. long (8–10″). The plumage of the male is completely black except for a broad scarlet marking on each wing. The female is chestnut colored on the upper parts, off-white on the lower, with dark bars. The beak is long and slender, and the legs are black. A similar species is *A. tricolor* with a darker red marking with white edges.
Habitat   Marshlands and cultivated land.
Distribution   North America.
Life and habits   This species, which has considerably enlarged its distribution area in recent years, often has gregarious habits. It almost always builds its nest in canebrakes, bushes or small trees near water; but in recent years it has also started nesting in cultivated areas. The nest is cup-shaped and woven with vegetable fibers; it contains 3–5 eggs (usually 4), which are incubated for 11 or 12 days solely by the female. The nestlings take to the air at 10 or 11 days. There are usually two broods a year. It feeds particularly on insects and other invertebrates in the warm months, and on seeds and crushed grit in autumn and winter.

10 AIX GALERICULATA
Mandarin Duck

Classification   Order Anseriformes, Family Anatidae.
Characteristics   About 42 cm. long (16″). The male has unmistakable coloring——wing feathers that are orange and look like vertical "sails," wide chestnut-colored "sideburns," a dark breast, a red beak, a blackish top of the head, and a large white marking behind and above the eye. The female has dull brownish-gray coloring, green wings and a blackish beak. Immature males and males in the postnuptial state resemble females, but the beak remains black, and not blackish.
Habitat   Ponds, inland water, lakes.
Distribution   Asia (especially China and Japan), artificially introduced to Europe.
Life and habits   Generally nests in hollows in trees. Lays, almost invariably, just one clutch of 9–12 eggs, which are incubated by the female for 28–30 days. The nidifugous nestlings are active and independent and follow the female, who takes care of them in the earliest stages.

11 ALAEMON ALAUDIPES
Hoopoe Lark

Classification Order Passeriformes, Family Alaudidae.
Characteristics About 20 cm. long (8″). It has a distinctive curved beak and a fairly long tail. It has dull coloring, gray-brownish in the upper parts, with a pale, streaked breast and white belly. The wings have a marked black-and-white pattern. The outer rectrices have white markings.
Habitat Desert and sandy regions with little or no vegetation, stony ground.
Distribution North Africa to southwestern Asia.
Life and habits It builds a crude nest usually on the ground, in the lee of a clump of grass or a bush. It lays 2–4 eggs, which are pale with large brown, green or pink spots. There is just one brood; there is little information about the incubation period and the rearing of the young. The Hoopoe Lark feeds on seeds and insects, particularly larvae that it pulls from the ground with its beak. A kindred species is Dupont's Lark (*Chersophilus duponti*), about 7″ long with a more barred coloring and an only slightly curved beak (less than *Alaemon alaudipes*), native of northern Africa.

12 ALAUDA ARVENSIS
Skylark

Classification Order Passeriformes, Family Alaudidae.
Characteristics About 18 cm. long (7″). The upper parts are brownish with close black stripes, and the lower parts are tawny white with broad dark stripes on the breast. In the tail the outer rectrices are white, as are the rear edges of the wings in flight. There is a small crest on the head. The young are dark brown in the upper parts with whitish spots on the feathers.
Habitat Open, grassy places, open country, steppe and heathland.
Distribution Europe, Asia and northwest Africa.
Life and habits It nests on the ground, in a hollow sheltered by clumps of grass; the nest is made of dry grasses and roots, and is well disguised as a result. It lays two or three clutches of 3 or 4 eggs (sometimes 5, rarely 7). The incubation period, for which only the female is responsible, lasts 11 days. The nidicolous nestlings are fed by both parents, leave the nest after 9 or 10 days and fly well at 20 days. The skylark feeds mainly on vegetable matter—grains of corn, seeds, buds, et cetera; in spring and summer it is insectivorous. During the nesting period it often takes to the air, climbing several hundred feet into the sky and singing into the wind; it then swoops back down to earth with its wings held tightly together, opening them just a few yards from the ground.

13 ALCA TORDA
Razorbill

Classification   Order Charadriiformes, Family Alcidae.
Characteristics   About 42 cm. long (16.5″). Its upper plumage is black, and its lower white. The secondary remiges have white tips that, in flight, form a white border on the rear edge of the base of the wings. A distinctive feature is the strong beak with the white line running along it. In the mating period there is also a white line that runs from the base of the bill to the eye. In winter the throat and sides of the neck turn from summer black to white. The upper parts of young birds are dark chestnut in color.
Habitat   Open sea, rocky crags, shingle beaches.
Distribution   Nests along the coasts of northern Europe and the northeastern coast of North America and Greenland, and is found wintering farther south.
Life and habits   It has gregarious habits, nesting in large colonies, often mixed with other, similar species like the Common Murre (*Uria aalge*), in rocks and crags and also in shingle on beaches. It lays a single egg (sometimes two) in cracks, holes and rocky ledges without building a nest. Incubation is the responsibility of both sexes and lasts for 25–35 days. The nestling is reared by both parents, and it leaves the nest at 12–15 days to reach the sea accompanied by an adult. It feeds on fish, crustaceans and mollusks.

14 ALCEDO ATTHIS
Eurasian Kingfisher

Classification   Order Coraciiformes, Family Alcedinidae.
Characteristics   About 16 cm. long (6″). It is an unmistakable bird because of its bright coloring and compact body with its long, tough, flattened beak. The upper parts have a coloring that, depending on the refraction of light, is either brilliant blue or emerald green; the lower parts are pale chestnut brown, the throat is white and the legs red. It can often be seen resting on branches or posts near water; from these perches it dives to catch its prey. It usually flies low over the water; its song is rapid, accompanied by bobbing movements of the wings.
Habitat   All watercourses (rivers, streams, canals, lakes), and marshland.
Distribution   Europe, Asia and North Africa.
Life and habits   For its nest it digs out a long tunnel on the banks of rivers, in piles of sand, et cetera; this is on a slight slope and 45–130 cm. in length (18–50″). The tunnel ends in a "chamber" that is the actual nest. In it the kingfisher lays 6 or 7 eggs (sometimes 4–8, rarely 10), which are incubated by both sexes for 19–21 days. The young are reared by both parents and leave the nest at 23–27 days. It feeds on fish, insects, worms and mollusks.

15 ALECTORIS GRAECA
Rock Partridge

Classification   Order Galliformes, Family Phasianidae.
Characteristics   About 35 cm. long (14″). Its upper plumage is gray-brown and the lower plumage is paler, tending to yellow on the belly, gray-brown on the breast and whitish on the sides with dark stripes. At a distance it is not easy to tell it apart from the Red-legged Partridge (*A. rufa*) and the Chukar Partridge (*A. chukar*). It has a well-defined black collar.
Habitat   Areas with a reasonable altitude, stony or rocky; also slightly wooded mountains. In winter it moves to lower altitudes.
Distribution   Southeastern Europe and southwestern Asia.
Life and habits   It nests on the ground among rocks and stony ground with sparse vegetation. On the average it lays a single clutch of 6–21 eggs (usually 8–14). The eggs are laid at intervals of 24–36 hours. Incubation is the task of the female and lasts 24–26 days. The nidifugous nestlings are reared by both parents and reach adult size in about 2 months. They remain together and form groups in autumn. It emits a call that sounds like *whit-whit-whit-pitchi-i,* and a staccato song in spring and autumn.

16 ALECTORIS RUFA
Red-legged Partridge

Classification   Order Galliformes, Family Phasianidae.
Characteristics   About 32 cm. long (13″), not easy to tell apart from the Rock Partridge (*A. graeca*) at a distance, but at close range has a wide reddish-brown collar that runs from the black line and ends up in the form of small pale markings. The upper parts are rust-brown, the breast is bluish gray, and the lower parts tend to pale yellowish; the sides are less closely striped than the Rock Partridge's.
Habitat   Cultivated areas, untilled land, hills, clayey, sandy or stony ground.
Distribution   Southwestern France, the Iberian peninsula, northwestern Italy, Corsica, and other offshore islands; reintroduced to England.
Life and habits   It nests on the ground in sparse vegetation and amid stones. It usually has a single brood, even though the female can lay two successive clutches in two different nests, one being incubated by the male and the other by the female. The clutch usually consists of 10–16 eggs—sometimes 7–20, and more rarely up to 28—which are incubated for a period of 23–25 days. The nidifugous nestlings stay together until the next reproductive season.

17 AMANDAVA AMANDAVA
Avadavat

Classification Order Passeriformes, Family Estrildidae.
Characteristics The Family Estrildidae is fairly closely related to the Ploceidae (weaverbirds). It includes species in which the design of the inside of the mouth is a distinctive feature, consisting of dark lines or dots on the palate, tongue and base of the beak, which are particularly obvious in young birds. The Avadavat is about 10 cm. long (4″). The male is quite brightly colored—reddish with chestnut-colored wings, a dark tail, small white spots on the body, and a reddish beak. The female has duller coloring: brownish gray with a dark tail and reddish beak. Both have a blackish marking around the eye.
Habitat Forests, marshlands, canebrakes, watercourses.
Distribution Southeast Asia.
Life and habits This bird is widely used for commercial purposes, as are many of the Estrildidae. It has been imported by man to many tropical islands, and to southern Egypt, from where it has now disappeared, and so on. Some individuals that have escaped from captivity have bred in the wild, in various European countries, including France, Germany and Italy. it feeds on vegetable matter.

18 AMAZONA AESTIVA
Turquoise-fronted Parrot

Classification Order Psittaciformes, Family Psittacidae.
Characteristics These are typically arboreal and climbing parrots that are from 26 to 47 cm. in length (10–18″), depending on the exact species. Their plumage is predominantly green. The ornithologist Kurt Kolar lists 26 species under the genus *Amazona*. The Turquoise-fronted Parrot is about 35–41 cm. long (14–16″), with a mainly green plumage with red and bluish markings on the wings; the head is pale yellow, except for the green nape and blue forehead.
Habitat Forests.
Distribution South America.
Life and habits It nests in hollows in trees, where it usually lays 2 eggs; these are incubated mainly by the female. Incubation lasts about 30 days. The diet consists principally of vegetable matter (seeds, nuts and fruit). Two species of *Amazona* are becoming increasingly rare—the St. Vincent Parrot (*A. guildingii*) which is about 41 cm. long (16″) and is found on the island of St. Vincent; and the Imperial Parrot (*A. imperialis*), which is the largest species, reaching 47 cm. in length (18″).

19 ANARHYNCHUS FRONTALIS
Wrybill Plover

Classification   Order Charadriiformes, Family Charadriidae.
Characteristics   It has grayish-brown plumage in the upper parts and pale lower parts, with a thin black bar just beneath the neck. The beak is distinctive and typical of the plovers, but the tip is twisted toward the right.
Habitat   Beaches, coastal regions and wetlands.
Distribution   New Zealand.
Life and habits   The Wrybill Plover is a truly distinctive bird because of the strange shape of the beak, which enables it to extract prey (various invertebrates) from beneath stones, and always from the same direction. The modifications occurring in the beaks and bills of various species of Charadriiformes are typical for their alimentary specialization; we should mention the Ruddy Turnstone (*Arenaria interpros*) and the Pied Avocet (*Recurvirostra avosetta*), which are discussed elsewhere, and the Spoon-billed Sandpiper (*Eurynorhynchus pygmaeus*), of northeastern Siberia, which has its bill flattened rather like a fish sluice and feeds in the same way as the Northern Shoveler (*Anas clypeata*).

20 ANAS ACUTA
Common Pintail

Classification   Order Anseriformes, Family Anatidae.
Characteristics   The male is about 66-70 cm. long (26-28″), and the female about 55-58 cm. (22-23″). With his nuptial plumage the male's head and neck are dark colored with a white band that runs down the sides of the neck as far as the breast; the sides and back are grayish, the wings green, the scapular feathers black; the subcaudal feathers are black, the abdomen white and the central tail feathers black and long. The female has a dull brownish coloring; she is slender, with a thin neck and pointed tail. The young and the males in their postnesting plumage resemble the females, but have darker upper parts.
Habitat   Tundra, lakes, marshlands, estuaries and coastal areas.
Distribution   Eurasia, America; also winters in Africa.
Life and habits   It nests in holes in the ground in low vegetation. It lays a single clutch of 6-12 eggs (more commonly, 7, 8 or 9), which are incubated by the female for 21-23 days. The nidifugous nestlings fly when they are about seven weeks old. The Common Pintail feeds on vegetable matter (seeds, algae, aquatic plants) as well as on invertebrates.
Note: In the photo the male is on the left.

21 ANAS CRECCA
Green-winged Teal

Classification Order Anseriformes, Family Anatidae.
Characteristics About 35 cm. long (14″), this is the smallest European duck. The European male has a horizontal white stripe on its scapular feathers, but the American male has a vertical white stripe in front of the wing. The head is chestnut-colored, with a green band that runs from the eye rearward and pale yellowish markings on both sides of the rump, which is black. The female is brownish; both sexes have green wings with a white edge.
Habitat Marshlands, ponds, estuaries, coasts, lakes, woodland clearings.

Distribution Europe, Asia, Africa, North America.
Life and habits It nests on the ground in vegetation, especially in marshland. It lays a single clutch of 8–12 eggs (sometimes as many as 16), which are incubated by the female, while the male loiters near at hand, for a period of 21–28 days. The nestlings are nidifugous and have blackish-gray beaks, legs and toes. The female, with the male close by, takes care of the young, which fly at about 44 days.
Note: The photo shows a male.

22 ANAS PENELOPE
Eurasian Wigeon

Classification Order Anseriformes, Family Anatidae.
Characteristics The male is about 49 cm. long (19″) with a chestnut-colored head, yellowish forehead, whitish-gray back and sides, pinkish-brown breast, and the subcaudal area black with white edging. The female is about 44 cm. long (17″) with uniform coloring, and is more tawny than other female ducks. Both male and female have a brown-gray beak with a black tip and when in flight show white-edged green wings and a pale-colored abdomen. The young resemble the female.
Habitat Lakes, rivers, heathland, marshland, lagoons, estuaries, coasts, and wooded areas.
Distribution Europe, Asia and Africa; rare in North America.
Life and habits It nests on the ground in vegetation and lays a single clutch usually of 7–8 eggs (more rarely 6–10). Incubation is the task of the female and lasts 22–25 days. The nidifugous nestlings are looked after by the female, with help from the male, and are independent by about 6 weeks. The Eurasian Wigeon feeds on an almost entirely vegetarian diet.
Note: The photo shows a male in the foreground.

23 ANAS PLATYRHYNCHOS
Mallard

Classification   Order Anseriformes, Family Anatidae .
Characteristics   The male reaches a length of 57 cm. (22″) and the female 49 cm. (20″). The male has a green head with a white collar, a brownish breast and pale grayish upper parts. The female is brownish and in flight shows a purplish-violet wing coloring between two white bars. The male usually has this eclipse plumage between September and June; in the July-August period he takes on the postnuptial plumage that makes him closely resemble the female.
Habitat   Marshlands, lakes, rivers, estuaries, lagoons, ponds.
Distribution   Europe, Asia, northwest Africa and North America.
Life and habits   It nests near water, in vegetation. It lays on average 10–12 eggs (more rarely 7–16), which are incubated by the female, when laying is over, for 28 or 29 days. The nidifugous young are looked after mainly by the female and fly after 7–8 weeks. The Mallard feeds mainly on vegetable matter (seeds, shoots, leaves, berries and grains), but also on insects, mollusks, crustaceans and worms.
Note: In the photo the male is the lower bird.

---

24 ANAS QUERQUEDULA
Garganey Teal

Classification   Order Anseriformes, Family Anatidae.
Characteristics   The male, which is about 40 cm. long (16″), has a broad white band that runs from the eye to the nape of the neck. The plumage is mottled brown on the breast and sides; the abdomen is white. There are long scapular feathers edged with grayish markings. The female is about 36 cm. long (14″) and has a uniform brownish coloring. In flight they show white-edged green wings and in the male the front part of the wings is bluish-gray. The young resemble the female.
Habitat   Marshland, lakes, ponds, boggy areas with plenty of vegetation.
Distribution   Europe, Asia, Africa (it makes a partial round-trip migration—i.e., one that takes different routes outward and back).
Life and habits   It nests on the ground in vegetation. It lays one clutch, usually of 8–11 eggs (sometimes 6–14), which are incubated by the female for 21–23 days. The nidifugous young are reared by the female and fly after 5–6 weeks. The Garganey's diet consists of animal and vegetable matter (small fishes, small amphibians, crustaceans, mollusks, insects, worms, shoots, leaves, roots and seeds).
Note: The photo shows a male.

25 ANASTOMUS LAMELLIGERUS
African Openbilled Stork

Classification Order Ciconiiformes, Family Ciconiidae.
Characteristics This bird is about 80 cm. long (31"); the coloring of the plumage is blackish with metallic highlights. The beak is distinctive; the two "halves" of the beak touch only at the base and the tip; in the central part, where the two halves do not touch, the upper part of the beak has horny formations like bristles. A similar species is the Asian Openbill (*Anastomus oscitans*), with white plumage, black wings and tail, and reddish-white feet.
Habitat Wooded regions, canebrakes, lakes and marshlands.
Distribution Africa.
Life and habits The specific structure of the beak prevents this species from catching amphibians or similar creatures, but this beak is very useful for prying open the shells of bivalve mollusks or for extracting the flesh from snails' shells. Openbills nest in trees, bushes and canebrakes. The Asian Openbill, which is locally distributed on the continent, nests in colonies of up to 60 pairs and, like the African species, claps its beak. In flight its neck is slightly bent.

26 ANHINGA ANHINGA
Anhinga or American Darter

Classification Order Pelecaniformes, Family Anhingidae.
Characteristics Very slender in appearance, with a very long neck, and long, pointed beak. It measures about 85–90 cm. in length (34–36"); its plumage is completely black, with white stripes on the wings. The plumage is similar in the two sexes, but the female is browner. The beak is yellow, and the feet are webbed.
Habitat Marshland, slow-flowing rivers, ponds.
Distribution Tropical and subtropical regions of America.
Life and habits In searching for food, it swims completely underwater except for its long neck and head. The nest is made with branches on trees jutting over water; in it the Anhinga lays 2–5 eggs (usually 3–4). Both parents are responsible for the incubation, which lasts 25–28 days. The nestlings are fed by both parents and remain in the nest for several weeks. This species nests in colonies, often together with other waterfowl. Food is taken exclusively in water and consists mainly of fish, but also of aquatic insects, amphibians and snakes. Its long neck (with more vertebrae than in other birds) can be jerked quickly forward, enabling this species to catch a wide variety of prey, using the beak like a harpoon.

29 ANSER ANSER
Graylag Goose

Classification   Order Anseriformes, Family Anatidae.
Characteristics   About 70–89 cm. long (28–35″) the male is larger than the female), it has a uniform brownish-gray coloring with pale-edged feathers in the upper parts; the tail is gray with a white tip and the tail coverts are white; the breast and abdomen are brownish gray, with a few small black spots; the beak is orange or red, and the legs and feet are pinkish. In immature birds the legs are more grayish, and there are no black spots on the breast.
Habitat   Marshlands, wetlands, estuaries, lakes, dry cultivated fields.
Distribution   Europe and Asia.
Life and habits   The Graylag Goose is the forebear of the domestic forms of goose that are farmed in large numbers nowadays. It has gregarious habits and flies in flocks often in the classic V formation. It generally nests in depressions in the ground in vegetation. It lays a single clutch of 3–8 eggs (usually 4, 5 or 6), which are incubated by the female for 27 or 28 days. The nidifugous nestlings become independent after about 8 weeks. The Graylag Goose feeds on vegetable matter (plants, tubers, grain, aquatic plants). It makes a striking loud, deep call that sounds something like a nasal *pink-pink*.

30 ANSER CAERULESCENS
Snow Goose

Classification   Order Anseriformes, Family Anatidae.
Characteristics   The male is about 78 cm. long (31″), and the female is about 70 cm. (28″). The subspecies properly defined as the Greater Snow Goose (*A. c. atlanticus*) has white coloring with black primary remiges, a red beak, pink legs and sometimes orange markings on the head. The coverts and base of the primary feathers are gray. Immature birds are brownish gray in the upper parts and grayish white in the lower parts; the beak and legs are gray. The subspecies known as the Lesser Snow Goose (*A. c. caerulescens*) has a bluish-gray coloration with white head and neck, with some individuals similar in coloration to the larger subspecies.
Habitat   Tundra, marshland, coasts, lakes, grassland, grassy fields.
Distribution   Siberia, North America, Greenland (it winters as far south as Mexico, China and Japan). Occasional visitor to northern Europe.
Life and habits   Usually gregarious, it nests on the ground in colonies. It usually lays 5–6 eggs, which are incubated by the female. The nidifugous nestlings are reared by both parents. The Snow Goose feeds mainly on vegetable matter (plants, berries, grain, wild rice, aquatic plants) but also on invertebrates. It is often to be seen in large flocks during the migratory season.

31 ANTHROPOIDES VIRGO
Demoiselle Crane

Classification Order Gruiformes, Family Gruidae.
Characteristics About 95 cm. long (37″), it is smaller than the Eurasian Crane (*Grus grus*); it has a tuft of crestlike white feathers behind each eye. The coloring of the plumage is bluish ash gray, while most of the neck and long breast feathers, together with the wing feathers, are black. The inner secondary coverts are long, extending to the tail. Like other cranes, it flies with its neck outstretched.
Habitat Open terrain, lowlands, fresh-water areas, marshland, steppe, cultivated areas.
Distribution Africa and Asia, accidental in Europe.
Life and habits It nests on the ground in vegetation and near water. It lays a single clutch of 1–3 eggs (most often 2). Both sexes, but mainly the female, incubate the eggs, which hatch after 28–30 days. The nidifugous nestlings are reared by both parents, who stay with them until they are thoroughly independent. The Demoiselle Crane feeds on vegetable matter, insects and other invertebrates.

32 ANTHUS CAMPESTRIS
Tawny Pipit

Classification Order Passeriformes, Family Motacillidae.
Characteristics About 16 cm. long (6″) it is more streamlined in appearance than other species in the genus *Anthus*. In the upper parts it is light brown, with pale lower parts, usually without any markings. It has a fairly conspicuous eyebrow. The legs, tending to yellowish, and the tail are both long. Immature birds have a striped breast.
Habitat Cultivated and waste areas, lowlands.
Distribution Europe, Asia and Africa.
Life and habits It nests on the ground in depressions screened by vegetation. It usually lays just one clutch but may lay two. There are usually 4 or 5 eggs (more rarely 6), which are incubated by both sexes, mainly by the female, for 13 or 14 days. The nidicolous nestlings are reared by both parents and leave the nest at about 12–14 days. It feeds on insects and other invertebrates.

33 ANTHUS PRATENSIS
Meadow Pipit

Classification   Order Passeriformes, Family Motacillidae.
Characteristics   About 14.5 cm. long (5.5″), it has brown coloring with darker stripes uppermost; in the lower parts it is paler, with numerous small stripes. The outer rectrices are white. The legs are brownish with a long hind claw. A similar species is the Tree Pipit (*Anthus trivialis*), which has a yellowish breast, pinkish legs and a short hind claw. Unlike the Meadow Pipit, the Tree Pipit will perch readily in trees, and its song is different from that of the Meadow Pipit.
Habitat   Grassland, heathland, marshland, tilled and irrigated meadows.
Distribution   Europe, Africa and Asia.
Life and habits   Nests on the ground in vegetation. Usually lays two clutches, with 3–7 eggs (ordinarily 3, 4 or 5). Incubation lasts about 11–15 days and is the responsibility of the female. The nidocolous young are reared by both parents and leave the nest after 10–14 days. The Meadow Pipit feeds mainly on insects and other invertebrates, and certain vegetable matter (such as seeds).

---

34 ANTHUS SPINOLETTA
Rock Pipit or Water Pipit

Classification   Order Passeriformes, Family Motacillidae.
Characteristics   About 16 cm. long (6″), it is slightly larger and slenderer than the Meadow Pipit (*A. pratensis*) and the Tree Pipit (*A. trivialis*), with a fairly long beak and darker legs than the other species in the genus *Anthus*. The mountain-dwelling subspecies (*A. s. spinoletta*) has white outer rectrices, whitish lower parts that are tinged with pink during the mating period, striped in autumn and winter, with a white eyebrow. The coastal subspecies (*A. s. littoralis, A. s. petrosus,* etc.) have darker coloring, with the lower parts closely striped and the outer rectrices grayish.
Habitat   Mountainous areas, coasts, muddy areas, seashores, inland waters, marshland.
Distribution   Europe, Asia, Africa and North America.
Life and habits   It nests on the ground, in depressions and hollows, sometimes in vegetation. It lays one or two clutches, usually of 4–6 eggs, which are incubated by the female for about 14 days. The nidicolous nestlings are reared by both parents and leave the nest at about 16 days. It feeds in particular on insects and other invertebrates.

35 APTENODYTES FORSTERI
Emperor Penguin

Classification   Order Sphenisciformes, Family Spheniscidae.
Characteristics   Up to 115 cm. long (45"), with the length of the feathers reaching 4.2 cm. (1.6"), the average weight is about 30 kg (66 lbs.). The plumage extends to the back. In the upper parts the coloring is black; lower down it is whitish with yellowish shadings. A distinctive feature is the coloring of the neck with the broad yellowish marking that makes it easy to tell apart from the King Penguin (*A. patagonica*).
Habitat   Coasts and open sea.
Distribution   Coasts of the Antarctic, especially those on the Ross Sea.
Life and habits   The Emperor Penguin rarely moves outside Antarctica. As described by ornithologist B. Stonehouse, the eggs are laid in autumn, when the offshore sea becomes iced over. The females then return to the sea, while the males look after the eggs, warming one another by standing close together. For about ninety days, 62–64 of which represent the effective incubation period, they remain without any food. When the young hatch from the eggs the females return and rear their own offspring. The males head for the sea to feed, and regain their normal weight within 14–22 days. The young develop very slowly.

36 APTENODYTES PATAGONICA
King Penguin

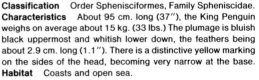

Classification   Order Sphenisciformes, Family Spheniscidae.
Characteristics   About 95 cm. long (37"), the King Penguin weighs on average about 15 kg. (33 lbs.) The plumage is bluish black uppermost and whitish lower down, the feathers being about 2.9 cm. long (1.1"). There is a distinctive yellow marking on the sides of the head, becoming very narrow at the base.
Habitat   Coasts and open sea.
Distribution   Subantarctic regions and cold temperate zones.
Life and habits   The King Penguin lays its eggs in the summer. The incubation is the responsibility of both parents and lasts 51–57 days. The newborn young, covered with fluffy down, are reared in colonies throughout the winter months. They are sometimes fed at intervals of 14 days. As described by ornithologist B. Stonehouse, who has made lengthy studies of their biology, King Penguins rear two young every three years. By the time they are a year old the young closely resemble adults. The King Penguin has been hunted for a long time for its plumage and oil.

39 APUS MELBA
Alpine Swift

Classification Order Apodiformes, Family Apodidae.
Characteristics About 21 cm. long (8″), it is larger than the Old World Swift (*A. apus*), with brown coloring and white lower parts, and a dark pectoral band. In flight it shows off its white throat and belly, and the dark pectoral band. It also has a forked tail.
Habitat Rocky regions, mountainous or coastal.
Distribution Southern Europe, Asia and Africa.
Life and habits Sociable by nature, it is found in large groups wheeling around its nesting places. In cracks in rocks and in the eaves of houses it builds a cup-shaped nest; it usually nests in colonies. It lays a single clutch of 1–4 eggs (usually 3 and sometimes 2), which are incubated by both sexes for 18–33 days. The nidicolous nestlings are reared by both parents and fly at 6–10 weeks. It feeds on insects, which it catches in flight.

40 AQUILA CHRYSAETOS
Golden Eagle

Classification Order Falconiformes, Family Accipitridae.
Characteristics About 82 cm. long (32″), with uniform dark brown coloring. The wingspread is more than 2 meters (6 ft.). Immature birds have white markings at the carpal articulation of the wing and at the base of the tail.
Habitat Mountains at various altitudes.
Distribution Europe, Asia, North Africa and North America.
Life and habits It nests in rocks and sometimes in trees, building a crude nest that is used for several years and is made with a large pile of branches, twigs and vegetable matter. As a rule the Golden Eagle builds several nests (2 or 3 and more, sometimes as many as 10) in a breeding area, and these are used in turn over the years. At intervals of 3 or 4 days it lays usually 2 eggs (more rarely 1 or 3). Incubation lasts 43–45 days and is usually the task of the female. The nidicolous young develop their plumage within 30–50 days and fly when they are about 63–70 days old. The Golden Eagle reaches sexual maturity at the age of 4 in most cases. It hunts mammals and small and medium-sized birds, and also eats carrion. The breeding area of the Golden Eagle can cover 10,000 hectares (25,000 acres).

41 AQUILA HELIACA
Imperial Eagle

Classification   Order Falconiformes, Family Accipitridae.
Characteristics   About 75 cm. long (30″), it has dark coloring, with a lighter marking on the nape of the neck, and a patch of white on the back (this is larger in the subspecies *Aquila heliaca adalberti*—the Spanish form). The young have a paler plumage, which is rather tawny, with markings on the lower parts. The tarsal bones are feathered.
Habitat   Lowlands, scrub and woods.
Distribution   The typical subspecies *A. h. heliaca* occurs in eastern Europe and central and western Asia; the subspecies *A. h. adalberti*, which is very rare, numbers some 60 pairs in southern Spain (according to Jesus Garzon Heydt) and a few individuals in northwestern Africa (S. P. Hills).
Life and habits   The Imperial Eagle nests in trees, usually laying 2 eggs (sometimes 3 and very rarely 4), which are incubated by both sexes for about 43 days. The young fly when they are 60 days old, and stay a further 2 or 3 weeks near the nest. It feeds on mammals (rabbits and rodents), reptiles and birds. The rare *adalberti* subspecies is the object of a conservation program being organized by the World Wildlife Fund and the Sociedad Española de Ornitologia.

42 AQUILA VERREAUXII
Verreaux's Eagle

Classification   Order Falconiformes, Family Accipitridae.
Characteristics   About 75–90 cm. long (30–35″), this is an impressive bird with very strong talons and beak. The plumage is entirely black, with a V-shaped white marking on the back, the base of the tail and the secondary wing coverts. The iris is brown. Young birds are reddish brown with light streaks and two white patches on the lower part of the wings. The female, whose wingspread reaches 2.10 meters (nearly 7 ft.) and weight 5.7 kg. (12.5 lbs.), is larger than the male, whose weight does not exceed 3.6 kg. (8 lbs.).
Habitat   Savanna, deserts and mountains.
Distributions   Central and southern Africa.
Life and habits   It frequents any type of open environment with few trees, as long as there are crags or cliffs for nesting. It ventures as high as 3,500 meters (11,500 ft.). Its nest is built on rocks with dry branches. Each pair has 1–3 nests. There are 1–3 eggs (as a rule, 2), which are hatched by both sexes for 43–46 days. The nestlings, which are born at intervals of 2 or 3 days, are fed by both adults, and they fly at 95–100 days. The diet of Verreaux's Eagle is made up of 80 percent mammals (coneys, mongooses and did-dik antelopes) and ground-dwelling birds up to the size of guineafowl.

43 ARDEA CINEREA
Gray Heron

Classification   Order Ciconiiformes, Family Ardeidae.
Characteristics   About 90 cm. long (35″), with ash-gray upper parts, black wing feathers, grayish-white lower parts, a dark stripe along the front of the neck, and the distinctive black crest ''hanging'' from the head. Immature birds are more uniform and grayer, without the black marking on the head and with a short crest.
Habitat   Marshland, lagoons, estuaries, wooded areas where there is water.
Distribution   Europe, Asia, parts of Africa.
Life and habits   It nests in colonies, generally high up in trees, and more rarely on the ground in bushes and canes, often with other species. It lays 2–7 eggs (more commonly 3–6) at intervals of about 2 days. Both parents incubate the eggs, for 23–28 days. The newborn young are looked after by both parents and stay in the nest for 50–55 days. The Gray Heron feeds on fish, amphibians, small aquatic mammals, small birds, mollusks, crustaceans, insects and vegetable matter.

44 ARDEA PURPUREA
Purple Heron

Classification   Order Ciconiiformes, Family Ardeidae.
Characteristics   About 79 cm. long (31″), resembles the Gray Heron, but is slenderer and smaller. The back and wings are dark slate-gray; the neck is reddish, streaked with black. The top of the head is black; the breast is chestnut, with black stripes at the sides. It has a black tuft at the nape of the neck, long dorsal feathers and similar feathers at the base of the neck. The young have a more sand-colored plumage, with a chestnut patch on the top of the head and tawny lower parts.
Habitat   Canebrakes, marshland, lagoons, ponds, wetlands.
Distribution   Europe, Asia and Africa.
Life and habits   It nests alone or in colonies on the ground, among reeds. At intervals of 3 days it lays 3–6 eggs (usually 4 or 5), which are incubated by both adults for 24–28 days. The nestlings are reared by both parents and can fly after approximately 42 days. They are independent at 60 days. The Purple Heron feeds on small birds, fish, amphibians, invertebrates and small mammals. It is less sociable than the Gray Heron.

45 ARDEOLA IBIS
Cattle Egret

Classification Order Ciconiiformes, Family Ardeidae.
Characteristics About 51 cm. long (20″), this small white heron has a tuft of longer tawny feathers on the top of the head and in summer on the back and throat. In winter its coloring is paler. The legs are yellow, orange or reddish in the mating season. The beak is yellow with a reddish base in the mating season. The young have blackish legs and a lighter beak.
Habitat Marshland, bogs and swamps, as well as wooded areas, grassland, plowed fields where there are herds of cattle and other mammals.
Distribution Southern Iberian peninsula, southern France, Asia and Africa, and from 1930 on, it has spread from British Guiana (where it arrived from Africa) up to North America.
Life and habits A gregarious bird, it nests in colonies with other species of heron. It lays 4–5 eggs (rarely 6), which are incubated by both sexes for 21–25 days. The nestlings remain in the nest for about a month. The Cattle Egret, in its search for insects, struts among grazing domestic animals; sometimes it will fly onto the backs of these animals, and even onto the backs of such wild beasts as elephants, hippopotamuses and rhinoceroses, to feed on the parasites it finds there.

---

46 ARDEOLA RALLOIDES
Squacco Heron

Classification Order Ciconiiformes, Family Ardeidae.
Characteristics About 45 cm. long (18″), it is a squat-looking bird, with light brown plumage; the wings are white, and there is a tuft of feathers on the head. The legs are greenish (they become red at the height of the mating season). The beak is greenish, is speckled black in winter, and becomes black and blue during the mating season. Young birds have a brown-streaked breast. When it is perched or at rest, a watcher can easily see the reddish-sandy color of the plumage; in flight the white of the wings, tail and rump is conspicuous.
Habitat Marshland, lagoons, ponds, wooded regions.
Distribution Southern Europe, southwestern Asia, Africa.
Life and habits Nests in marshland vegetation, in trees, undergrowth or on the ground. It lays a single clutch, of 4–6 eggs (rarely 7), which are incubated by both sexes for 22–24 days. The nidicolous nestlings are reared by both parents and stay in the nest for about 32 days. The Squacco Heron feeds on fishes, insects, larvae, worms and plants.
Note: The photo shows a male in the mating season.

47 ARDEOTIS KORI
Kori Bustard

Classification   Order Gruiformes, Family Otididae.
Characteristics   Larger than the Great Bustard (*Otis tarda*), this species reaches an over-all length of 100–130 cm. (40–50″) and has a streamlined body and fairly long legs. The plumage is brown with black in the upper parts, white in the lower, and a whitish to grayish neck. On the head there is a black marking and a tuft of dark feathers. The beak and legs are yellowish. Three of the other species of bustard are the Arabian Bustard of North Africa to Asia Minor (*A. arabs*); Denham's Bustard (*Neotis denhami*) found in East Africa; and the rare Great Indian Bustard of India (*Choriotis nigriceps*), whose weight can reach 20 kg. (45 lbs.) and wing span 2.50 m. (100″).
Habitat   Steppe and savanna.
Distribution   Africa.

Life and habits   During the mating season the males raise their tails to show off the white lower feathers, and remain motionless with the body vertical and the wings dangling. In addition they puff out their throat, which can swell to four times its normal size. It nests in hollows in the ground. Kori Bustards are called "rubber turkeys" by Boers, because they have a fondness for the rubbery resin of acacia trees; they also feed on plant matter and invertebrates.

---

48 ARENARIA INTERPRES
Ruddy Turnstone

Classification   Order Charadriiformes, Family Charadriidae.
Characteristics   About 22 cm. long (9″). Its coloring, particularly in summer, is very bright with dark red-brown upper parts and black markings that make the facial pattern a distinctive one. In winter the coloring is deep brown, with a white throat. The legs are orange, and the beak is tough and black.
Habitat   Marshland, rocky and shingly coasts, inland waters, tundra.
Distribution   Europe, North, Central, and South America, North Africa and northern Asia, wintering on all tropical coasts.
Life and habits   Its common name comes from its habitual upturning of stones, pebbles and shells in its search for the invertebrates on which it feeds. It nests on the ground amid vegetation. It lays a single clutch usually of 3–5 eggs (ordinarily 4), which are incubated by both sexes, but mainly by the female, for 22 or 23 days. The nidifugous nestlings are reared by both parents. It feeds on insects, crustaceans and mollusks.

49 ARGUSIANUS ARGUS
Great Argus Pheasant

Classification   Order Galliformes, Family Phasianidae.
Characteristics   About 2 meters long (80"), it weighs about 10–11.5 kg. (23–26 lbs.) and is an unmistakable bird. In the male the secondary remiges are longer than the primaries (a unique condition in birds). There are 12 rectrices, with two very long central ones (about three times as long as the others). The skin on the head and neck, in the male, is usually bare and blue colored. On the occiput the female has a tuft of very fine feathers. The general coloring of the plumage is brownish. The Great Argus is the only galliform without the uropygial gland.
Habitat   Wooded areas.
Distribution   Malaysia, Borneo and Sumatra.
Life and habits   In an area with a diameter of 4–5 meters (12–15 ft.) the male shows himself off during courtship. He unfurls his handsome plumage to attract the female. She usually lays 2 eggs, which are incubated for 24 or 25 days. The nidifugous nestlings stay for some time with their mother, following her every movement quite closely. The adult dimensions are reached within about a year. Ornithologist H. Sigurd Raethel mentions a Great Argus that lived in captivity for thirty years.

50 ASIO FLAMMEUS
Short-eared Owl

Classification   Order Strigiformes, Family Strigidae.
Characteristics   About 37 cm. long (14.5"), it has light tawny-colored plumage; the lower parts have wide stripes. In flight the wings are long with barred coloring and a large dark marking at the carpal bones. It often comes to rest on the ground and usually flies low.
Habitat   Open areas, lowlands, heathland, marshland.
Distribution   Europe, Asia, Africa, North America, Central and South America.
Life and habits   It usually hunts at nightfall, but has also been seen in full daylight. It makes sounds that are like a *boo-boo-boo* or a *kee-aw*. It nests on the ground amid vegetation. It lays one or two clutches, usually of 4–8 eggs (more rarely 3, and up to 14 when there is plenty of food available). Incubation lasts about 24–28 days and is the task of the female. The nidicolous nestlings are fed by the female, while the male actually hunts the food; they leave the nest at 12–17 days and fly after about 10 more days. It feeds on small mammals, birds and insects.

51 ASIO OTUS
Long-eared Owl

Classification   Order Strigiformes, Family Strigidae.
Characteristics   About 35 cm. long (13.5"), its upper parts are speckled gray-tawny in color and the lower parts are tawny with broad stripes and thin bars. There are two small but distinctive tufts of feathers on the head; the eyes are yellow. In flight it differs from the Short-eared Owl (*A. flammeus*) in that the underwing is generally darker.
Habitat   Coniferous forests, mixed woodland.
Distribution   Europe, Asia, North Africa and North America.
Life and habits   Nests in hollows in trees, in old nests that have been abandoned by crows and rooks (Corvidae), and in squirrels' nests, rarely on the ground. It lays one clutch of 3–8 eggs (ordinarily 4 or 5), which are as a rule incubated by the female for 25–30 days. The nidicolous nestlings are fed by the female, while the male actually hunts the food; the young leave the nest at 23 or 24 days. The Long-eared Owl feeds on small mammals, birds and invertebrates.
Note: The photo shows a nestling being brooded by the adult.

---

52 ATHENE NOCTUA
Little Owl

Classification   Order Strigiformes, Family Strigidae.
Characteristics   About 21 cm. long (8.5"), this small bird has a large head, barred brownish upper parts that are speckled with white, and dark-striped, whitish lower parts.
Habitat   Open areas, lowlands, rural regions.
Distribution   Europe, North Africa and Asia.
Life and habits   It nests in hollows in trees, in rocks and in old buildings. It lays one and sometimes two clutches of 2–8 eggs (usually 3, 4 or 5), which are incubated by the female for 28–29 days. The nidicolous nestlings are reared by both parents and can leave the nest at about 4 weeks, even though they cannot fly until about 5 weeks. The Little Owl feeds on small rodents, small birds and various invertebrates (insects and slugs). It makes a distinctive plaintive cry like *kiu-kiu* and a sharper *werro*.

53 AYTHYA FERINA
Common Pochard

Classification Order Anseriformes, Family Anatidae.
Characteristics The male, which is about 46 cm. long (18"), has a reddish-chestnut head, pale gray back, and sides with lighter markings; the breast and both surfaces of the tail are black. The female, which is about 42 cm. long (16"), has an over-all dark brown coloring with lighter cheeks, throat, and base of the beak. The legs are grayish, and the beak is black with a pale blue stripe. In its postnuptial plumage the male resembles the female.
Habitat Lakes, marshland, estuaries.
Distribution Europe and Asia.
Life and habits It nests amid vegetation near water. It lays a single clutch of 6–11 eggs, and occasionally as many as 18. Incubation is the task of the female and lasts 24–26 days. The nidifugous nestlings are reared by the female, who looks after them until they are independent—at 7–8 weeks. The Common Pochard feeds mainly on plant matter (roots, leaves, shoots, seeds, etc.) as well as on invertebrates (insects, worms and crustaceans), amphibians and small fish.

54 AYTHYA FULIGULA
Tufted Duck

Classification Order Anseriformes, Family Anatidae.
Characteristics The male, which is about 42 cm. long (16"), has black plumage with white sides, and a black tuft on the head. The female, about 38 cm. long (14"), and young birds are dark brown. In flight the Tufted Duck looks black with white underside, and black head, neck, breast, wing edges and tail. The legs are grayish; the beak is dark blue in the male and grayish in the female.
Habitat Lakes, marshland.
Distribution Europe, Asia and Africa.
Life and habits It nests on the ground amid vegetation, near water. It lays a single clutch of 5–12 eggs, occasionally 14 (up to 18 have been recorded). The female incubates them for 23–25 days. The nidifugous nestlings are looked after by the female and are able to dive a few hours after being born; they fly at about 6 weeks. The Tufted Duck feeds on plant matter (berries, aquatic plants, etc.) and animals (invertebrates, mollusks, small fish.)

55 BALAENICEPS REX
Shoebill

Classification   Order Ciconiiformes, Family Balaenicipitidae.
Characteristics   About 120 cm. long (47″), this is a distinctive bird; the plumage is blackish gray, the beak is extraordinarily deep and wide (hence the very enlarged skull). On the upper part of the head there is a short tuft of feathers.
Habitat   River banks, marshland.
Distribution   Africa, localized.
Life and habits   An agile flier, it sometimes uses upward currents for gliding. On the ground and in flight the beak is usually rested on the breast. It is predominantly solitary by nature, although it has been sighted in small groups (up to 7 individuals). It feeds generally on fish, amphibians and invertebrates (such as mollusks) and will eat by night too. The nest is a platform of vegetable matter, made amid aquatic plants, where 2 or 3 eggs are laid. The nidifugous young are covered with soft down.

56 BALEARICA PAVONINA
Crowned Crane

Classification   Order Gruiformes, Family Gruidae.
Characteristics   The Gruidae are very distinctive birds, with long legs and slender necks. They range in size from 90 to 150 cm. (35–60″). In flight, cranes have their head and neck outstretched, unlike herons (Ardeidae), which fly with their neck in an S-shaped position. The Crowned Crane is about 95 cm. long (37″), with dark plumage, tending to blackish, with yellowish-white markings on the wings. In the face and behind the eyes there is a white patch. A distinctive feature is the tuft of feathers on the head. There are two subspecies: *B. p. pavonina* and *B. p. ceciliae*, although various scholars include *B. regulorum* (with a further two subspecies) in this species as well.
Habitat   Open terrain, savanna.
Distribution   Africa.
Life and habits   The Crowned Crane is one of the few Gruidae that roost in trees. The nest is built on the ground or in low scrub and bushes; it usually lays 2 eggs. As mentioned by W. Makatsch, cranes change their plumage once a year, except for the remiges, which are shed every two years simultaneously, preventing flight for a few weeks, while the Crowned Crane loses its remiges gradually and as a result can always fly. The Crowned Crane feeds on invertebrates and vegetable matter.

57 BOMBYCILLA GARRULUS
Bohemian Waxwing

Classification   Order Passeriformes, Family Bombycillidae.
Characteristics   About 18 cm. long (7″), the Bohemian Waxwing weighs on average 55 grams (2 ounces). Its upper parts are gray, with a brownish head, a yellow-tipped tail, and a black marking on the throat and behind the eye. The lower parts are pinkish brown. The wings are various shades of yellow, with white tips. The young, which have no black patches on the head, are striped on the lower parts.
Habitat   Coniferous and birch forests.
Distribution   Europe, northern Asia, and mainly western North America.
Life and habits   The southern boundary of the breeding area of this species is Latitude 62–63 degrees North. The nest is made in trees (often conifers) and is built with twigs, lichens and plants, into a cup shape. There is one clutch a year of 5 eggs, which are incubated solely by the female for 13 or 14 days. The nidicolous nestlings are fed and helped by both parents and fly at 15–17 days. It feeds mainly on berries and fruit, but also on insects, which form a substantial part of the diet of the young. A distinctive feature of this species is the invasions (migratory movements) that recur at intervals of several years and are probably due to overpopulation that develops in places where there have been consecutive years of ideal conditions for reproduction.

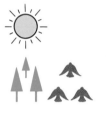

58 BOTAURUS STELLARIS
Old World Bittern

Classification   Order Ciconiiformes, Family Ardeidae.
Characteristics   About 76 cm. long (30″), it has extremely mimetic coloring, with the upper parts dark golden tawny, closely barred black, and lighter lower parts likewise barred dark reddish brown. The top of the head is black and the legs pale green. The young resemble the adults, but have a more uniform coloring. It adopts a distinctive mimetic position among reeds with its body extended and neck and beak turned upward. It is not often seen in flight; but, when in the air, it displays wide, rounded wings.
Habitat   Canebrakes, marshland, lagoons.
Distribution   Central and southern Europe, northwestern and southern Africa, and central and western Asia.
Life and habits   It is shy, it lives alone, and it is generally most visible in twilight hours. It nests amid reeds. It lays 3–7 eggs (ordinarily 4, 5 or 6) at intervals of 2 or 3 days, and these are incubated by the female, once the first egg is laid, for about 25 or 26 days. The nestlings leave the nest at 2 or 3 weeks and become independent at about 8 weeks. The male may be polygamous. The Old World Bittern feeds on small mammals and birds, fishes, crustaceans, insects, other invertebrates and plant matter. It makes a raucous sound and has a deep song that can be heard over considerable distances.

59 BRANTA CANADENSIS
Canada Goose

Classification   Order Anseriformes, Family Anatidae.
Characteristics   It is 90–100 cm. long (35–40″) and weighs 4–6 kg. (9–14 lbs.). The head, neck and tail are black; the breast and belly are brown-gray; the upper parts are brown. On each side of the head there is a broad white patch that runs down to the throat.
Habitat   Fields near freshwater marshes, lakes with wooded shores.
Distribution   North America; introduced into northern Europe.
Life and habits   It nests on small islets covered with bushes in lakes and marshland, forming colonies with the nests built at a certain distance from one another. The nest is made in a hollow in the ground and is lined with plant matter and down. Each year there is a single clutch of 2–11 eggs (usually 5 or 6), which are incubated solely by the female for 28–30 days. Both adults look after the goslings, which leave the nest soon after hatching and fly at 9 weeks, although they remain with their parents for some time after that. Their diet consists of grasses and plants, seeds and other vegetable matter, together with mollusks, small fish and amphibians. This species, coming originally from North America, was successfully introduced into Europe in the late eighteenth century and now breeds in Great Britain and Sweden.

---

60 BRANTA LEUCOPSIS
Barnacle Goose

Classification   Order Anseriformes, Family Anatidae.
Characteristics   It measures 58–67 cm. in length (23–26″), and its wing span reaches 127 cm. (50″); it can weigh up to 2.2 kg. (5 lbs.). The upper parts are gray with black and white bars, the lower parts are white. The head, neck and breast are black; the face and forehead are white.
Habitat   Brackish marshland, prairie, tundra, rocky riverbanks.
Distribution   Arctic regions of Europe and Asia, Greenland.
Life and habits   Gregarious by nature, it builds its nest in a hollow in the ground and lines it with down. The single clutch each year has 3–6 eggs, which are incubated by the female for 24 or 25 days. The nidifugous nestlings leave the nest shortly after hatching and head toward the nearest water. Helped by the parents, they fly at 7 weeks. This species feeds mainly on aquatic plants, marine algae and a small amount of mollusks and crustaceans. It is a migratory species and winters in certain parts of central and northern Europe, often near the coast. The large flocks that gather in the winter months feed under cover of night.

61 BRANTA RUFICOLLIS
Red-breasted Goose

Classification Order Anseriformes, Family Anatidae.
Characteristics It is 50–55 cm. long (20–22″), with a wing span of 120 cm. (48″) and a weight of about 1.6 kg. (3.5 lbs.). The coloring of the upper plumage and the lower shows a combination of black and white (in particular, there is a strip or band on the sides, and conspicuous undertail and a white mark on the cheeks). The neck and breast are rich reddish. Immature birds have paler coloring.
Habitat Coastal tundra and grassy steppe.
Distribution Northern Asia and eastern Europe.
Life and habits The breeding habitat is situated in grassy steppes along rivers, and in coastal tundra. The nest is made in a shallow hollow on the ground and is lined with plant matter and down. There is a single clutch each year of 4 or 5 eggs, which are incubated solely by the female, while the male acts as a sentry near the nest. The nidifugous nestlings follow their parents about outside the nest. The diet consists mainly of grasses and grains. The population of this species is quite reduced and according to an estimate by the Council for Bird Preservation (1973) the flock of 30,000–40,000 geese which winters in Rumania represents the bulk of the total population.

---

62 BRANTA SANDVICENSIS
Hawaiian Goose

Classification Order Anseriformes, Family Anatidae.
Characteristics It is about 60–70 cm. long (24–28″), and its plumage has a combination of brown, gray, black and white coloring; the head is covered with black feathers, and the beak and legs are black. It has long legs and strong toes. It adapts to life on the slopes of volcanoes.
Habitat Semiarid slopes of volcanoes with sparse vegetation of the scrubby type, between 1,500 and 2,500 meters (5,000 and 8,000 ft.) above sea level.
Distribution On the island of Hawaii in that archipelago; on the slopes of the volcanoes Mauna Kea, Mauna Loa and Hualalai. Reintroduced in 1962 to the Haleakala crater on the island of Maui in the Hawaiian archipelago.
Life and habits The Hawaiian Goose lays 4–6 eggs in hollows in the ground near bushes and grass. It feeds on grasses and berries. It is a very rare goose and has been in danger of extinction. In 1950 only about 50 were still living in the wild; the ornithologist Peter Scott caught a male and two females and reared them at the Wildfowl Trust in England. A further 800 geese have been raised from these three specimens—200 individuals have been reintroduced to Hawaii and 180 have been given to major zoos for rearing in captivity. There are at present more than 1,000 individuals.

63 BUBO BUBO
Eurasian Eagle Owl

Classification Order Strigiformes, Family Strigidae.
Characteristics About 65–70 cm. long (26–28″), this is a large owl with tawny brown upper parts and dark brown markings, and tawny lower parts with black streaks. The female is larger than the male. There are distinctive tufts on the ears. The eyes are orange. Its wing span can reach 1.5 meters (60″). The male weighs 2.7 kg. (6 lbs.), and the female weighs 3.2 kg. (7 lbs).
Habitat Forests, rocky areas, woods.
Distribution Europe, Asia and North Africa.
Life and habits It nests at various altitudes, from lowlands to mountainous regions. Environmental constants in its nesting area are the presence of rocky crags and cliffs, woodland and cultivated areas. The nest is built in rocks and, in special rare cases, on the ground or in a tree. It lays a single clutch of 1–6 eggs (ordinarily 2 or 3), which are laid at intervals of 3 or 4 days and incubated by the female for 34–36 days. The nestlings are fed by both parents. They leave the nest at 6–10 weeks. The Eurasian Eagle Owl, from preference, hunts at dusk and dawn——mammals (mice, rats and rabbits, etc.), birds (even species as large as the Capercaillie) and snakes, lizards, frogs, fish and large insects.

64 BUBO LACTEUS
Milky Eagle Owl

Classification Order Strigiformes, Family Strigidae.
Characteristics A large bird with an over-all length of 53–61 cm. (21–24″). The plumage is a uniform gray-brown color, paler and closely barred with black on the lower parts. Two dark stripes mark the off-white facial disk. The iris is dark brown. The wing span is about 1.5 meters (60″) and the female is slightly larger than the male.
Habitat Forests with clearings.
Distribution Central and southern Africa.
Life and habits The environments most frequented are forests along riverbanks, including dense forests where the Eurasian Eagle Owl does not normally live. The nest is built in a hollow in a tree, but more often than not in a nest that has been abandoned by a large bird of prey. It lays 1–3 eggs (usually 2), and they are incubated for a few weeks by both sexes. The nestlings are helped by the parents for several weeks after they have learned to fly. If a predator approaches the nest, the adults put on showy displays, pretending to be injured, thus luring the invader away from the nest and its helpless occupants. This owl feeds on quite large prey, caught on the ground in clearings or at the edge of a wood or forest: hares, coneys, birds as large as francolins, snakes, fruit-eating bats and large insects.

65 BUBO VIRGINIANUS
Great Horned Owl

Classification   Order Strigiformes, Family Strigidae.
Characteristics   About 43–53 cm. long (17–21″). This large bird has two distinctive horn-shaped tufts at either side of the head. The plumage is dark brown in the upper parts with black markings, and lighter brown with black bars in the lower. The iris is bright yellow. There is a lot of variation in the color of the plumage, which tends to be darker or lighter than that described. Sixteen geographical types have been identified.
Habitat   Forests, deserts, scrub and rocky terrain.
Distribution   North and South America.
Life and habits   This is a very adaptable species and is found in all types of habitat. It nests in the abandoned nests of birds, in hollows in rocks and sometimes on the ground. It lays 1–5 eggs (usually 2–3), which are incubated for 35 days by both parents. Because the eggs are laid over a few days the nestlings do not hatch simultaneously; they can fly at the age of 9 or 10 weeks. This species feeds on lots of different animals—from insects to hares and birds the size of ducks or partridges, through a wide range of rodents, small carnivorous mammals and even fish.

66 BUCEPHALA CLANGULA
Common Goldeneye

Classification   Order Anseriformes, Family Anatidae.
Characteristics   It is 38–43 cm. long (15–17″). The male's nuptial plumage has a white neck and white lower parts, a black back with white stripes, and a black head with a white patch on each cheek. The female's upper parts and sides are gray. The head is brown and unmarked, and there is a white collar, which is not present in young and immature birds.
Habitat   Lakes and rivers in wooded areas (northern taiga and coastal regions).
Distribution   Europe, Asia and North America.
Life and habits   The nest is built in hollows in tree trunks (sometimes in a rabbit's burrow) near water. There are 6–11 eggs laid at intervals of approximately 36 hours; these are incubated solely by the female for 27–32 days. The nidifugous ducklings soon leave the nest and head for the nearest water, helped by the female. They fly at 8 weeks. Goldeneyes, which winter on larger lakes and often at sea as well, feed mainly on mollusks, crustaceans, worms and small fish, as well as vegetable matter. Food is searched for beneath the surface of the water and these ducks will dive to a depth of nearly 7 meters (23 ft.). The males' courtship displays, which consist of a series of ritual attitudes made in or on the water, usually start at the end of January.

67 BUCEROS BICORNIS
Great Hornbill

Classification   Order Coraciiformes, Family Bucerotidae.
Characteristics   This is a large and very distinctive bird with black plumage and large white stripes on the wings and tail. The neck is whitish yellow in color, the sides of the face black. As with all the Bucerotidae, the beak is large and strong, curving slightly downward, with an odd structure, known as a casque, on the upper half. There are differences between males and females in the beak coloring and in the ring around the eye as well as the eye itself. The skull of the Great Hornbill, together with the casque, weighs about 320 grams (11 ounces). There are two subspecies—*B. b. homrai,* which is about 120 cm. long (47"), with the beak, in the male, up to 29.5 cm. in length (11.6"), and *B. b. bicornis,* which is smaller, with the male's beak reaching 25 cm. (10"). A related species is the Rhinoceros Hornbill (*B. rhinoceros*).
Habitat   Forests and woods.
Distribution   Southeast Asia.

Life and habits   It nests in hollows, like all the other species of hornbill; the male "bricks in" the hollow, leaving just a slit through which to feed the female and young, and to eject droppings. It feeds on fruit, invertebrates and small vertebrates.

68 BUCORVUS LEADBEATERI
African Ground Hornbill

Classification   Order Coraciiformes, Family Bucerotidae.
Characteristics   The ground hornbills can reach an over-all length of 110 cm. (44") and a weight of 3.5–4 kg. (7.7–8.8 lbs.). The tarsal bones are fairly well developed. The side areas of the head and throat are bare, and the nostrils are protected by a tuft of feathers that keep blades of grass from intruding inside them. The plumage is black with white on the wings. It has a tough beak, with a not very large casque. The bare parts are reddish (bluish red in females). The beak is about 17 cm. long (7") in males, 15.5 (6.5") in females. The Abyssinian Ground Hornbill (*B. abyssinicus*), the males of which have a bill of about 22 cm. (9"), is considered by some ornithologists to be a subspecies of *B. leadbeateri.*
Habitat   Savanna and steppe.
Distribution   Africa.
Life and habits   The ground hornbills make their own nest in trees (mainly baobab trees) and are the only Bucerotidae that do not wall the female into her nest. They usually lay 2 eggs, which are incubated for about one month by the female. The nidicolous nestlings remain in the nest for about three more months. They then stay close to their parents for a further nine months. Sexual maturity is reached at about 3 years of age.

69 BUPHAGUS AFRICANUS
Yellow-billed Oxpecker

Classification   Order Passeriformes, Family Sturnidae.
Characteristics   The subfamily Buphaginae, in the family
Sturnidae, has species with short, tough beaks, short legs,
strong, pointed claws, and a pointed tail. The Yellow-billed Oxpecker, about 21 cm. long (8.5″) has brownish-black plumage,
pale yellowish in the lower parts, with a grayish head and a
strong yellow bill with a reddish tip. The oxpeckers' bills have
very sharp edges, designed to remove ticks and rummage
through the hides of large African mammals (elephants and rhinoceroses). The other species of oxpecker is the Red-billed
Oxpecker (*B. erythrorhynchus*), which too has brownish plumage, a red bill and a circle of bare yellow skin around the eye.
Habitat   Steppe and savanna.
Distribution   Africa.
Life and habits   Oxpeckers congregate on the hides of un-
gulate (hoofed) mammals, where they feed on parasites and
insects buzzing around them; in some cases they act as
"watchdogs," warning the mammal of approaching danger.
They nest in hollows in trees (and in the eaves of houses),
usually laying 3–5 eggs, which are incubated for 11–12 days.
The nidicolous young stay in the nest for about 28–29 days.

70 BURHINUS OEDICNEMUS
Eurasian Stone Curlew or Thick-knee

Classification   Order Charadriiformes, Family Burhinidae.
Characteristics   About 40 cm. long (16″), it has brown-
striped mimetic coloring. In flight it shows a white marking on
the wings and a double bar; seen from beneath, the wings are
very pale colored with a dark hind edge. The head is roundish,
the eyes yellow, the beak yellow and black, and the legs yellowish. It often moves about on the ground, helped by its cam-
ouflage. Its flight pattern is straight, generally low, with the legs
jutting out behind the tail. The young resemble the adults.
Habitat   Stony, sandy areas, barren hills, areas with sparse
vegetation, marshland, cultivated areas.
Distribution   Central and southern Europe, southwestern and
southern Asia, North Africa.
Life and habits   Solitary by nature in the nesting period (during migration it is possible to see quite large flocks), it nests on
the ground in holes or shallow hollows. This species lays a single clutch (rarely 2), generally of 2 eggs (rarely 3), laid on alternate days; these are incubated by both parents for 25–27
days. The nidifugous young are reared by both parents and
become independent at about 6 weeks. It feeds on various invertebrates and sometimes on the young of pheasants and
partridges, small mice, et cetera.

71 BUTEO BUTEO
Eurasian Buzzard

Classification Order Falconiformes, Family Accipitridae.
Characteristics About 51–58 cm. in length (20–23″), with a wing span of up to 1.35 meters (53″). Its weight varies from 0.5 to 1.2 kg. (1.1–2.6 lbs.), with females being the heavier. The plumage goes through several phases (reddish, pale, blackish, etc.) but is essentially brown in the upper parts, off-white in the lower parts, with close bars and brown markings. The iris is brownish yellow and the legs yellow. The young differ from the adults in the coloring of the plumage.
Habitat Forests, woods, medium-altitude mountains, wooded countryside.
Distribution Europe and central and northern Asia.
Life and habits It almost always builds its nest in trees (sometimes among rocks in treeless areas). There is one clutch a year of 3–4 eggs laid at intervals of 2–3 days. These are incubated by both parents (mainly by the female) for about 33–35 days. The nidicolous nestlings fly at 40–45 days, helped and still fed by the two parent birds, which take care of their young for a long time after they have left the nest. Buzzards catch a wide variety of prey, mainly rodentlike mammals (up to the size of a rabbit), small and medium-sized birds and reptiles. They also feed on carrion.

72 BUTEO JAMAICENSIS
Red-tailed Hawk

Classification Order Falconiformes, Family Accipitridae.
Characteristics About 50–65 cm. long (20–26″), it has a wing span of 130–145 cm. (51–57″). The upper parts are brown, the tail a rufous color, while the lower parts are whitish with dark bars. The female (average weight 1.2 kg., or 2.6 lbs.) is slightly larger than the male (average weight 1 kg., or 2.2 lbs.). There are variations in the coloring of the plumage, which may be lighter or darker. A similar species is Swainson's Hawk (*B. swainsoni*).
Habitat Deserts, cultivated and wooded areas, rocky hills.
Distribution North and Central America.
Life and habits Usually a nonmigratory species, it may migrate from colder regions. It is very eclectic in its choice of habitat, nesting from sea level to medium-altitude mountains in every type of environment. The nest is built with branches and twigs in trees, in cacti or among rocks, and it often is used in successive years. The eggs (1–3 in number and sometimes 4) are incubated for 28–32 days by both sexes. The young fly at about 45 days, and for several weeks the parents continue to teach them how to hunt. In its diet it is also an adaptable bird of prey, feeding mainly on rodents and rabbits when possible, but also on snakes and medium-sized ground-dwelling birds.

73 BUTORIDES VIRESCENS
Green Heron

Classification Order Ciconiiformes, Family Ardeidae.
Characteristics This small bird is about 45–55 cm. long (18–22″) and, like all herons, has long, rounded wings, long legs and a slender, pointed beak. The lower parts of the body are tawny brown, except for the throat, which is white. The back and wings are gray-green, and darker on the back itself. The legs are yellow. Brown immature birds have light and dark bars. On the head there is a short tufted crest of feathers, which is raised when the bird is alarmed.
Habitat Marshland, freshwater and brackish ponds.
Distribution North America and Central America.
Life and habits This bird has migratory habits and winters in the northern areas of South America. It nests in small colonies or on its own in trees near water. The nest is made of dry branches and is lined with green plants. In it are laid 3–6 eggs (usually 4 or 5), which are incubated by both parents for 19–21 days. The adults look after and feed their young together; the nestlings fly at 21–23 days. When in search of food it will remain motionless in shallow water, ready to spear any prey that comes within range of its sharp beak. Its diet consists of small fish, amphibians, aquatic insects and other small creatures.

74 CALCARIUS LAPPONICUS
Lapland Longspur

Classification Order Passeriformes, Family Emberizidae.
Characteristics About 14 cm. long (6″), it weighs about 24 grams (slightly less than 1 ounce). In its nuptial plumage the male's head, breast and sides are black; there is a white stripe on the eye and cheek, and the nape of the neck is chestnut colored; the upper parts are striped brown and the lower, white. The female is uniformly brown uppermost and resembles young birds and males in their winter plumage. The outer edges of the tail are white.
Habitat Tundra, grasslands on seacoasts.
Distribution Arctic regions of Europe, Asia and America.
Life and habits The nest is built in a cup-shaped depression in the ground and is lined with grass, moss, hair and feathers. The single annual clutch of 5–6 eggs, laid at intervals of a day, is incubated mainly by the female for 10–14 days. The nidicolous young are fed by both parents, and they fly at the age of 12–15 days. This species searches for food on the ground and feeds mainly on the seeds of herbaceous plants, and in the summer months, though to a lesser extent, on insects which are part of the diet for the nestlings. The Lapland Longspur migrates to coastal lowland areas with herbaceous vegetation in more southerly regions, where it winters, and also takes on gregarious behavioral patterns.

75 CALIDRIS ALBA
Sanderling

Classification Order Charadriiformes. Family Scolopacidae.
Characteristics About 20 cm. long (8″), it has very pale plumage in autumn and winter; the head and lower parts are white, while the upper parts are grayish brown. In summer the head, neck, upper parts and top of the breast are brown speckled with black; the lower parts are white. In flight it shows a white wing band, which stands out against the otherwise dark-colored wings.
Habitat Sandy and shingly coastal areas, marshland, tundra with sparse vegetation.
Distribution Breeds inside the Arctic Circle, and winters farther south in America, Africa, Asia, Europe and Australia.
Life and habits It is often seen in dense groups. It nests in depressions and hollows in the ground, which it covers with dried leaves and other plant matter. Sanderlings lay a single clutch of 4 eggs (in exceptional cases 3), which are incubated by both parents, but mainly the female, for 23–24 days. The nidifugous young are reared by both parents and are independent at the age of 23–24 days. The Sanderling feeds on invertebrates (insects, worms, crustaceans and mollusks.)
Note: In the photo the Sanderlings are in the center.

76 CALIDRIS ALPINA
Dunlin

Classification Order Charadriiformes, Family Scolopacidae.
Characteristics About 19 cm. long (7.5″), it has dark brown coloring uppermost and pale plumage in the lower parts; the belly is black. There are some thin stripes on the upper breast. The beak is slightly curved downward at the tip. In winter the coloring is dark gray, and the belly is white. In flight it shows a white band on the wings and white on the sides of the upper part of the dark-colored tail.
Habitat Marshland, lagoons, wetlands, coastal regions.
Distribution Europe, Asia, North Africa and North America.
Life and habits It nests on the ground, in peat bogs and brackish marshland. It lays just one clutch of 2–6 eggs (normally 4), which are incubated by both parents for 21 or 22 days. The nidifugous nestlings are reared by both parents, but primarily by the female; they become independent at about 25 days. The Dunlin feeds on invertebrates (mollusks, worms, insects, etc.) and plant matter.

77 CALIDRIS CANUTUS
Red Knot

Classification   Order Charadriiformes, Family Scolopacidae.
Characteristics   About 25 cm. long (10″). In the spring and summer months the upper parts of the plumage are black-speckled chestnut; the head and lower parts are rust colored. In the winter plumage the coloring is ash gray uppermost, and white in the lower parts. The Knot has a "tough," squat look about it, with short neck, beak and legs. The white wing band and white rump are visible in flight.
Habitat   Wetlands or stony ground with sparse vegetation, sandy or muddy coastlands, estuaries and marshland.
Distribution   Arctic Circle; it winters farther south in Asia, Africa, Europe and America.
Life and habits   It nests in depressions or hollows in the ground among lichens. It lays 3 or 4 eggs (most often 4), which are incubated by both parents for about 20–25 days. The nidifugous nestlings are reared mainly by the male and become independent after about 3 weeks. It feeds on invertebrates and vegetable matter. Knots are often seen in large flocks on sandy and muddy coasts. It makes a *twit-wit* sound and a low *nut* sound.

78 CALIDRIS MINUTA
Little Stint

Classification   Order Charadriiformes, Family Scolopacidae.
Characteristics   About 14.5 cm. long (5.5″). In summer its uppermost coloring is brownish; and lower down it is white. In winter the upper parts are grayish and the lower remain white. The legs are black. In flight it shows white sides on its rump and in winter a sort of pale V on its back. A similar species is Temminck's Stint (*C. temminckii*), slightly larger, with more grayish coloring than the Little Stint and has pale-colored legs.
Habitat   Tundra, grasslands, marshland, coastal areas.
Distribution   Northern Europe and northern Asia, wintering farther south.
Life and habits   It nests on the ground in hollows and depressions, laying a single clutch usually of 3 or 4 eggs (more commonly 4), which are incubated mainly by the female. The nidifugous nestlings are reared by both parents. It feeds on invertebrates (insects, worms and mollusks) and seeds.

79 CALLIPEPLA SQUAMATA
Scaled Quail

Classification   Order Galliformes, Family Phasianidae.
Characteristics   Small in size and rather squat in appearance, with sturdy legs that can move about on the ground with great agility. It is about 25–30 cm. long (10–12″). The plumage is brown-gray with gray and white markings on the front parts, giving it its "scaled" look. The sexes are similar.
Habitat   Arid areas and semiarid regions, prairies.
Distribution   North America (western U.S. and Mexico).
Life and habits   During the nesting season it is a solitary species, but in autumn and winter it gathers in large flocks. When threatened by a predator, this quail escapes over the ground, using its camouflaged coloring. It nests in hollows in the ground, which it lines with grass and feathers. The clutch of 9–16 eggs (usually 12–14) is incubated for about 21 days by the female, who takes care of the young. We do not know exactly when the nestlings can fly, although they leave the nest almost as soon as they have hatched, and feed themselves. Their diet consists of 30 percent insects and the rest seeds and other vegetable matter.

80 CALYPTE ANNA
Anna's Hummingbird

Classification   Order Apodiformes, Family Trochilidae.
Characteristics   About 8.5 cm. long (3.3″). This hummingbird has red markings on the top of its head and throat; the upper parts are dark grayish green and the lower, white with darker sides; females have a more greenish coloring uppermost.
Habitat   Scrub, woodland, gardens.
Distribution   California, Arizona and extreme northern Mexico.
Life and habits   It nests in a small cup-shaped nest covered with lichens in trees or bushes. The clutches of almost all hummingbirds have almost invariably 2 eggs (rarely 1 or 3), which are incubated for 14–21 days. The young leave the nest on average at about 22–23 days. The American ornithologist F. G. Stiles has made a 3-year study in California of the biology of this small nectar-eating hummingbird and finds that it is a very aggressive species, which fiercely defends the flowering shrubs that are the source of its food; its reproductive cycle is closely allied to the flowering of plants. In addition, the recent proliferation of flowering shrubs in California gardens seems to be responsible for the growth in numbers of *C. anna*.

81 CAPRIMULGUS EUROPAEUS
Eurasian Nightjar

Classification Order Caprimulgiformes, Family Caprimulgidae.
Characteristics It has long, pointed wings, weak legs and a wide, flat beak. On average about 24 cm. long (10″), it weighs 80 grams (2.85 oz). The sexes are virtually identical, with a remarkably well camouflaged brown plumage speckled tawny and brown. The male, in flight, shows white markings at the tip of its wings and outer rectrices.
Habitat Clearings in woodland, arid terrain with sparse vegetation, sand dunes.
Distribution Europe, Asia and northwest Africa.
Life and habits Nocturnal by nature, it spends the daylight hours resting motionless on the ground or on a branch, well camouflaged with its surroundings. The nest is built on the ground in a bare hollow, in which it places nothing else. There are two annual clutches of 2 eggs each, incubated by both parents (the female usually being in charge during the day) for 18 days. The down-covered and partly nidifugous nestlings are looked after and fed by both parents. They fly at 16–18 days. These migratory birds feed at night, swallowing flying insects—coleopterans, moths, dragonflies and dipterans (flies)—as they fly along, thanks to the size of their mouth.

82 CARDINALIS CARDINALIS
Cardinal

Classification Order Passeriformes, Family Fringillidae.
Characteristics About 18–22 cm. long (7–9″), it has a long crest on its head and a short, conical beak with which it breaks open seeds and grain. The plumage is brick red all over, except for the throat and the base of the beak, which are black. The female, likewise crested, is less brightly colored than the male; her upper parts are brown and the lower are light brown.
Habitat Open terrain and cultivated land with trees and bushes, parks.
Distribution North America (central and eastern states) and the Hawaiian Islands, where it has been introduced.
Life and habits This species in recent years has spread to the north. Its nest is built in bushes or small trees, and it is in the shape of a small cup woven with plants. The Cardinal lays 3–6 eggs (more commonly 3 or 4), which are incubated for 12 days, possibly by both parents. The young leave the nest at about 14 days. Every year 2 or even 3 clutches are reared. Cardinals feed mainly on plant matter (berries and seeds), but also on insects and other invertebrates. Both adults collaborate in looking after the young, as is the case with similar species.

83 CARDUELIS CARDUELIS
Eurasian Goldfinch

Classification   Order Passeriformes, Family Fringillidae.
Characteristics   About 12 cm. long (5″). Sexes similar. Bright coloring. The upper parts are tawny brown, the rump white, the lower parts chestnut; the distinctive wings are black barred with yellow. The head has a small black, white, and red mask. Young birds have grayish-chestnut upper parts and whitish lower parts.
Habitat   Woods, parks, gardens, meadows, fields with thistles.
Distribution   Europe, western Asia, northwest Africa.
Life and habits   It nests in the branches of trees, sometimes in hedgerows and bushes. The cup-shaped nest is built by the pair with roots, twigs, moss, lichens, et cetera. In it they lay 4–7 eggs (sometimes only 3); these are incubated by the female, who is fed by the male, for 12–14 days. The nidicolous nestlings leave the nest after 13–15 days. The Eurasian Goldfinch lays 2 clutches each year, and sometimes 3. It feeds on seeds—particularly thistle seeds—but its diet also includes insects and various invertebrates. The male courts the female by swaying his body from side to side, holding his wings open and making them beat quickly.

---

84 CARDUELIS CHLORIS
Eurasian Greenfinch

Classification   Order Passeriformes, Family Fringillidae.
Characteristics   About 14 or 15 cm. long (6″). The coloring of the upper parts is brownish olive-green, the lower parts yellowish green with grayish shades. There is yellow on the wings and rectrices. In spring the yellow and green are brighter. The female's upper parts are more brownish and the lower grayer. The young resemble the female, but have white streaks above and below. The flight is undulating.
Habitat   Woods, gardens, parks, orchards.
Distribution   Europe, Asia, northwest Africa.
Life and habits   It nests in trees, hedgerows and bushes, where it builds a crude nest, cup-shaped, which is very soft inside. It lays 4–6 eggs (rarely 3 or 8), which are incubated by the female and fed by the male, for 13 or 14 days. The nidicolous young stay in the nest for 13–16 days. They are reared by both parents and fed on regurgitated food. Greenfinches lay two clutches a year (rarely 3). They feed on seeds, with a preference for oily varieties, as well as on blackberries, the shoots of fruit trees, and sometimes insects.

85 CARDUELIS SPINUS
Eurasian Siskin

Classification   Order Passeriformes, Family Fringillidae.
Characteristics   About 11 cm. long (4.5″), it weighs 12–14 grams (approx. 0.5 oz.). The beak is short and tough, designed for an essentially granivorous diet. In the male the plumage is greenish yellow, with brown stripes on the sides and a yellow rump. The top of the head and chin are black. The female and young are grayer, with almost-white lower parts and no black on the head.
Habitat   Gardens, cultivated land, woods (especially coniferous).
Distribution   Europe and northern Asia.
Life and habits   The nest is built in the branches of conifers and is a small cup made with grasses, moss, wool and horsehair. It lays two clutches a year. These have 2–5 eggs each, laid at intervals of one day. The incubation is the task of the female alone and lasts 11–14 days. The nidicolous nestlings are looked after by both parents for 13–15 days, after which they can fly. The diet consists essentially of coniferous seeds (fir), broadleaf seeds (alder), and thistle seeds. But the young are fed insects at least in their earliest days. In winter Siskins usually are gregarious and often combine with other finches in the search for food.

86 CARIAMA CRISTATA
Crested Seriema

Classification   Order Gruiformes, Family Cariamidae.
Characteristics   This species of the family Cariamidae are characterized by a long neck and long legs, dense plumage and a long tail. The Crested Seriema is the largest, reaching an over-all length of about 1 meter (40″). The plumage is yellowish brown, with darker shades uppermost and lighter lower parts; the tail is black and white, the beak and legs are reddish orange. Around the eyes there is a pale blue area. On the head there is a tuft of stiff feathers.
Habitat   Wooded areas.
Distribution   South America.
Life and habits   The Cariamidae are mainly ground-dwelling birds; they are good runners, but poor fliers. They feed on vegetable matter (fruit) and animals (from invertebrates to snakes). The Crested Seriema lives on heights up to 2,000 meters (6,500 ft.) in temperate mountainous regions, as mentioned by C. C. Olrog. It usually lives in pairs and in small groups in autumn and winter. It nests in forks in trees, usually laying 2–3 eggs, which are incubated by both parents for about 24 days.

87 CASUARIUS CASUARIUS
Two-wattled Cassowary

Classification Order Casuariformes, Family Casuaridae.
Characteristics The Two-wattled Cassowary measures (to the back) about 1 meter (40″); the length of the tarso-metatarsus (leg) is 30 cm. (12″), and the weight can reach 85 kg. (190 lbs.). The very strong legs have three toes (the claw on the inner toe is straight and can be up to 10 cm. long (4″)). The head is surmounted by an appendage that is like a helmet and is curved sharply upward. On the front of the neck there are two glabrous (smooth) caruncles. Other species include the One-wattled Cassowary (*C. unappendiculatus*) and the Little Cassowary (*C. bennetti*).
Habitat Lowland plateaus (Little Cassowary lives also in mountainous regions up to 3,000 meters) (10,000 ft).
Distribution Northern Australia and New Guinea.
Life and habits It feeds mainly on fruit and small animals (the intestine is very short—shorter than the Emu's). In 1957 the first living cassowary arrived in Europe (Amsterdam). It is a solitary bird; in the mating season males and females gather in small family groups. The nest is a depression in the ground covered with plant matter. In it, it lays 3–8 eggs. Incubation lasts 49–56 days and is the task of the male, which also takes care of the young.

88 CENTROCERCUS UROPHASIANUS
Sage Grouse

Classification Order Galliformes, Family Tetraonidae.
Characteristics A large bird, it is about 70 cm. long (27.5″). The tail feathers are long and pointed. The male has a black breast and throat and long white feathers lower down. The smaller female does not have the showy white lower plumage. During their nuptial displays the males have two brightly colored sacs of bare yellow skin on either side of the crop.
Habitat Prairie with herbaceous vegetation and sagebrush.
Distribution Western North America.
Life and habits This species is closely allied in both diet and nesting to the sage plant. Usually gregarious, the males gather in spring in areas designed for collective nuptial courtship (arenas, or *leks*); here they parade before the females and display their tail feathers and puff out their vocal sacs. The nest is made in a hollow in the ground surrounded by sage. In it the Sage Grouse lays 7–15 eggs (usually 9–12), which are incubated for about 22 days by the female, who takes care of the young on her own. The nidifugous nestlings can fly after 1 or 2 weeks. The diet consists of the leaves, shoots and flowers of sage, various other plants and insects.

89 CEPHALOPTERUS ORNATUS
Umbrellabird

Classification Order Passeriformes, Family Cotingidae.
Characteristics Up to 51 cm. long (20″), this is an odd bird. The plumage is black, and only the beak (particularly the lower jaw) is light colored. The head has a black plume of feathers with metallic highlights; this plume juts over as far as the tip of the beak. In addition there hangs from the throat and breast a membranous structure that can be 33–40 cm. long (13–16″). This saclike appendage on the throat can be dilated; ornithologist Wilhelm Maise likens it to a fir cone with its scales opened. Among the other species of Cotingidae are the strange bellbirds (belonging to the genus *Procnias*) which are 20–26 cm. long (8–10″), one species of which, the Three-wattled Bellbird (*P. tricarunculata*), has three caruncles on its forehead and on the sides of the base of the beak.
Habitat Forests.
Distribution From Costa Rica to Bolivia and Brazil.

Life and habits The Umbrellabird makes loud sounds like mooing or bellowing, which is why it is also known as the *bullbird*. This is possible because of a considerably enlarged windpipe (trachea). The sac on the throat dangles while the bird emits its calls during courtship displays. These habits have been studied in depth by ornithologist Helmut Sick. It feeds on fruit.

90 CERTHIA FAMILIARIS
Brown Creeper

Classification Order Passeriformes, Family Certhiidae.
Characteristics Streamlined in appearance, with a long, slender and slightly curved beak, it measures 12 cm. long (5″) and weighs about 7–10 grams (about 0.3 oz.) The plumage is brown with tawny stripes on the upper parts, snowy white on the lower. The adults and the young are similar in appearance. A similar species is the Short-toed Tree Creeper (*C. brachydactyla*) which lives in Europe (central-southern areas) and northwest Africa, but steers clear of mountainous areas. It is hard to tell the two apart; the latter has grayish lower parts.
Habitat Woods and forests (coniferous and broadleaf).
Distribution Europe and Asia, in the central and southern regions, and North America.

Life and habits The nest is made of blades of grass, roots and moss, by both sexes, in a cleft in the trunk or branch of a tree, and often in a crack in the bark. There are two broods each year. The clutch can be 3 to 9 eggs, but is usually 6, which are incubated solely by the female for 14 or 15 days. The nidicolous young are looked after by both parents and fly at 14–16 days. Brown Creepers look for food—which consists of invertebrates—by climbing up and down tree trunks with their strong legs, ranging from the foot of the trunk to the tips of branches.

91 CERYLE RUDIS
Lesser Pied Kingfisher

Classification   Order Coraciiformes, Family Alcedinidae.
Characteristics   About 25 cm. long (10″), this is an unmistakable bird. The male has black upper parts with white-edged and white-streaked feathers particularly on the tail and wings. The lower plumage is white with two silver-gray pectoral bands. The coloring of the female is very similar to that of the male, but the female has only one breast band, with a break in the middle. The beak and legs are black. Young birds have a more uniform coloring. Among the other species of Alcedinidae is the Belted Kingfisher (*Ceryle alcyon*), which is up to 37 cm. long (14.5″) and is found in North America.
Habitat   Lakes, rivers, coastal areas.
Distribution   Africa and Asia.
Life and habits   It digs a tunnel some 30 cm. long (12″), which ends with the laying chamber; here it lays from 2 to 6 eggs (but usually 4), which are incubated by both sexes. The nestlings are reared and fed by both parents too.

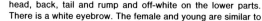

92 CETTIA CETTI
Cetti's Warbler

Classification   Order Passeriformes, Family Sylviidae.
Characteristics   It is about 14 cm. long (6″) and weighs 13–15 grams (0.5 oz.); the plumage is reddish brown on the head, back, tail and rump and off-white on the lower parts. There is a white eyebrow. The female and young are similar to the male. The wings are short and rounded; the fairly long tail is often held upright.
Habitat   Canebrakes and low, dense vegetation near water.
Distribution   Southern Europe, northwest Africa and western Asia.
Life and habits   The nest, shaped like a rather crude cup, is made with dried leaves and lined with horsehair, feathers and the inflorescences of reeds; it is built by the female in bushes or reeds not far from the ground. Each year there are one or two clutches. These consist of 3 to 5 eggs each (usually 4), which are incubated solely by the female for 13 days. The nidicolous nestlings are looked after by both parents and leave the nest at 12 days, already capable of making short flights. The male is probably polygamous. The diet consists of insects and other invertebrates (including small mollusks), with a few seeds thrown in. The young are fed entirely on animal food.

93 CHARADRIUS ALEXANDRINUS
Snowy or Kentish Plover

Classification   Order Charadriiformes, Family Charadriidae.
Characteristics   About 16 cm. long (6.5"), it has a short beak and fairly long, strong legs; Average weight is 40 grams (1.4 ounces). The upper parts are light chestnut, and the lower are white, except for a small black mask across the eye and two black patches on the sides of the breast. The female and young bird have slightly duller coloring. The legs are black.
Habitat   Seacoasts and brackish lagoons, expanses of sand and mud near water, marshland.
Distribution   Europe, Asia, Africa, Australia and America.
Life and habits   The nest is built in a slight depression in the ground and is thinly covered with twigs and plant matter. There are probably two broods a year. It usually lays 2 to 4 eggs (usually 3), which are incubated by both adults for 24 days. The nidifugous nestlings are covered with camouflaging down. They find their own food, but are watched over and looked after by the parents. They fly at 25 days. The diet consists of insects, worms, mollusks and crustaceans found on the ground. If a predator approaches the nest, the adults try to attract attention to themselves by feigning helplessness in order to draw the predator away from the eggs or young.

94 CHAUNA TORQUATA
Southern Crested Screamer

Classification   Order Anseriformes, Family Anhimidae.
Characteristics   The Anhimidae are gooselike birds with long, strong legs and unwebbed toes. They weigh about 2 or 3 kg. (4.5–6.5 lbs.). On the bones of the metacarpus there are two pointed spurs—an odd feature in Anseriformes. In addition the male sex organ is rudimentary. For some time those birds were classified as Rallidae or Ciconiidae, but they are currently considered to have originated from the same ancestors as the Anatidae. Species of the genus *Chauna* have 12 rectrices. The Southern Crested Screamer is about 90 cm. long (35"), with distinctive grayish plumage that is darker uppermost, a black collar, a yellowish beak, red areas around the eyes and red legs, and a small tuft of feathers on the head.
Habitat   Marshlands, along watercourses.
Distribution   Southern South America.
Life and habits   They generally live in groups and despite the absence of webbing are fine swimmers. They feed mainly on plant matter. They build a nest near water in which 5 or 6 eggs are laid; these are incubated by both sexes. The nestlings are nidifugous. Natives raise Crested Screamers as domestic birds.

95 CHIONIS ALBA
Snowy Sheathbill

Classification   Order Charadriiformes, Family Chionididae.
Characteristics   The family Chionididae includes two species, which weigh abut 600 grams (21 oz.) and are about
38–42 cm. (15–16″). They have short beaks, reinforced by a
bony structure situated above the upper mandible; the legs are
also short; the face is partly naked and is covered with
"warts." At the wing angle there is a rudimentary spur, which
is used as a weapon. The plumage is white and covers the gray
down beneath. They live in the cold regions of the Antarctic,
which is why beneath the skin there is a fatty layer about 1 cm.
(0.4″) thick, which gives them a rather chubby look. The other
species is the Black-billed Sheathbill (*Chionis minor*).
Habitat   Coastal areas and ice floes.
Distribution   Antarctic.
Life and habits   These birds are well adapted to life in the
cold. As well as being protected by their layer of fat, they can
ruffle up their feathers, stand on one leg and hide in cracks in
rocks. They feed on invertebrates, vegetable matter, birds'
eggs and residue. They build their nests, which are sometimes
3 feet deep, of grass, algae and snail's shells; they lay 2–4
eggs, which are incubated by both parents for about 28 days.

---

96 CHIROXIPHIA CAUDATA
Swallow-tailed Manakin

Classification   Order Passeriformes, Family Pipridae.
Characteristics   The family Pipridae includes species whose
dimensions range from as small as 8.5 cm to 16 cm. (3.3–6.3″),
with the tarsi almost invariably covered with shields and a slender beak; the males have very brightly colored plumage. They
are distinctive birds because of their "dances" during their
nuptial displays. These dances occur on leafless branches and
are accompanied by calls and noises made by beating the
wings, or screeching and snorting noises produced by the secondary remiges, which are particularly designed for this because of the thickening of the rachis, the reinforced outer vex-
illi (vanes), the calamus detached from the ulna and attached to
it by special muscular bonds. The Swallow-tailed Manakin has
blue plumage, with black on the wings and head, the top of
which is reddish.
Habitat   Forests.
Distribution   Southern South America.
Life and habits   Pipridae live generally in the forest between
1 and 5 meters from the ground (3–16 ft.). They feed on vegetable matter (berries) and invertebrates. The female builds the
nest, incubates the 2 eggs, and looks after the nidicolous
young. The males do their typical nuptial dances bending the
head, jumping up and down in the same spot, and pivoting
through 180 degrees, depending on the species.

97 CHLIDONIAS HYBRIDA
Whiskered Tern

Classification   Order Charadriiformes, Family Laridae.
Characteristics   About 33 cm. long (13″), it has a summer plumage showing a black head and white cheeks and throat, dark gray, almost blackish, lower parts, white inner-wing coverts, and red legs and beak. In winter the front and upper parts are white, the top of the head has black and white stripes. Immature birds have brown-gray upper parts. A similar species is the White-winged Black Tern (*C. leucopterus*), which in summer has a black head, abdomen, breast and inner-wing coverts and wings white on the upper surface.
Habitat   Lagoons, ponds and marshes.
Distribution   Europe, Asia, Africa and Australia.
Life and habits   It nests in colonies, gathering reeds and other plant matter on the water and mooring them to the aquatic vegetation. It lays 2 to 4 eggs (usually 3), which are incubated by both sexes but mostly by the female. The young are raised by both parents. The Whiskered Tern, like its related species, feeds mainly on aquatic insects.

98 CHLIDONIAS NIGER
Black Tern

Classification   Order Charadriiformes, Family Laridae.
Characteristics   About 25 cm. long (10″). The nuptial plumage is unmistakable——the back, tail, wings and lower parts (with the exception of the undertail, which is white) are gray-black, and the legs are black. In winter the lower parts are white, there is a blackish area on the head, and the upper parts are grayish. The young have a blackish mark on top of the head, the upper parts being chestnut gray and the lower white.
Habitat   Marshland, ponds, lagoons, lakes and rivers.
Distribution   Europe, western Asia and North America.
Life and habits   It nests in colonies, building a crude jumble of reeds and water plants on the actual water near marshland vegetation. Here it lays a single clutch, usually of 3 eggs (sometimes 2 or 4), which are incubated by both adults, but mainly by the female, for 14–17 days. The young are reared by both parents and fly at about 3–4 weeks. The Black Tern feeds mainly on aquatic insects.

99 CICONIA ABDIMII
Abdim's Stork

Classification   Order Ciconiiformes, Family Ciconiidae.
Characteristics   About 75 cm. long (30″), this is a small stork; the plumage is black, uppermost, and the hind part of the back is white, as are the lower tail coverts. The head and neck are greenish black, the face is light reddish, the lower parts are white, and the beak and legs are greenish. A distinctive African species is the Yellow-billed Stork (*Ibis ibis*), which is up to 105 cm. long (41″), having white plumage with satiny shades, the edges of the wings and tail being black with highlights, the beak being yellow and the legs and face red.
Habitat   Open terrain, grasslands, near villages.
Distribution   Africa.
Life and habits   Abdim's Stork often forms large colonies, and in some areas nests on the roofs of huts. As described by ornithologist Kai Curry-Lindahl, in his fine work on migration (1977), Abdim's Stork has a most spectacular migratory movement—it nests in Africa north of the Equator, then moves across the equatorial rain forest and the savanna until it finally reaches South Africa.

---

100 CICONIA CICONIA
White Stork

Classification   Order Ciconiiformes, Family Ciconiidae.
Characteristics   Up to 102 cm. long (40″). Plumage is white, with the scapulars, wing coverts, primaries and secondaries black. The legs and beak are brilliant red. In young birds the plumage is white, with brown on the wings; the beak and legs are reddish brown. It often stands on one leg. In flight, its neck is outstretched, and not drawn back in an S like a heron's.
Habitat   Grasslands, lowlands, marshland, nesting in trees and on buildings.
Distribution   Breeds in central and eastern Europe, Spain, Turkey, Asia Minor, central and eastern Asia, and northwest Africa. Winters south to South Africa, where it breeds rarely.
Life and habits   It uses the same nest for many years. This consists of a large platform of twigs and branches. It nests in trees, and on all sorts of buildings (remember the familiar picture of storks on the roofs of many European houses). It lays 1–7 eggs (ordinarily 3–5), which are incubated for 25–30 days. The young are cared for by both parents and leave the nest at 53–55 days. During the nuptial displays it makes distinctive noises by rhythmically clapping its beak.

101 CICONIA NIGRA
Black Stork

Classification   Order Ciconiiformes, Family Ciconiidae.
Characteristics   It has a wing span of 2 meters (6.5 ft.) on average and an average weight of 3 kg. (6.6 lbs.). It is about 96 cm. long (38"). The plumage of the adult is black with green and purple highlights on the back, wings, neck and head; the other parts are white, with the beak and legs red. The young have duller coloring, and a gray-green beak and legs.
Habitat   Marshland, grassland and rocky terrain in wooded areas.
Distribution   Europe, Africa and Asia.
Life and habits   It usually nests in large trees, more rarely on ledges or in hollows in cliffs, in very rugged areas near water. The nest is used year after year and is made of dry branches and plant matter. There is a single clutch of 3–5 eggs (usually 4), laid at 2-day intervals. The eggs are incubated by both adults for 30–35 days. Then both parents look after the nidicolous young, which fly at 63–71 days. The diet of the Black Stork consists of worms, small fish, aquatic insects, amphibians and reptiles, which it finds in marshy areas. This species, with its rather solitary nature, is migratory and winters in Africa and southern Asia, and a few even remain to breed in South Africa.

102 CINCLUS CINCLUS
Eurasian Dipper

Classification   Order Passeriformes, Family Cinclidae.
Characteristics   About 17 cm. long (7"), it weighs on average 60 grams (2.1 ounces). It is squat looking, with a short tail. The upper parts are black, the breast is white, the belly is chestnut-colored or brown, depending on the subspecies. The sexes are similar in appearance. The young are gray uppermost, speckled gray and white in the lower parts.
Habitat   Torrents and streams in hills and mountains.
Distribution   Northwestern Africa, Europe and northern Asia.
Life and habits   The nest is built by both adults in rocks, in the roots of trees (near water), and often behind a waterfall. It is made with moss and dry leaves. There are two, and sometimes three, clutches each year. Each has 3–8 eggs (most commonly 5), laid at one-day intervals and incubated by the female for 15–18 days. The nidicolous young are helped by both parents and fly at 19–25 days. Dippers search for food along banks and among pebbles, and on the bottom of torrents, diving for a few seconds with its legs, wings and tail used as flippers. The diet is mainly aquatic insects and their larvae, small crustaceans, worms and small fry. A film of air around the plumage (which is endlessly preened and smoothed with the beak) keeps the feathers from absorbing water.

103 CIRCAETUS CINEREUS
Brown Harrier Eagle

Classification   Order Falconiformes, Family Accipitridae.
Characteristics   About 73–78 cm. long (28–31″), this large bird has a wing span of about 1.8 meters (71″). The female is slightly larger than the male. The plumage is uniformly chestnut colored on both upper and lower parts. The iris is yellow. Immature birds are paler than adults, with light-colored stripes.
Habitat   Savanna, wooded areas with large clearings.
Distribution   Central to southern Africa.
Life and habits   It nests at different altitudes, from lowlands to mountainous plateaus up to 2,500 meters (8,000 ft.). The nest is build at the top of acacia or euphorbia trees with dry branches. A single egg is laid and is incubated solely by the female for 40–52 days (most commonly 45). The nestling is fed first by the female alone and then by the male as well, and flies at about 100–109 days. When hunting, the Brown Harrier Eagle uses two basic techniques: one consists in flying low over grassy areas, ready to pounce on prey, the other in sighting the prey from a perch (in a tree or on a pole), and catching up with it with a few powerful movements of the wings. About three quarters of the diet consists of reptiles, especially snakes (including poisonous species like cobras), and the rest consists of birds of medium size that are caught on the ground.

104 CIRCAETUS GALLICUS
Short-toed Eagle

Classification   Order Falconiformes, Family Accipitridae.
Characteristics   About 63–69 cm. long (25–27″). Its coloring varies considerably; it is generally gray-brown uppermost and light in the lower parts; the head and upper breast are brown. In flight it shows the light-colored lower parts (white with brown bars, the number differing from individual to individual) and barred tail. Typical features are the orange-yellow iris and head that looks quite sturdy compared with the body. The young resemble the adults, but are lighter in color.
Habitat   Scrubby vegetation, not very wooded open terrain, woods with large clearings and rocky reliefs.
Distribution   Central and southern Europe, northeast Africa, central and southern Asia.
Life and habits   It nests in trees and prefers evergreens (only occasionally nests on rocks). It lays a single clutch of one egg; this is usually incubated by the female, who is fed by the male, for about 47 days. The nestling leaves the nest at about 60 days and flies at 70–75 days. The diet of the Short-toed Eagle consists mainly of reptiles, particularly snakes and lizards. It will sometimes even eat vipers and other poisonous snakes.

105 CIRCUS AERUGINOSUS
Marsh Harrier

Classification Order Falconiformes, Family Accipitridae.
Characteristics About 48–55 cm. long (19–22″). The female is larger than the male. The plumage is dark brownish. The adult male has an ash-gray tail, secondaries and certain wing coverts that contrast sharply in flight with the black primaries; its lower parts are dark reddish. The female is dark brown with pale back and head. The young resemble the female.
Habitat Marshland, canebrakes, wetlands in general, open countryside and grassy areas near water.
Distribution Europe, Asia and Africa.
Life and habits It generally nests on the ground in vegetation, in canebrakes. The nest is a mound of reeds and twigs and is made mainly or entirely by the female, who lays 3–8 eggs (usually 4 or 5). Incubation is the task of the female, who is fed by the male, and lasts about 33–38 days. The young fly at 35–40 days and follow the parents for a further 2 or 3 weeks. The Marsh Harrier feeds on amphibians, reptiles, small mammals and small birds.
Note: The photo shows a female.

106 CIRCUS PYGARGUS
Montagu's Harrier

Classification Order Falconiformes, Family Accipitridae.
Characteristics About 40–45 cm. long (16–18″). The upper plumage of the male is ash gray, with a dark bar halfway along the wing, black outer remiges, and lighter lower parts. The female is brownish with a white mark at the top of the tail, and more reddish lower down. The young resemble the female. Similar species include the Northern Harrier (*C. cyaneus*), in which the male is like the male of Montagu's Harrier but without the dark wing bar, while it has a black rear-wing edge and is paler in color in the lower parts; and the Pallid Harrier (*C. macrourus*), which is much paler in color and has no bars on the wings. The females of these two species are brown, with white at the top of the wing.
Habitat Marshland and heathland.
Distribution Europe, Asia and Africa.
Life and habits It nests on the ground amid vegetation. It lays 3–10 eggs (usually 4 or 5), at intervals of 1–3 days; incubation period, once the first egg has been laid, is 27–30 days for each egg. The young fly at 35–40 days. Montagu's Harrier feeds on amphibians, reptiles, small birds and mammals.

107 CISTICOLA JUNCIDIS
Fan-tailed Warbler

Classification   Order Passeriformes, Family Sylviidae.
Characteristics   It is 10 cm. long (4″) and weighs 8–9 grams (about 0.3 oz.), has a slender, streamlined appearance, with a thin beak designed for an insectivorous diet. The plumage is brown on the upper parts, with tawny and reddish stripes. The lower parts are off-white with reddish patches on the sides and breast. The tail is short and rounded. Adults of the two sexes are similar, as are the young.
Habitat   Dry terrain or wetlands, grassland, cereal fields.
Distribution   Southern Europe, Africa, Asia and Australia.
Life and habits   The nest is built in tall, dense grass, not far from the ground and often near water. It is in the shape of an elongated cup woven with grasses and cobwebs. It lays 2 and even 3 clutches annually, each one with 4–6 eggs. They are incubated for 11–12 days (it is not known exactly whether both parents collaborate in this task) and the nestlings remain in the nest for 12–14 days, after which they are ready to make short flights. It is probable that both adults look after their young. The diet consists of small insects (dipterans, coleopterans, orthopterans). These warblers are easily seen flying about not far from the ground over their own territory, making their persistent shrill song.

108 CLAMATOR GLANDARIUS
Great Spotted Cuckoo

Classification   Order Cuculiformes, Family Cuculidae.
Characteristics   About 39–45 cm. long (16–19″), with a maximum weight of 220 grams (8 oz.). The adult plumage is brown uppermost with white markings, and cream colored in the lower parts. The long tail has large white patches, and the head has a crest of gray feathers. The young, which do not have the crest, have reddish primary feathers.
Habitat   Mediterranean *maquis*, olive groves, wooded lowlands.
Distribution   Southern Europe, Africa and the Middle East.
Life and habits   The Great Spotted Cuckoo is a parasitic species, laying its eggs in the nests of Corvidae (for Europe and Turkey five host species have been identified: the Rook, the Common Raven, the Eurasian Jay, the Azure-winged Magpie and, above all, the Black-billed Magpie). The female lays 1 or 2 eggs in the host's nest, removing 1 or 2 of the host's eggs, and repeats this operation in 4 or 5 nests. The eggs hatch after 14 days and the young are raised with the young of the owner. The nestlings fly at 24 days and are still fed for some time by the adopted parents. The diet consists in particular of the grubs of the processionary moth and various insects (orthopterans, coleopterans and hemipterans).

109 COCCOTHRAUSTES COCCOTHRAUSTES
Hawfinch

Classification   Order Passeriformes, Family Fringillidae.
Characteristics   It is 17.5 cm. long (7″) and weighs an average of 55 grams (2 oz.), the very high-set and strong beak is gray-blue; the wings are black with a white band on the shoulder; the rump and tip of the tail are white. The remaining upper parts are brown, apart from the throat, which is black. The lower parts are pink-chestnut. The young are brown with a yellow patch on the throat.
Habitat   Broadleaf and coniferous woods, parks and orchards.
Distribution   Europe, Asia, and northwest Africa.
Life and habits   The nest is a cup of twigs, small roots and lichens, and it is built in trees almost exclusively by the female. There is usually one clutch a year (sometimes 2) of 2–7 eggs (most commonly 5), which are incubated for 12–14 days by the female, with occasional help from the male. The nidicolous nestlings are fed by both parents and fly at 10–14 days. Thanks to the tough beak (which can develop on average a thrust of 45 kg. (100 lbs.), the Hawfinch can break open even the hardest seeds. The diet consists of berries, seeds, nuts, et cetera. Sedentary by nature, this species may make erratic movements and actual local migrations.

110 COCHLEARIUS COCHLEARIUS
Boat-billed Heron

Classification   Order Ciconiiformes, Family Ardeidae.
Characteristics   This is a distinctive bird with a wide and flattened beak about 7 cm. long (3″) and about 5 cm. wide (2″) ending in a hook (for many years this beak was the object of discussion among experts, who did not consider it right to include this species in the Family Ardeidae). In the upper parts the plumage has a grayish color, lower down it is light with reddish and pale yellow shades at the sides. The top of the head is black with a dark tuft of feathers. Immature birds are predominantly brown.
Habitat   Along watercourses, lakes, marshland.
Distribution   Tropical areas of the Americas.
Life and habits   It has mainly crepuscular and nocturnal habits. The tuft of feathers on the nape of the neck is raised during courtship rituals. While the tuft is raised males and females clap their beaks, then the male wheels about the female, who flattens herself on the ground and stretches out her neck. Boat-billed Herons generally live alone or in pairs. With their strange beaks, they feed mainly on aquatic invertebrates.

111 COLAPTES AURATUS
Northern Flicker

Classification Order Piciformes, Family Picidae.
Characteristics About 30–35 cm. long (12–14"), it has a long pointed beak, very strong legs and tail with which it supports itself while climbing on tree trunks. The plumage of the upper parts is brown with black bars, white on the rump, black on the wings and tail. The lower plumage is off-white with a streak of scarlet on the nape of the neck and black markings on the belly. The lower surface of the wings is yellow to salmon. The appearance of the male is distinct from that of the female in that the male has a black stripe across each cheek.
Habitat Woods, cultivated land, forests along watercourses.
Distribution North America.
Life and habits It usually feeds climbing on tree trunks, but often descends to the ground to eat ants. It nests in holes in trees and in buildings, often high above the ground. It lays 5–10 eggs, which are incubated by both adults for 11–12 days. The nestlings, which are fed by both parents, leave the nest at 25–28 days. The diet consists largely of ants, then other insects and a little wild fruit, with berries and seeds.

112 COLINUS VIRGINIANUS
Common Bobwhite

Classification Order Galliformes, Family Phasianidae.
Characteristics A small bird, about 25 cm. long (10") and squat looking. Its plumage is brown, and paler with white bars on the lower parts. The body is dark; there is a slight crest with an eyebrow, and a white marking on the throat. In the female these white parts are yellowish ocher. There are considerable variations of coloring in the different populations.
Habitat Cultivated land and grassland with scrub.
Distribution North America.
Life and habits This species, which has been introduced into many areas outside America, has adapted well to open habitats that have scrubby hedgerows for nesting purposes; the nest is well hidden amid vegetation and is lined with grass. The female, who is reluctant to leave the nest even when threatened, lays 12–20 eggs (usually 14–16). These are incubated by both parents for 23–24 days. The nidifugous nestlings fly within two weeks after hatching. The diet of the bobwhite consists mainly of vegetable matter of all sorts (seeds, shoots, berries) and a small proportion of insects, which form the basic food of the young.

113 COLIUS STRIATUS
Speckled Mousebird

Classification   Order Coliiformes, Family Coliidae.
Characteristics   The Coliidae are birds characterized by a crest of feathers, soft plumage, long rectrices that are up to 25 cm. long (10″), and toes, the first and fourth of which can be pointed forward or backward. They are called mousebirds because of their brownish-gray plumage and their way of moving swiftly in bushes like mice. Their gray-brown plumage is crossed with not very noticeable darker stripes. Depending on the various subspecies, it may have the upper mandible black and the lower one silvery, or a yellow marking at the base of the beak.
Habitat   Forests along rivers.
Distribution   Africa.
Life and habits   They live in small family groups of 5–7 individuals, and sometimes in flocks of more than 30. They build cup-shaped nests in bushes or hedgerows. They usually lay 2–5 eggs, which are incubated by both sexes for 11–12 days. The nidicolous nestlings fly at 2½ weeks. The young remain with their parents and are independent at about 2 months.

114 COLUMBA LIVIA
Rock Pigeon

Classification   Order Columbiformes, Family Columbidae.
Characteristics   About 33 cm. long (13″), it has uniform gray plumage with green and purple highlights on the neck. On each wing there are two black bands, crosswise, and a black band at the tip of the tail. The rump is white, and the legs are purplish red. The plumage is similar in adults and young. This species is the forebear of the Domestic Pigeon from which, by artificial selection, numerous domesticated varieties have been obtained (carrier or homing pigeons, fantail pigeons, etc.).
Habitat   Rocky seacoasts, inland areas, city parks, farms, and suburbs.
Distribution   Europe, North Africa and Asia; introduced in North America.
Life and habits   Gregarious by nature, it usually nests in colonies in hollows and in caves in cliffs. The nest is a crude affair of twigs and vegetable matter, built by both adults. Each year there are 2 or 3 clutches, each with 2 eggs (sometimes 3), which are incubated by both parents for 17–19 days. The nidicolous nestlings are fed by both parents with a milky secretion from the crop. They fly at 30–35 days. The diet of pigeons consists of plant matter (seeds, grains, berries and green shoots).

115 COLUMBA PALUMBUS
Wood Pigeon

Classification   Order Columbiformes, Family Columbidae.
Characteristics   About 41 cm. long (16″). The upper plumage is gray, except for a white patch on each side of the neck and on each wing. The breast is pinkish. The tail ends with a broad black band, while the legs are purplish red. The plumage of young birds is paler.
Habitat   Chiefly broadleaf and coniferous woods, and city parks.
Distribution   Europe, western and southern Asia, northwestern Africa.
Life and habits   The nest is built with dry twigs in trees, very rarely on building exteriors, rocks or on the ground. Each year there are 2 or 3 clutches (possibly even four, according to some ornithologists). Usually 2 eggs are laid, rarely 1; both sexes incubate the eggs for 17 days. The nidicolous nestlings are looked after by both parents and fly at 28–35 days. Wood Pigeons feed on plant matter (seeds, grains, berries and acorns). The nuptial display consists in bowing and reciprocal caressing by both male and female, accompanied by gentle pecking of each other's plumage. The courtship aerial display includes a swift ascent into the air, followed by repeated clapping of the wings and a glide with the wings held still.

116 CORACIAS GARRULUS
Eurasian Roller

Classification   Order Coraciiformes, Family Coraciidae.
Characteristics   It is about 28 cm. long (11″) and weighs on average 140 grams (5 oz.). The beak is very tough, and the wings are quite broad. The plumage, which is alike in the two sexes, is blue with a reddish back and dark blue wings and tail. The young are duller in coloration.
Habitat   Open forests, countryside with wooded areas, Mediterranean *maquis*.
Distribution   Southern Europe, northwestern Africa and western Asia.
Life and habits   The nest is built in holes in tree trunks, in hollows in rocks and in buildings, and it may have either a thin lining of grasses and feathers or no lining at all. There is one clutch annually of 4–5 eggs (sometimes 7), which are incubated by both parents for 18–19 days. The nidicolous young are looked after and fed by both adults and fly at 26–28 days. From a perch on a branch or other elevated place, the Eurasian Roller plunges down onto its prey. It feeds mainly on insects (large coleopterans and orthopterans), other invertebrates, small rodents, amphibians, reptiles and birds. The male makes a nuptial flight up into the air, where he performs a series of acrobatics, dives and pirouettes, and utters a succession of raucous calls.

117 CORAGYPS ATRATUS
Black Vulture

Classification   Order Falconiformes, Family Cathartidae.
Characteristics   About 55–68 cm. long (22–28″), it is completely black, including the bare skin on the face. In flight it clearly shows a white marking on the lower surface of the wings, near the tips. It can reach a weight of 1.9 kg. (4.2 lbs.) and a wing span of about 1.5 meters (60″).
Habitat   Open land with scattered trees.
Distribution   North and South America (from the southern U.S. to central Patagonia).
Life and habits   It lives in warm regions with open woods and avoids the higher mountains and desert areas. The nest is built, often in colonies, on the ground and sometimes on buildings. There are 1–3 eggs (nearly always 2), laid at intervals of 2 days; they are incubated by both parents, who also jointly care for the young; these leave the nest after about 10 weeks. The diet consists essentially of carrion, sometimes eggs and fruit of the oil palm. Occasionally they kill small ground-dwelling creatures. Because the long, thin beak is rather weak, this bird of prey is forced, when it comes to feeding, to wait until other stronger species of vulture have torn open the skin of the carcass.

118 CORVUS ALBICOLLIS
African White-necked Raven

Classification   Order Passeriformes, Family Corvidae.
Characteristics   The Family Corvidae includes birds whose size ranges from 18 to 70 cm. in length (7–28″), with 10 primaries and 12 rectrices (with the exception of one species that has 10). The plumage is generally dullish in color, although some species do have bright coloring. The various species of this family fall conveniently into seven groups—jays, magpies, ground jays, nutcrackers, crows, choughs and the species *Ptilostomus ater*, which is a self-contained group. In the crow group there are species with predominantly blackish coloring and a tough beak with bristles. The African White-necked Raven, about 50 cm. long (20″), has blackish plumage with a white patch on the nape.
Habitat   Rocky areas, scrub.
Distribution   Eastern and southern Africa.
Life and habits   The White-necked Raven nests in hollows in cliffs. More rarely it may nest in trees. The parents rear the nestlings, which are nidicolous, until they are independent. When the young have been reared, the adults roam about in pairs, often gathering in large groups of up to 100 individuals. The White-necked Raven feeds on mice, rats and large insects.

119   CORVUS CORAX
Common Raven

Classification   Order Passeriformes, Family Corvidae.
Characteristics   About 51–63 cm. long (20–25″), it has a
wing span of about 1.20 meters (47″). It weighs on average
1–1.3 kg. (2.2–3.0 lbs.). The entire body is black, with metallic
highlights in good light conditions. The beak is huge and black,
as are the legs. The tail is quite long and wedge shaped. The
young resemble the adults.
Habitat   Mountainous regions, rocky seacoasts.
Distribution   Europe, Asia, North Africa and North America.
Life and habits   It frequents rocky regions with trees, often
high above sea level; also arid areas. The nest is usually built in
cracks and ledges in cliffs, more rarely in trees, and consists of
a large collection of dry branches, lined with wool and horsehair; it is built by both adults. The single annual clutch consists
of 3–7 eggs (ordinarily 4, 5 or 6), which are laid at intervals of
1–2 days and are incubated for 20 or 21 days by the female.
Both sexes look after the nidicolous young, which can fly at 5-6
weeks. The food comprises a large variety of animal matter
(carrion, small mammals and birds, large insects, and reptiles)
and vegetable matter (fruit and seeds). In its nuptial flight, both
members of the pair carry out numerous aerial acrobatics.

120   CORVUS CORONE
Carrion Crow

Classification   Order Passeriformes, Family Corvidae.
Characteristics   It measures 43–46 cm. in length (17″), has
a wing span of 92–100 cm. (36–40″) and weighs around
450–580 grams (16–21 oz.). There are two subspecies (which
some consider to be two distinct species)—the Carrion Crow
(*C. c. corone*) which is a uniform black color, and the Hooded
Crow (*C. c. cornix*), which is gray except for the black head and
wings. In areas in which the two overlap there are hybrid offspring with intermediate characteristics, but in all cases the
young resemble the adults.
Habitat   Cultivated land, open and wooded terrain.
Distribution   Europe and northern Asia.
Life and habits   It usually nests in trees, and sometimes in
rocks. The nest is a structure of dry branches lined with wool.
There is a single clutch each year, with 4–6 eggs (rarely as
many as 7), which are incubated by the female for 18–20 days;
the nidicolous nestlings are fed by both adults and fly at 4 or 5
weeks. This species is very eclectic in its choice of habitat and
diet; in fact it feeds on seeds, fruit and other plant matter as
well as on insects, mollusks, worms, small vertebrates and
carrion. Gregarious by nature, it is a nonmigratory species.
Note: The photo shows the subspecies *C. c. corone*.

121 CORVUS FRUGILEGUS
Rook

Classification Order Passeriformes, Family Corvidae.
Characteristics On average, this species is 44 cm. long (17″), with a wing span of 90 cm. (35″) and a weight of about 450 grams (16 oz.). The plumage is black, with violet highlights. By the base of the beak there is a patch of bare gray skin, which is not present in young birds, where it is covered by black plumage. The beak is dark gray.
Habitat Wooded countryside.
Distribution Europe and Asia (it also has been introduced to New Zealand).
Life and habits Nests in colonies called rookeries, in trees at the edge of woods. The nest, which is cup-shaped and made of dry branches lined with grass, wool and leaves, is built by both adults. There is one clutch a year of 3–5 eggs (sometimes up to 9), laid at intervals of one day. The female alone incubates them for 16–20 days. The nidicolous nestlings fly at 29–30 days, after having been looked after and fed by both parents. The Rook feeds mainly on cereal crops, fruit, berries, insects, worms, carrion and even the eggs and chicks of small birds. The nuptial displays start in midwinter; in a tree or on the ground, the male, with drooping wings and extended tail, bows repeatedly forward toward the female, offering her food with his beak.

122 CORVUS MONEDULA
Eurasian Jackdaw

Classification Order Passeriformes, Family Corvidae.
Characteristics About 30 cm. long (12″), it weighs on average about 220 grams (8 ounces), but males are slightly larger than females. The plumage is uniformly black, except for a gray patch on the back of the neck, which is less marked in young birds. The tough beak is black, as are the legs.
Habitat Open woodland, wooded countryside, cliffs by the sea, urban areas.
Distribution Europe, northwestern Africa, western Asia.
Life and habits Jackdaws are gregarious by nature and nest in colonies in holes in trees, on cliffs and on buildings. The nest consists of a cup-shaped structure of twigs lined with wool and horsehair. The one annual clutch of 2–9 eggs (usually 4, 5 or 6) is incubated exclusively by the female for 17 or 18 days (the eggs are laid at intervals of one day). The nidicolous nestlings are reared by both parents, and the fledglings fly after 28–32 days. The diet is made up of animal and vegetable matter. The social behavior of jackdaws, which has been closely studied by the ethologist K. Lorenz, is quite involved; there are numerous calls and postures having to do with pair formation and the creation and maintenance of a hierarchy of dominance within the colony.

123 COTURNIX COTURNIX
Migratory Quail

Classification Order Galliformes, Family Phasianidae.
Characteristics It is about 17.5 cm. long (7″); its upper parts are brownish, with irregular black markings and tawny and cream-colored cross bars. In the male the center of the chin and the throat are black or dark brown. At the base of the throat is a U-shaped marking. The breast is brownish, the lower parts light colored. The female has a white throat and small black markings on her breast. The upper feathers have a central, pale, arrow-shaped stripe.
Habitat Cultivated land, grassland, untilled fields.
Distribution Europe, Asia and Africa.
Life and habits It nests on the ground in hollows among vegetation. it lays a single clutch (sometimes 2, but as happens with many species the second clutch may be a substitute one if the first has been lost or destroyed) of 7–12 eggs (sometimes 6–18), which are incubated by the female for 16–21 days. The nidifugous nestlings develop their feathers quickly and can fly at 19 days. The quail's diet consists mainly of vegetable matter, but also includes various invertebrates, particularly when rearing the young.

---

124 CRAX RUBRA
Great Curassow

Classification Order Galliformes, Family Cracidae.
Characteristics The family Cracidae is made up of species of arboreal birds limited to the tropical and subtropical regions of the Americas. They have a slender body, long legs, short, rounded wings, and a fairly long tail, the length of which in some species can be slightly more than that of the wings. The beak is sturdy, slightly curved, and often having a protuberance, varying in shape, on the upper part. On the foot the well-developed hind toe is on the same level as the others when it runs. The Great Curassow is about 95 cm. long (37″); the male is predominantly black, with a crested head; the ventral area is whitish and there is a yellow protuberance on the upper jaw of the beak. The female's plumage is rust-brown or yellowish, and there is no protuberance; she has a crest with black and white markings on the head.
Habitat Forest.
Distribution Mexico to northwestern South America.
Life and habits It makes a nest of plant matter in trees and lays 2 eggs. It roosts in trees, but spends much of its time on the ground feeding on plant matter (fruit and seeds). During courtship the male emits a hollow-sounding call.

125 CREX CREX
Corn Crake

Classification   Order Gruiformes, Family Rallidae.
Characteristics   About 26.5 cm. long (10.5″). Its coloring is tawny gray, with blackish markings uppermost, and pale below with sides and undertail barred with reddish brown. The wings are chestnut. The breast and cheeks are grayish. The female's coloring is duller. Young birds have less distinctly barred sides and do not show any gray.
Habitat   Meadows, grasslands, cultivated fields, marshland with plenty of vegetation.
Distribution   Europe, Asia and Africa.
Life and habits   Mainly solitary by nature, and active in twilight, it spends a lot of time among tall grasses. It nests amid vegetation on the ground. It lays one clutch, sometimes two, usually of 8–12 eggs (sometimes 6–14). Incubation is principally the task of the female and lasts about 14 or 15 days. The nidifugous nestlings are reared by both parents (or by just the female) and can fly after about 5 weeks; they have complete plumage by 7–8 weeks. It feeds on invertebrates, seeds, green plants and grain.

126 CUCULUS CANORUS
Old World Cuckoo

Classification   Order Cuculiformes, Family Cuculidae.
Characteristics   It has a long tail and narrow, pointed wings. About 32 cm. long (13″), it weighs about 110 grams (4 oz.). The male has gray-blue upper parts, and white lower parts with black bars. The female has two distinct phases—one gray, like the male; the other reddish, in which the upper parts are reddish, with dark barring, and the lower parts are white, with black bars and tawny shades. The young go through both phases, regardless of the sex.
Habitat   Clearings in woodland, cultivated fields.
Distribution   Europe, Asia and Africa.
Life and habits   This species is parasitic, and the females are polyandrous. Every female, which specializes in a single host species (probably the one which reared it) lays 8–10 eggs a year (up to 25 in artificial conditions), each one in a nest made by the host bird, and removes one of the latter's eggs. The cuckoo's eggs (resembling those of the host species) hatch after 12 and a half days of incubation, and the nestling quickly sees to the job of flicking the other eggs or legitimate nestlings out of the nest. Fed and looked after by its adopted parents, it flies at 20–23 days. The Old World Cuckoo feeds on insects (especially the larvae of lepidopterans).

127 CURSORIUS CURSOR
Cream-colored Courser

Classification   Order Charadriiformes, Family Glareolidae.
Characteristics   About 23 cm. long (9″), it has a wing span of up to 50 cm. (20″), a long, slightly curved beak, very pale sand-colored plumage, with the exception of the primary feathers and the lower surface of the wings, which are black. Over the eye there is a white eyebrow. The legs are creamy yellow. Young birds have the upper parts barred with brown and the breast is speckled with black.
Habitat   Sandy or stony desert or semidesert.
Distribution   Africa, western Asia.
Life and habits   This species lives in sandy and stony terrain with sparse herbaceous vegetation, with which it is perfectly camouflaged. The nest is made in a low, unprotected hollow in dry ground, completely exposed to the sun. There are one or two (in some cases) clutches a year. There are usually two eggs (rarely three), which are incubated by both parents for an unknown period of time. The nidifugous nestlings leave the nest the day after they are born and follow their parents about; the parents supply them with food. We do not know exactly when the young can fly. The Cream-colored Courser catches its prey on the ground after a hot pursuit; its diet consists mainly of insects, but also includes small lizards.

---

128 CYANOPICA CYANUS
Azure-winged Magpie

Classification   Order Passeriformes, Family Corvidae.
Characteristics   This species is about 35 cm. long (14″). Its plumage has a distinctive coloring: the head has a black "cap" down to the nape of the neck; the wings are azure, the upper parts brownish gray, and the lower parts pale with gray-brown sides.
Habitat   Woods, gardens, *maquis,* with cork oak, pines and holm oak.
Distribution   There are three isolated populations: one in southern Spain and Portugal, one in northern Mongolia and Transbaikalia and a third in eastern Siberia, China and Japan. The causes of this very disjunctive range are not well known, but they must have something to do with the climatological changes of the glacial and postglacial periods.
Life and habits   Its nest is built in a fork of a tree. It lays 5–7 eggs (sometimes as many as 9), which are incubated by the female for about 20 days. The nestlings are reared by both parents and are fed on regurgitated food. it lays a single clutch each year. It feeds on seeds, insects and other small creatures.

129 CYGNUS ATRATUS
Black Swan

Classification   Order Anseriformes, Family Anatidae.
Characteristics   An unmistakable bird because of its plumage, which is entirely black, except for the wing tips, which are white and visible only in flight. The beak is red, with a small white marking. In proportion, the neck seems longer than in other swans. Its wing span is about 2 meters (80″).
Habitat   Marshland, expanses of water.
Distribution   Australia; introduced into New Zealand in the latter half of the nineteenth century.
Life and habits   Gregarious. It breeds in large nests, which can be up to a meter (40″) in diameter. It usually lays 5–6 eggs, which are incubated by both sexes for about 40 days. The nestlings have grayish down. By the end of the first year, the plumage turns from brownish gray to the black of adults. The Black Swan feeds mainly on vegetable matter. Because of their beauty, many zoos and parks keep Black Swans, thus supporting the sad trade of the wild species.

130 CYGNUS OLOR
Mute Swan

Classification   Order Anseriformes, Family Anatidae.
Characteristics   About 150 cm. long (60″), much of which is accounted for by the neck, and a wing span of up to 230 cm. (90″), it can weigh between 10 and 23 kg. (22–50 lbs.) The adult plumage is completely white; the legs are black and the beak orange and black. The young are gray-brown, with the front of the neck white and the beak gray.
Habitat   Marshes, freshwater lakes, seacoasts.
Distribution   Europe and Asia; introduced into North America.
Life and habits   Pairs are solitary and are very aggressive toward other pairs; the nest is built on dry land, but also in the water amid bog vegetation. It consists of a large platform of plant matter, with a central hollow lined with down. There is one clutch a year of 4–12 eggs (more commonly 5, 6 or 7), which are incubated mainly by the female for 34–38 days. The nidifugous nestlings follow their parents into the water and fly at about 4 months. The young reach sexual maturity at about 3–4 years of age. The diet of this species consists mainly of aquatic plants, mollusks and small fish. In the nuptial display the male and female intertwine their necks and mutually preen the head feathers, interrupting the ceremony every so often to plunge the head into the water and then extend the neck.

131 DACELO GIGAS
Laughing Kookaburra

Classification Order Coraciiformes, Family Alcedinidae.
Characteristics About 42–47 cm. long (16–18″), weighing about 380 grams (14 oz.), with a beak up to 8–10 cm. long (3–4″), this is a large kingfisher with dark plumage uppermost, whitish lower parts, white on the wings and a fairly long tail barred black and reddish. There is a dark stripe on the forehead and on the sides of the head. The strong, large beak has a dark upper mandible and a light lower one. A similar species is the Blue-winged Kookaburra (*Dacelo leachii*), which is 22 cm. long (17″).
Habitat Woods, parks and gardens.
Distribution Australia and Tasmania.
Life and habits It nests in hollow trunks or holes in trees, or in arboreal termite nests that have been emptied out. It usually lays 2–4 eggs, which are incubated for about 25 days by both parents. The nidicolous nestlings remain in the nest for about 30 days, after which, although outside the nest, they are fed by the parents for up to 40 additional days. It is called the *Laughing* Kookaburra because of its loud cry, which resembles laughter; this cry is heard mainly in the early morning or shortly after sundown. It feeds on invertebrates, lizards, small birds and snakes.

132 DAPTION CAPENSIS
Cape Petrel

Classification Order Procellariiformes, Family Procellariidae.
Characteristics About 35 cm. (14″) long, almost as large as a Herring Gull, it has a distinctive plumage with black and white upper parts, dark wings with a white marking. The head, sides of the face, and neck are black. The lower parts are white. The beak and legs are black. Young birds resemble adults.
Habitat Rocky islands, coasts, open sea.
Distribution Southern oceans; outside the mating season it may be found north of the Equator, but very rarely.
Life and habits It can dive up to 10–15 meters (35–50 feet); it often approaches or follows ships. It nests on crags in the Antarctic islands in the southern summer from December to March. It lays a single clutch, with a single egg, in the shelter of rocks. After the reproductive period, the Cape Petrel starts its movement of postnuptial dispersion, which takes it north, sometimes even beyond Latitude 25 degrees S. It feeds on fish and other marine creatures.

133 DELICHON URBICA
House Martin

Classification   Order Passeriformes, Family Hirundinidae.
Characteristics   About 12–13 cm. long (5″) and weighing
between 16–25 grams (0.6–0.9 oz.). The plumage of the head,
back, wings and tail is blue-black. The lower parts and the
rump are white. The tail is forked. The two sexes and the young
are similar. The rather short legs make it difficult for this bird to
move on the ground.
Habitat   Cultivated land near buildings and rocky walls,
urban areas.
Distribution   Europe, central and northern Asia, northwestern Africa.
Life and habits   In the Alps this species breeds as high as
2,200–2,400 meters (7,200–7,900 feet) and ventures much
higher in search of food. The nest is built in a small colony
under the eaves of buildings or in natural rock walls. It is a
hemisphere of mud and blades of straw (picked from the
ground). Each year there are two or three clutches, each of
which has 2 to 6 eggs (usually 4 or 5). Incubation is undertaken
by both sexes for 13–19 days. The adults look after and feed
their young together; the nidicolous chicks fly at 19–25 days.
The young of the first clutch may stay near the nesting area
and help to feed the nestlings of the last clutch. House Martins
feed on insects (mainly dipterans) caught in flight.

134 DENDROCOPOS MAJOR
Great Spotted Woodpecker

Classification   Order Piciformes, Family Picidae.
Characteristics   About 23 cm. long (9″), it has a black back
with white markings on the shoulders, a black tail, a black top
of the head, a yellowish patch on the forehead and, in adult
males, a red patch on the nape of the neck. (In the young of
both sexes the top of the head is red.) The pale-colored face
has a black stripe around it. The lower parts are white, and the
lower tail coverts red. Similar species are the Middle Spotted
Woodpecker (*D. medius*), the Lesser Spotted Woodpecker (*D.
minor*), the Syrian Woodpecker (*D. syriacus*) and the White-
backed Woodpecker (*D. leucotos*).
Habitat   Mixed woodland, parks and gardens.
Distribution   Europe, Asia, northwestern Africa.
Life and habits   Like other woodpeckers, it nests in holes in
trees, laying a single clutch usually of 4–7 eggs (sometimes of
3 or 8), which are incubated by both sexes, but mainly by the
female, for about 16 days. The nestlings leave the nest at
18–21 days. The Great Spotted Woodpecker feeds on invertebrates living in wood and also on pine seeds. The tapping with
the hard beak on trees also indicates the occupation of its own
territory.

135 DENDROCOPOS VILLOSUS
Hairy Woodpecker

Classification   Order Piciformes, Family Picidae.
Characteristics   About 24 cm. long (10″), it is usually completely white (or pale gray on the belly) with black tail and wings, the latter speckled with white (particularly easy to see in flight). On the head there is a black marking that terminates in a patch of scarlet on the nape, which is absent in the female; a pattern of black lines on the white cheeks completes the head coloring. Twenty-one geographical varieties have been described, 12 of which are present in North America north of Mexico. A similar, but smaller, species is the Downy Woodpecker (*D. pubescens*).
Habitat   Every type of wood and forest.
Distribution   North America south to western Panama.
Life and habits   As a rule this species is nonmigratory, but in winter there can be a considerable shift to more southerly regions. It nests in holes in dead trees, often some way up from the ground. It lays 3–6 eggs (usually 4), which are incubated by both sexes, and both rear the young. We do not know exactly how long incubation lasts, nor at what age the nestlings can fly. The diet consists mainly of insects and spiders and, to a lesser extent, fruit and seeds. The strong beak enables woodpeckers to probe the bark of trees for insects (mainly wood-eating) and their larvae.

---

136 DENDROICA FUSCA
Blackburnian Warbler

Classification   Order Passeriformes, Family Parulidae.
Characteristics   A small bird, 12–13 cm. long (5″), with a long thin beak designed for an insectivorous diet. The upper parts are black, with the exception of an orange marking on the head, orange eyebrows, and two broad yellow bands on the back. The throat and breast are orange-red, and the belly and sides lighter, with black stripes. Females, immatures and non-breeding males all have duller winter plumage.
Habitat   Coniferous woods.
Distribution   North America.
Life and habits   This is a migratory species that leaves its coniferous woods (pine, fir and larch) in northern parts in the autumn and winters in the forests of Central and South America as far south as Peru. The nest is built solely by the female with twigs, roots, and the fluff of plants on the horizontal branch of a conifer. This warbler lays 4 (and sometimes 5) eggs, which are incubated by the female for 12–13 days. The nestlings, which are fed by both adults, fly after an additional 12 or 13 days. We do not know whether this species lays two clutches a year, but this is the case with similar species. The diet consists mainly of insects and spiders caught among the foliage and on branches, plus a smaller proportion of wild berries.

137 DICRURUS MACROCERCUS
Black Drongo

Classification   Order Passeriformes, Family Dicruridae.
Characteristics   The Dicruridae, known as *drongos*, form a family of Passeriformes that includes species with a tough beak, slightly curved at the tip, surrounded by long bristles. The over-all length falls beteen 17 and 37 cm. (7–14.5"), omitting the rectrices. The plumage is usually black (except in two species) with metallic highlights; the legs are short. The Black Drongo has brilliant iridescent black coloring with a long forked tail. The Greater Racket-tailed Drongo (*D. paradiseus*) is about 36 cm. long (14"), with black plumage, a crest on the head, and a tail with two very long rectrices that end in a spatula shape.
Habitat   Open terrain, lowlands, forests.
Distribution   Southern Asia.
Life and habits   The ornithologist Charles Vaurie mentions how these birds are solitary by nature, tree-climbing and have an insectivorous diet. They breed in very small, flat nests, generally in the forks of branches, sometimes as high as 15 meters (50 feet) from the ground. Bertram F. Smythies describes how these birds usually lay 3–4 eggs (less frequently 2 or 5). Drongos often perch on the cattle and catch insects in mid-air.

---

138 DIOMEDEA EPOMOPHORA
Royal Albatross

Classification   Order Procellariiformes, Family Diomedeidae.
Characteristics   The Royal Albatross, together with the Wandering Albatross (*D. exulans*), has the largest wing span of all the seabirds, ranging from 200 to more than 320 cm. (80–125"). It weighs 7–8 kg. (15–18 lbs.). This species has a mainly white coloring. The Short-tailed Albatross (*D. albatus*), also known as Steller's Albatross, was once present in large numbers in all the islands in the Bonin Archipelago southeast of Japan. At the present time it is only to be found on the island of Torishima; a census carried out in April 1962 recorded the existence of only 47 individuals.
Habitat   Open sea, islands.
Distribution   Western Pacific.
Life and habits   According to ornithologists who have studied the reproduction pattern of the albatrosses, particularly L. E. Richdale, Royal Albatrosses return to their place of birth after 4–7 years, and it is thought that their first attempts at nesting may fail because they have not reached complete sexual maturity. Nesting takes place in colonies on the ground, in nests made of mounds of vegetable matter. A single egg is laid and incubated by both parents for about 79 days. The nestling is reared by both parents and flies at the age of about 263 days (almost 9 months).

139 DIOMEDEA EXULANS
Wandering Albatross

Classification Order Procellariiformes, Family Diomedeidae.
Characteristics The wing span of the Wandering Albatross may exceed 3 meters (10 feet), while the bird itself may be more than 1 meter long (40″). The general coloring of the plumage is whitish, with grayish black on the wings. The young are brown, with white on the front of the head.
Habitat Islands in the Southern Hemisphere.
Distribution Seas in the Southern Hemisphere when non-breeding.
Life and habits It breeds, sometimes in isolation, in nests on the ground made of mounds of vegetable matter. It lays one egg, incubated in turns by the two parents for a period of about 70–80 days. The nestling is looked after by both adults until it can fend for itself, which happens after about 5 weeks. The first flight takes place after about 278 days. Because of the long period needed to rear the nestling, the Wandering Albatross usually breeds every two years. Albatrosses have a complex set of courtship ceremonies, in which the male holds his tail open like a fan, wings outstretched, and head and neck extended, with the tip of the beak often hidden among the scapular feathers, while he makes strange noises. In the Wandering and Royal albatrosses sometimes up to 8 males may take part in certain courtship ceremonies.

140 DIOMEDEA IMMUTABILIS
Laysan Albatross

Classification Order Procellariiformes, Family Diomedeidae.
Characteristics Albatrosses have nasal tubes that are typical of the Procellariiformes; they are not very conspicuous, are not joined, and are situated on the sides of the upper part of the beak. The remiges are very long (the ulna has 27–40 secondary remiges). The Laysan Albatross, which is about 80 cm. long (31″) has white plumage with dark wings.
Habitat Open sea, islands.
Distribution Central Pacific.
Life and habits Albatrosses glide, making use of ascending currents which are caused by air masses colliding with the sea. They often soar above the sea's surface, or swim. Like many seabirds, albatrosses drink salt water, getting rid of much of the salt by means of nasal glands situated in a cranial cavity above the eye sockets. Younger albatrosses, in the event of danger, spurt out foul-smelling intestinal secretions. Albatrosses feed mainly on cephalopods (cuttlefish, octopus, etc.) but also on fish, crustaceans, various wastes, a few vegetable substances, and sometimes even hunt other seabirds. They move a considerable distance and often fly far from the southern seas. The Laysan Albatross reproduces annually, laying a single egg.

143 DROMAIUS NOVAEHOLLANDIAE
Emu

Classification Order Casuariiformes, Family Dromaiidae.
Characteristics The Emu has an over-all height of about 180 cm. (70″); to the top of the back it measures about 100 cm. (40″); it can weigh up to 55 kg. (120 lbs.) and have a beak up to 12 cm. long (5″). The body is very bulky, the coloring of the plumage brownish. The feet have three toes. The Emu has no uropygial gland, and the male sex organ is retractable. The Emu of Kangaroo Island (*D. minor*), measuring about 80 cm. to the shoulder (31″), is now extinct.
Habitat Scrubby steppe.
Distribution Australia.

Life and habits The nest is a hollow in the ground near a shrub, and it is covered with leaves, grass, et cetera. Various females lay 15–25 eggs, which are incubated by the male for 52–60 days, depending on the interruptions made by the male to find food and water. The nestlings, which have a distinctive white and brown-striped plumage, achieve complete development and sexual maturity within 2 or 3 years. The Emu can run at speeds of up to 50 kph. (30 mph.). The predecessors of today's Emus lived in Australia during the Upper Pleistocene, about 50,000–100,000 years ago. The Emu eats fruit and seeds.
Note: The photo shows two young birds.

---

144 DRYOCOPUS MARTIUS
Black Woodpecker

Classification Order Piciformes, Family Picidae.
Characteristics About 45 cm. long (18″), it has a uniform black plumage. The top of the male's head is red and slightly crested. In females the red in this area is limited to a marking on the rear of the head. The beak is light colored.
Habitat Forests and woods (conifers, ash, poplar, cherry, alder and birch).
Distribution Europe and Asia.
Life and habits Originally this bird lived in vast broadleaf forests where there were many old trees, either fallen or rotting; now it is found in coniferous woods as well as mixed woods. It emits a strong *kle-ea*, as well as a *kr-ri—kr-ri—kr-ri—kr-ri* and a *choc—choc—choc*, as described by G. Mountfort. It nests in hollows in trees. It lays a single clutch generally with 4–6 eggs (sometimes 9), which are incubated by both parents for about 12–14 days. The nidicolous nestlings are fed by the parents with regurgitated food, and they leave the nest at 24–28 days. The Black Woodpecker feeds mainly on ants, as well as other insects living in the bark and wood of trees.

145 DUMETELLA CAROLINENSIS
Gray Catbird

Classification   Order Passeriformes, Family Mimidae.
Characteristics   About 20–22 cm. long (8–9″). Its plumage is a uniform gray, except for the black cap and a chestnut patch on the undertail. The sexes are similar. The name of this bird comes from the call, which resembles a *miaow*. The beak is long and slender.
Habitat   Open forests, shrubby areas, gardens and parks.
Distribution   North America.
Life and habits   This is a fairly common bird and is often found near houses. Migratory by nature, in summer it reaches the most northerly limits of its distribution area (southern Canada). The nest is made with twigs, leaves and stems of plants, in bushes, vines or small trees. The clutch usually has 2–6 eggs (ordinarily 4), which are incubated by the female and the male for 12–15 days. The nestlings, which are reared by both parents, leave the nest at 9–15 days. There are usually two clutches a year. A good 50 percent of the Gray Catbird's diet consists of vegetable matter (berries, fruit and seeds) and the rest of insects, spiders and other invertebrates. The nestlings are fed exclusively on animal matter.

146 EGRETTA GARZETTA
Little Egret

Classification   Order Ciconiiformes, Family Ardeidae.
Characteristics   The Little Egret is about 56 cm. long (22″); its plumage is completely white. In summer the adults have a crest of white feathers and elongated white scapular feathers. The beak is dark; the legs are dark with yellow feet.
Habitat   Lagoons, ponds, marshlands, wooded areas near water.
Distribution   Parts of Europe, southern Asia, Africa and Australia.
Life and habits   It nests in colonies, often with other species, building its nest among bushes or in trees. At intervals of 1 or 2 days it lays 3–6 eggs (but ordinarily 4), which are incubated for 21–25 days. The newborn young are reared by both parents and leave the nest after about 30 days. The Little Egret feeds on small fish, mollusks, worms, crustaceans, insects and larvae.

147 ELANUS CAERULEUS
Black-winged Kite

Classification   Order Falconiformes, Family Accipitridae.
Characteristics   About 32 cm. long (12.5″) and weighs on average 230 grams (8 ounces). This kite has long wings and a forked tail. The head is white, as are the lower parts and tail. The upper parts are pale blue-gray with the exception of the "shoulders," which are black. The iris is purple-red and the legs are yellow. Immature birds are brown-gray uppermost, and white lower down, with brown stripes and reddish tones.
Habitat   Open terrain with sparse trees, savannah, semi-desert.
Distribution   Southern Europe, Africa and Asia.
Life and habits   The Black-winged Kite is found at altitudes of 3,000 meters (10,000 feet) and prefers arid habitats with sparse trees. It builds a nest of dry branches in lone trees. There is one clutch a year. This has 3 or 4 eggs (sometimes 5), which are incubated almost exclusively by the female for 26 days. The nestlings, which differ considerably in size because the eggs in the clutch are laid at intervals of 2 or 3 days, are looked after by both parents and fly at about 5 weeks. It feeds mainly on small mammals, with small birds and insects caught sometimes in mid-air.

148 EMBERIZA CALANDRA
Corn Bunting

Classification   Order Passeriformes, Family Emberizidae.
Characteristics   It measures 18 cm. in length (7″) and weighs on average 60 grams (2 oz.), the male being slightly larger than the female. The upper plumage is ocher colored, with dark stripes; the lower feathers are off-white with black markings. The young are more or less the same as the adults.
Habitat   Cultivated land, untilled land that is wooded.
Distribution   North Africa, Europe and western Asia.
Life and habits   The nest is made on the ground amid thick grass and thistles, sometimes in bushes, and consists of a cup-shaped structure of grass stalks, horsehair and small roots. There are usually 1 or 2 clutches a year (rarely 3); these have 1–7 eggs (most often 4, 5 or 6), which are incubated solely by the female for 12–14 days. The female takes care of the nidicolous young, which fly at about 12 days, with the occasional assistance of the male, which has been observed to be polygamous. The Corn Bunting feeds on the seeds of herbaceous plants and cereal crops, and insects (the latter being important in the young birds' diet). In the nuptial display the male sings in the air, then lands near the female and performs a dance with its wings drooping and vibrating and its tail extended. In some zones this species shows a migratory pattern, in others it is nonmigratory.

149 EMBERIZA CIRLUS
Cirl Bunting

Classification   Order Passeriformes, Family Emberizidae.
Characteristics   This species is 16 cm. long (6.5″) and weighs about 20 grams (0.7 ounces). The male's lower parts are lemon yellow with a black throat and striped sides. The olive-green head has black and yellow stripes. The upper parts are chestnut colored. The female and young have duller plumage.
Habitat   Cultivated land, wooded countryside.
Distribution   Southern Europe, Asia Minor and northwestern Africa.
Life and habits   The nest is built in bushes (sometimes on the ground or in a small tree) and is cup-shaped and made of grasses, moss and roots. There are 2 or 3 clutches a year, each of which has 4 eggs. These are incubated exclusively by the female for 11–13 days. The nidicolous nestlings are fed and reared mainly by the female and fly at 11–13 days. The Cirl Bunting feeds mainly on seeds, but also on insects. In the nuptial display the male adopts attitudes like those of the male yellowhammer (*E. citrinella*) and presents the female blades of grass with its beak, but does not help to build the nest itself. Usually nonmigratory, in some regions it does make migratory movements.

150 EMBERIZA CITRINELLA
Yellowhammer

Classification   Order Passeriformes, Family Emberizidae.
Characteristics   About 16 cm. long (6.5″), weighing on average 30 grams (1 oz.). The upper plumage is brown, with lighter and darker stripes, while the head and lower parts are lemon yellow, with brown stripes on the sides. The outer tail rectrices are white. The females and young have less extensive yellow and are paler.
Habitat   Cultivated land, wooded countryside.
Distribution   Europe and Asia.
Life and habits   The nest is made in bushes, in hedgerows and in tall, thick grass. The female alone makes a cup-shaped nest of grass and moss (lined with horsehair). Each year there are 2 or 3 clutches, each with 3–5 eggs (sometimes 2 or 6), which are incubated by the female for 11–14 days. The nidicolous nestlings are fed and reared by both parents and fly at 16 days. The Yellowhammer feeds mainly on seeds, cereals and, to a lesser extent invertebrates (insects and arachnids). At the beginning of the mating season the pairs isolate themselves from the small flocks that form in winter to look for food, and start their nuptial displays, during which the male, with head held high (the beak pointing at the sky), tail erect and wings half-open and vibrating, performs a dance around the female.

151 EMBERIZA HORTULANA
Ortolan Bunting

Classification Order Passeriformes, Family Emberizidae.
Characteristics This bunting is 16 cm. long (6.5″) and weighs on average 24 grams (0.85 oz.). The male's lower parts are tawny orange, the throat is yellow, and the head and breast olive green. The upper parts are brown, streaked with black. The female has dark markings on the breast, while the young are darker, with lower striping. Among similar species we find Cretzschmar's Bunting (*E. caesia*), the male of which has a gray head and breast, and reddish throat; this species is found in the eastern parts of the Mediterranean.
Habitat Cultivated land, wooded countryside.
Distribution Europe, Africa and western Asia.
Life and habits The cup-shaped nest, made of grasses and small roots, is built in grass and sometimes on the ground, by the female alone. The two annual clutches have 4–6 eggs each, incubated only by the female for 11–14 days. The nidicolous young are fed by both parents and fly at 10–15 days. The diet of this species consists of the seeds of herbaceous plants and insects, the latter being the main ingredient for the young. It is a migratory species, migrating in winter to the southern parts of its distribution area.

---

152 EMBERIZA SCHOENICLUS
Reed Bunting

Classification Order Passeriformes, Family Emberizidae.
Characteristics This Bunting is about 15 cm. long (6″). The male has a black head and throat, with a white half-collar on the nape and sides of the neck. The upper parts are reddish black, and the rump is gray. The lower parts are whitish, barred with blackish brown on the sides. The female has a pinkish-brown head striped with black, and a whitish chin and throat. The young resemble the female, but are more striped on the upper parts.
Habitat Marshlands, canebrakes, lakes, wetlands.
Distribution Europe, northern and central Asia.
Life and habits It nests on the ground or just above it, in clumps of grass in wetland areas. The nest is cup-shaped, made of plant matter; in it the Reed Bunting lays usually 4 or 5 eggs (more rarely 6 or 7), which are incubated by the female for 12–14 days. It lays 2–3 clutches a year. The nidicolous nestlings are reared by both parents and stay in the nest for 10–13 days. The Reed Bunting feeds mainly on seeds and on various invertebrates (small mollusks, spiders, grubs, insects and their larvae). It is, on the whole, nonmigratory, though some populations migrate. It has a zigzag flight.

153 EPHIPPIORHYNCHUS SENEGALENSIS
Saddle-billed Stork

Classification   Order Ciconiiformes, Family Ciconiidae.
Characteristics   This species is about 150 cm. long (60″); its wing span may reach 240 cm. (95″) and its weight may reach 6 kg. (13 lbs.). The plumage is white; the rump, head and neck are black, as are the wings, which also have bluish highlights. The long, red and black beak has a yellow "plate," or saddle. Young birds are brownish gray. An allied species is the Wood Stork (*Mycteria americana*), an American bird with white plumage and a sleek, bluish-black head, neck and feet. Another allied species is the Black-necked Stork (*Xenorhynchus asiaticus*), which is found from India to Australia and is colored like the Saddle-billed Stork, but lacks the bright beak.
Habitat   Along the shores of lakes and watercourses; marshlands.
Distribution   Africa.
Life and habits   It usually nests alone in trees or bushes, gathering in small groups in marshland and on the shores of lakes. It feeds on fish, and aquatic animals (invertebrates). It lays 3 eggs.

---

154 EREMOPHILA ALPESTRIS
Horned Lark

Classification   Order Passeriformes, Family Alaudidae.
Characteristics   It is about 17 cm. long (7″); its upper plumage is pinkish brown with dark stripes; the sides are reddish gray, the wings dark brown, the tail brown with white at the edges. The head and front of the neck are yellow, with a black band and two tufts of dark feathers on the head. The lower parts are pale, and there is black from the top of the breast to the base of the neck.
Habitat   Tundra, steppe, coastal regions and marshland.
Distribution   Europe, Asia, North Africa and North America.
Life and habits   It nests on the ground amid vegetation or stones. It lays two clutches, each containing 2–7 eggs (most commonly 4), which are incubated by the female for 10–14 days. The nidicolous nestlings are reared by both parents and leave the nest at 9–12 days. The Horned Lark feeds on invertebrates (mollusks, crustaceans and insects) and plant matter (seeds, shoots and buds).

155 ERITHACUS RUBECULA
European Robin

Classification   Order Passeriformes, Family Turdidae.

Characteristics   About 13.5 cm. long (5.3″) and weighing on average 16 grams (0.6 oz.), the sexes are similar and have olive-green upper parts, an orange-colored breast and a white belly. The young are brown with reddish and tawny markings and streaks.

Habitat   Woods, parks, wooded countryside with shrubby vegetation.

Distribution   Europe, Asia Minor.

Life and habits   This species is somewhat eclectic in its choice of habitat and in winter frequents canebrakes in marshy areas and meadows. The nest is made by the female amid shrubs and roots of trees and in hollows in rocks in wooded areas. It is a cup-shaped structure made with plant matter, feathers and horsehair. Each year there are two or three clutches, each with 3–9 eggs (usually 5 or 6), which are incubated solely by the female for 12–15 days. The nidicolous nestlings are fed by both parents and fly at 12–15 days. The diet consists of insects, other invertebrates, berries and seeds (these latter particularly in winter). Robins show marked territorial behavior, even outside the reproductive period. A frequent aggressive posture consists in raising the tail, spreading the wings and showing off the brightly colored breast (see photo).

---

156 EUDOCIMUS RUBER
Scarlet Ibis

Classification   Order Ciconiiformes, Family Threskiornithidae.

Characteristics   This is a magnificent bird with bright red plumage and a long downward-curving beak. Young birds have a pinkish-brownish plumage, particularly on the head, neck and wings. A similar species is the White Ibis (*E. albus*), which is found from southern U.S. To Peru.

Habitat   Along riverbanks and lakesides, marshlands.

Distribution   South America, including Trinidad.

Life and habits   Sometimes the Scarlet Ibis will pair up with a White Ibis, which is why various ornithologists, and the specialist Hans Kumerloeve in particular, consider them as belonging to the same species. It nests in mangrove or other trees, in fairly large colonies. The male finds the materials for building the nest, and the female actually builds it. The Scarlet Ibis usually lays 2 eggs (the White Ibis 3 or 4), which are incubated for 21–23 days. The nidicolous nestlings are reared by both parents and leave the nest at about three weeks. Sexual maturity is reached at about 2 years. The Scarlet Ibis has been indiscriminately hunted and is protected in many areas today.

157 EUDROMIA ELEGANS
Elegant Crested Tinamou

Classification Order Tinamiformes, Family Tinamidae.
Characteristics At one time the tinamous were included in the order Galliformes, particularly because of their resemblance to the guineafowl (Numididae). They are about 20–53 cm. long (8–21"), with the weight ranging from 450 to 2,300 grams (1–5 lbs.). The Elegant Crested Tinamou has a very mimetic plumage, with long feathers on the head. The wings are short, so like all the Tinamidae, this species is not often seen in the air. It has no hind toe.
Habitat Scrubland, undergrowth, steppe and lowlands.
Distribution South America.
Life and habits The Tinamidae feed mainly on vegetable matter (small fruit, seeds, plus berries, leaves, flowers and roots) and also on invertebrates (insects, mollusks). They are ground-dwelling birds; they rarely fly. They are shy by nature and live an isolated life except in the mating season. Males and females are polygamous and polyandrous respectively. The nest is made on the ground, with the incubation falling to the male, who leaves the nest daily to find food. The nestlings leave the nest after a day and follow the male around. Depending on the species, they lay 1–16 eggs, which are incubated for 16–22 days.

158 EUDROMIAS MORINELLUS
Eurasian Dotterel

Classification Order Charadriiformes, Family Charadriidae.
Characteristics About 22 cm. long (9"), it has a distinctive springtime plumage; upper parts are brownish gray tending to black, white cheeks and throat, and a brown breast crossed by a white band, orange-chestnut lower parts with a blackish belly, white undertail and yellow legs. The autumn and winter plumage is duller, without the bright summer contrasts. The young have a coloring like the adult in winter.
Habitat Tundra, hills without vegetation, stony areas with sparse vegetation at high altitudes, grassland, coastal regions and marshes.
Distribution Local in Europe, North Africa and northern Asia.
Life and habits In arctic regions it nests on the tundra, in the more southerly parts of its distribution area in mountainous regions. The nest is a hole dug in the ground, sometimes crudely lined with moss and lichens. It lays 2–4 eggs (most commonly 3), which are incubated almost exclusively by the male for 21–26 days. The nestlings are nidifugous. They are generally reared by the male and are independent at about 4 weeks. They feed mainly on insects.

159 EUDYPTES CRESTATUS
Rockhopper Penguin

Classification   Order Sphenisciformes, Family Spheniscidae.
Characteristics   This penguin is about 55 cm. long (22″) and weighs 2.5 kg. (5.5 lbs.). The feathers reach a length of 2.9 cm. (1.1″). The members of the genus *Eudyptes* are characterized by having a tuft of feathers above the eyes, and a strong, reddish beak. In most species the males are larger than the females, and the young have smaller tufts. The Rockhopper Penguin has black upper parts and white lower parts. The feet have strong claws, which enable it to climb over rocks when waves wash it ashore. This species moves by hopping on both feet, hence the name.
Habitat   Seas, coasts.
Distribution   Islands around Antarctica and Heard Island in the subantarctic belt.
Life and habits   It nests in large colonies, laying 2 or 3 eggs. The species of the genus *Eudyptes* leave their nesting area in late summer or autumn and move to the open sea for 3–5 months, probably moving directly north. The adults then return to the same nest and the young to the same colony where they were born.

160 EURYPYGA HELIAS
Sun Bittern

Classification   Order Gruiformes, Family Eurypygidae.
Characteristics   About 41 cm. long (16″) and weighing about 220 grams (8 ounces), it has soft, compact plumage like that of the Strigiformes. The coloring of the plumage is grayish brown in the upper parts, with black bars (finer at the tail), a brownish neck, a black head with white stripes, a brownish breast and pale lower parts. The neck and legs are quite long.
Habitat   Forests, near watercourses.
Distribution   From southern Mexico to northern South America.
Life and habits   It generally leads a solitary life or lives in pairs. It takes on a specific position with the wings and tail completely extended; this is in effect a threatening posture, although for a long time it was interpreted as being part of the nuptial display. It makes a fairly crude nest of branches and twigs in which it usually lays 2 eggs, which are incubated by both sexes for about 27 days. Based on observations made in captivity, the nestlings seem to stay in the nest for 21 days. François Haverschmidt mentioned that this gruiform feeds on invertebrates (mollusks and insects).

161 FALCO BIARMICUS
Lanner Falcon

Classification   Order Falconiformes, Family Falconidae.
Characteristics   About 42 cm. long (16.5″), this falcon weighs on average 570 grams (20 ounces), and has a wing span of up to 110 cm. (44″). The female is larger than the male. The plumage is brown in the upper parts, whitish on the lower parts with black markings. The top of the head is reddish, and there are two fairly thin black "whiskers." In immature examples the plumage is darker and more speckled.
Habitat   Open terrain, rocky terrain, deserts and semi-deserts.
Distribution   Africa, Mediterranean basin.
Life and habits   The nest is usually made in hollows in cliffs or in the old nest of another bird (raven, eagle, etc.). No material is added by the pair, and the single annual clutch of 3–4 eggs (sometimes 5) is laid on the bare rock. These are incubated by both sexes for 31–38 days; they both take care of the young, which are nidicolous and fly at 45 days although they remain near the nest with their parents for a further four weeks. The diet consists mainly of birds, mammals, reptiles and insects. The prey is caught both in flight (with the same technique as that of the Peregrine Falcon) and on the ground by a swift dive. In the nuptial display the male dives over the female, who, in flight, may turn on to her back and present her talons to her mate.

162 FALCO MEXICANUS
Prairie Falcon

Classification   Order Falconiformes, Family Falconidae.
Characteristics   It is a nimble bird with a long body, measuring about 43 cm. (17″). The coloring of the upper parts is dark brown; the lower parts are white with brown markings and a brown "mustache" stretching from the eye across the cheek. It reaches a weight of 0.8 kg. (1.75 lbs.) The female is slightly larger than the male.
Habitat   Arid plains and steppes with crags.
Distribution   North America (from British Columbia to Mexico).
Life and habits   The regions frequented by this bird of prey are usually arid and treeless, but with high ground and rocky crags suitable for nesting. The eggs——3–6, but usually 4 or 5——are laid in a bare hollow in the rock or in the nest of a raven. Both sexes incubate them for about 31 days. The nestlings, which hatch on successive days, are fed by both parents and leave the nest after 40 days. The diet consists mainly of medium-sized and small birds, often caught in flight, mammals, and occasionally lizards and large insects. This is a nonmigratory bird of prey, when living in more temperate zones, and migratory elsewhere.

163 FALCO PEREGRINUS
Peregrine Falcon

Classification   Order Falconiformes, Family Falconidae.
Characteristics   About 43 cm. long (17″), it has dark upper parts—dark gray-blue or dark brown, depending on the subspecies—and reddish-white lower parts, with close black bars. The female is larger and darker uppermost, and more barred in the lower parts. The top and sides of the head are dark, with a large dark "mustache." The young are browner, with the lower parts striped instead of barred. In flight it looks compact with long pointed wings; it is a speedy, agile flier. There are various subspecies of Peregrine Falcon: the ornithologist Dementiev lists 22.
Habitat   Open rocky land, rocky coasts, also wooded areas and moorland.
Distribution   Virtually worldwide.
Life and habits   It nests on rocks, more rarely in trees in the old nests of other large birds. It lays a single clutch with 2–6 eggs (usually 3 or 4), which are incubated for 28–29 days by both sexes. The young fly at 35–42 days and depend on their parents for about an additional 2 months. The diet of the Peregrine Falcon has a wide range; it feeds from preference on birds and small mammals. Many populations are threatened by pollution, environmental alterations and poaching.

164 FALCO RUSTICOLUS
Gyrfalcon

Classification   Order Falconiformes, Family Falconidae.
Characteristics   A large, strong-looking bird, 50–59 cm. long (20–24″), with a wing span of 130 cm. (51″). The female, whose average weight is 1.7 kg. (3.75 lbs.), is larger than the male, whose average weight is 1.1 kg. (2.4 lbs.). There are color phases: in the dark phase the adults have gray upper parts and white lower parts with black markings; on the head there are two black "whiskers"; in the light phase the plumage is completely white, with a few black markings. The iris is brown, and the legs are yellow. But there are also intermediate phases between these two.
Habitat   Rocky sea coasts, tundra.
Distribution   Arctic regions of Europe, Asia and America.
Life and habits   The nest is built on sea cliffs and among rocks, and sometimes in the nest of other large birds. It does not reproduce regularly each year, and this seems to depend on the climatic conditions (which influence the physical state of adults in winter) and the availability of food in summer. The clutch has 2–7 eggs (usually 3 or 4), which are laid at intervals of three days and are incubated by the female for 28–29 days. The nidicolous nestlings are helped by both parents and fly at 46–49 days. The Gyrfalcon feeds mainly on ptarmigan (genus *Lagropus*), seabirds, waterfowl, and mammals.

165 FALCO SPARVERIUS
American Kestrel

Classification   Order Falconiformes, Family Falconidae.
Characteristics   About 25–30 cm. long (10–12″), it has long, narrow wings and a fairly long tail. The male's upper parts are hazel-colored, except for the wings, which are gray with black markings. The head is white with gray and hazel on the nape and three black stripes on each cheek. The lower parts are ocher, speckled with black. The females and the young are slightly different with less brightly colored plumage. The male's average weight is 0.1 kg. (3.5 oz.), the female's is 0.11 kg. (3.9 oz.).
Habitat   Desert areas and open land with few trees.
Distribution   North and South America.
Life and habits   This fairly adaptable species, which is also frequent in urban areas, flies nimbly and fast, with a pattern that is interrupted every so often when the bird "hovers"—that is, remains in place in the air while rapidly flapping its wings to maintain its altitude. The nest is built in a hollow in a tree or on ledges of a building. The American Kestrel lays 3–7 eggs (usually 4 or 5), which are incubated mainly by the female for 29–30 days. The nestlings can fly at about 30 days. This species feeds mainly on insects in summer and mice and small birds in winter.

166 FALCO SUBBUTEO
Eurasian Hobby

Classification   Order Falconiformes, Family Falconidae.
Characteristics   About 38–48 cm. long (15–19″). The male weighs on average 180 grams (6.4 oz.), and the female 225 grams (8 oz.). The wing span is about 80 cm. (31″). In adults the upper parts are dark gray, and the lower parts are off-white with close black stripes. The undertail area and the plumage at the base of the legs are reddish. On each cheek there is a black "mustache." The iris is brown, the legs yellow. In immature birds the plumage is browner uppermost, and there is no reddish coloring on the lower parts.
Habitat   Wooded countryside, moorland, clearings in woods.
Distribution   Europe, Asia, northwestern Africa.
Life and habits   The Eurasian Hobby does not build its own nest; instead it uses an old nest made by a corvid or other falconiform, in a tree. The single annual clutch has 2 or 3 eggs, laid at intervals of 2 or 3 days. Incubation, undertaken mainly by the female, lasts 28 days. The nidicolous nestlings stay in the nest in the care of both parents for 28–32 days, at which stage they can fly. The prey, which is caught mainly in the air thanks to the agility and speed of this species, is mainly small birds, insects and sometimes bats.

167 FALCO TINNUNCULUS
Old World Kestrel

Classification   Order Falconiformes, Family Falconidae.
Characteristics   This species is about 34 cm. long (13″) and weighs on average 200 grams (7 oz.), the female being slightly larger than the male. Its wing span can reach 80 cm. (31″). In the male the upper parts are chestnut colored with black markings, the lower parts tawny with black markings. The head and tail are gray, the head has a black "mustache" running across each side, and the tail ends in a black and white tip. In the females and young the upper parts, including the head and tail, are brown with dark bars. The legs are yellow, and the iris is brown.
Habitat   Open land, cultivated fields, rocky sea coasts.
Distribution   Europe, Asia and Africa.
Life and habits   This species is quite eclectic in its choice of habitat and can be found even high up in mountains. The nest is built in hollows in rocks, on ledges of buildings and on tree trunks; and often in a tree in the abandoned nest of another bird. There is one clutch a year of a maximum of 9 eggs (but usually 4 or 5), laid at intervals of 2 or 3 days, and incubated mainly by the female for 27–29 days. The nidicolous nestlings are reared by both parents and fly when they are 27–39 days old. The diet consists of small mammals, caught with short swoops, small birds, reptiles and insects.

168 FICEDULA HYPOLEUCA
Pied Flycatcher

Classification   Order Passeriformes, Family Muscicapidae.
Characteristics   About 13 cm. long (5″), weighs about 13 grams (0.5 oz.). The male's plumage is black in the upper parts and white in the lower parts. The sides of the tail, the forehead, and part of the wings are also white. Uppermost, the female is gray-brown, and lower down it is off-white. The young resemble the female, but have browner shades and are more reddish.
Habitat   Broadleaf and coniferous woods.
Distribution   Europe, North Africa.
Life and habits   The nest is often made near water, in natural holes in tree trunks or in holes made by woodpeckers, and in holes in buildings. The inside of the nest is lined by the female with leaves, moss and lichens. The single annual clutch has from 1 to 11 eggs (but the larger clutches usually belong, in all probability, to two females; more commonly there are between 4 and 7). The eggs are incubated by the female for 12–13 days. The nidicolous young are reared by both adults and fly at 13–16 days. The Pied Flycatcher feeds on insects, caught both amid foliage and in flight. The male, which may be polygamous, defends its possession of the hole used for reproduction and, by a series of postures, invites the female to visit it and set up home.

169 FRANCOLINUS JACKSONI
Kenya or Jackson's Francolin

Classification Order Galliformes, Family Phasianidae.
Characteristics The francolins are galliforms, with various similarities with the common partridges (genus *Perdix*)—such as the strong legs (which, in the male, have 1 or 2 sharp spurs) and the short, slightly rounded tail with 14 rectrices. As mentioned by ornithologist Heinz Sigurd Raethel, there are 34 species of francolins in Africa and 5 in southern Asia. Jackson's Francolin has a uniform dark brown coloring, red beak and legs, and rust-colored lower parts with white stripes. The male is larger than the female.
Habitat Prefers mountainous forests and stands of bamboo.
Distribution Kenya on Mount Kenya, in the Aberdare Mountains, on the Kinangop Plain and in the Mau Forest.
Life and habits Francolins are ground-dwelling birds and also nest on the ground. The Gray-winged Francolin (*F. afer*), living in scrubby steppe and agricultural zones of Africa, lays 5–9 eggs in a well-camouflaged nest; these are incubated for 18–20 days by the female. The very beautiful Black Francolin (*F. francolinus*), which was once present in Sicily and Italy (having probably been introduced in the Middle Ages to Spain, Sicily and Greece), lays 6–8 eggs on the ground, and incubates them for 21–23 days.

170 FRATERCULA ARCTICA
Atlantic Puffin

Classification Order Charadriiformes, Family Alcidae.
Characteristics About 30 cm. long (12″), this unmistakable bird has a summer beak that is red, blue and yellow with a triangular and laterally compressed shape, while in winter the beak is smaller (the Puffin sheds part of it) and, in the process, loses the bright coloring, remaining gray-brown with a yellowish tip. The plumage is black and white, and the legs are bright orange. The young have a smaller, blackish beak.
Habitat Rocky and grassy areas on islands and coasts; open sea.
Distribution Coasts of northern Europe, Iceland, Greenland and northeastern North America.
Life and habits It nests in colonies in burrows already dug by rabbits or shearwaters, or in holes that it digs in the earth among rocks or in grassy areas. It lays one clutch, usually with just 1 egg (sometimes 2), which is incubated mainly by the female for 40–43 days. The nidicolous nestlings stay in the nest for 40 days, after which they move to the sea at about 47–51 days.

171 FREGATA MAGNIFICENS
Magnificent Frigatebird

Classification   Order Pelecaniformes, Family Fregatidae.
Characteristics   About 101 cm. long (40"). The name Frigate derives from this bird's "piratical" habit of flying off with the food of other seabirds. The Magnificent Frigatebird has a wing span of more than 2.5 meters (100"); the male has black coloring with purplish highlights; on the chin there is a brilliant red sac of bare skin which, during courtship, is puffed up like a balloon. The female has brownish-black coloring; the lower parts are pale. The young have white head, neck and lower parts. Similar species are the Greater Frigatebird (F. minor) and the Lesser Frigatebird (*F. ariel*).
Habitat   Open sea, tropical coastal waters, small islands.
Distribution   In the Atlantic (Gulf of Mexico, Caribbean and Cape Verde Islands) and along the American Pacific coast.
Life and habits   It usually nests in colonies, building a nest made of twigs and dry branches interwoven, in a tree or sturdy bush. It lays a single matt-white egg which is incubated by both sexes for about 40 days. The young develop a full plumage within 4–5 months. Frigatebirds feed on fish and other marine animals.

172 FRINGILLA COELEBS
Eurasian Chaffinch

Classification   Order Passeriformes, Family Fringillidae.
Characteristics   About 15 cm. long (6"). The male has a black forehead, a gray-blue top of the head and nape, and a chestnut and white back which is yellowish green lower down. The sides of the head and neck, the throat and the breast are reddish, while the undertail is whitish. The upper parts of the female are greenish gray-brown, and the lower are brownish gray. The young resemble the females, with whitish flashes on the nape and a brownish-green rump.
Habitat   Woods, gardens, parks, cultivated and wooded areas.
Distribution   Europe, Asia, northwestern Africa.
Life and habits   It builds a cup-shaped nest of moss, lichens, grass and feathers, et cetera, in which it lays one or two clutches a year with 2–8 eggs (more commonly 4 or 5) in each. The eggs are laid at intervals of a day: incubation starts with the laying of the last egg, and is the task of the female, lasting around 11–13 days. The nidicolous nestlings are raised by both parents and leave the nest at 12–15 days. The Chaffinch's diet is mostly granivorous, consisting mainly of seeds, the pulp of fruit, and plant matter; it also eats invertebrates.

173 FRINGILLA MONTIFRINGILLA
Brambling

Classification   Order Passeriformes, Family Fringillidae.
Characteristics   About 15 cm. long (6″) and weighing on average 24 grams (0.85 oz.), it has a fairly strong beak. In its summer plumage the male has a black head and back, white rump and white wings on both surfaces. The shoulders and breast are orange. The female is brown with stripes on the upper parts, with a paler orange coloring. The young and males in winter resemble the female.
Habitat   Birch and coniferous woods, cultivated land.
Distribution   Europe and northern Asia.
Life and habits   The nest is built usually in a conifer (rarely in bushes) and is cup-shaped and made of moss, bark, lichens, wool, et cetera. The female builds it. The single annual clutch has 5–8 eggs, laid at intervals of a day and incubated solely by the female for 11 or 12 days. The nidicolous nestlings are reared by both parents and fly at 11–13 days. The food, which is obtained from the ground, consists mainly of seeds, berries and insects (particularly prominent in the diet of the chicks). In winter this species migrates southward and becomes gregarious, forming flocks of many thousands of individuals, which use collective nocturnal dormitories.

174 FULICA ATRA
Old World Coot

Classification   Order Gruiformes, Family Rallidae.
Characteristics   About 38 cm. long (15″). Its plumage is slate black with a white beak and frontal plate. In flight it shows a narrow white edge on the secondary remiges. The legs and feet are greenish. Young individuals have a brownish-gray coloring with whitish throat and breast.
Habitat   Lakes, rivers, marshlands, lagoons.
Distribution   Europe, Asia, Africa, Australia.
Life and habits   It nests on the ground or on water amid vegetation. The nest is a crude structure of dry branches, leaves and plant matter, often floating on the water's surface amid vegetation. It lays two clutches, sometimes three, with 5–15 eggs (but usually between 6 and 9), which are incubated by both sexes for about 21–24 days. The nidifugous nestlings are reared by both parents and become independent at about 8 weeks of age. It feeds on grass, seeds, aquatic plants and invertebrates (mollusks, worms, insects). It makes short, shrill calls—"*tewk*" and "*kt—kowk.*"

175 FULMARUS GLACIALIS
Northern Fulmar

Classification Order Procellariiformes, Family Procellarii-dae.

Characteristics About 47 cm. long (18.5"). Its upper parts are blackish gray; the head, neck and lower parts are yellowish white. The tubular beak is typical of the Procellariiformes. There is also a dark phase with dark coloring in the lower parts as well. The flight pattern is a gliding one, describing various circles. It takes off from the water by seemingly walking on the surface for a certain distance; it dives occasionally.

Habitat Open sea, small islands and rocky crags, sometimes flattish coastal areas as well.

Distribution Northern Europe, Greenland, northern North America, and it sometimes moves south.

Life and habits It nests in colonies on rocky coasts. It lays a single clutch with one egg (rarely 2). The female incubates it for 55–57 days, together with the male. If bothered, the young, like the adults, spurt a jet of oily fluid from their beak, which has a strong musk smell. The young leave the nest after 46–51 days. Fulmars feed on mollusks, crustaceans, fish, waste, and the carcasses of sea animals. During courtship the pair face each other, extending their necks and dangling their heads with their beaks open and making guttural calls.

176 FURNARIUS RUFUS
Rufous Ovenbird

Classification Order Passeriformes, Family Furnariidae.

Characteristics About 19 cm. long (7.5"), it weighs about 75 grams (2.7 oz.). It is a predominantly brownish bird, darker uppermost, with reddish mainly on the tail, and paler coloring lower down. The beak is long and slender; there is a white stripe over the eye, the legs are dark, and the tail is long.

Habitat Meadows, open wooded areas.

Distribution South America.

Life and habits The Rufous Ovenbird makes a nest near a vantage point in its own territory, ranging from 2 to 30 meters above the ground (6–100 feet). Sometimes the nest is built on top of an already existing one, with up to 4 nests being built on top of one another. The nest is an odd structure of four walls made with small lumps of clay encrusted and joined together on the outside with straw and cattle manure, and on the inside with blades of grass. As described by ornithologist Helfried Hermann, the construction of the nest usually takes 10–16 days. A single pair may build up to four nests at the same time. Some nests found weighed between 2 and 6.75 kg. (4.5 and 15 lbs.). The clutch has 3 or 4 eggs, which are incubated for 14–18 days; the nidicolous nestlings leave the nest at about 21–26 days.

177 GALERIDA GRISTATA
Crested Lark

Classification   Order Passeriformes, Family Alaudidae.
Characteristics   About 17 cm. long (7″), weighing about 40 grams (1.4 oz.). The upper parts are sand colored, with dark stripes, and the lower cream colored, with brown stripes on the breast. On the head is a crest of dark feathers. The young are more or less the same as the adults. Among similar species we find the Thekla Lark (*G. theklae*), which has a more speckled breast and lives in North Africa, the Iberian peninsula and in some parts of France.
Habitat   Cultivated land, arid steppe.
Distribution   Africa, Europe, Asia.
Life and habits   This species lives in arid regions with sparse herbaceous vegetation. The nest is built on the ground and is cup-shaped, made with dry grasses and horsehair by both members of the pair. Each year there are two or even three clutches, each of which has 3–5 eggs (sometimes as many as 6), which are incubated solely by the female for 12–13 days. The nidicolous nestlings are fed by both adults and fly at about 18 days. The diet consists mainly of vegetable matter (grass seeds) but also of insects, which are important in the diet of the young. The male Thekla Lark delimits his territory by singing both on the ground and in the air.

178 GALLINAGO GALLINAGO
Common Snipe

Classification   Order Charadriiformes, Family Scolopacidae.
Characteristics   About 26 cm. long (10″). Its plumage is brownish, blackish and reddish with cream stripes uppermost, and pale stripes on the head. The beak is long and straight, and is held in a down-facing position when it flies. The sides of the tail have a little white on them. It has a distinctive zigzag flight pattern.
Habitat   Marshes, wetlands, paddy fields.
Distribution   Europe, Asia, Africa, America.
Life and habits   During the nuptial display, it makes diagonal flights during which the rectrices are held very wide apart and produce a vibrating sound. It lays one clutch (rarely 2) with usually 4 eggs (sometimes 3), which are incubated by the female for about 18–20 days. The nidifugous nestlings are reared by both parents and can fly at about 19 or 20 days. It makes a harsh *scha-ap* sound when it is driven into the air. Snipe feed on invertebrates (worms, insects, larvae, mollusks and crustaceans) as well as on plant matter.

179 GALLINULA CHLOROPUS
Moorhen or Common Gallinule

Classification Order Gruiformes, Family Rallidae.
Characteristics About 32 cm. long (12.5″), weighing on average 250 grams (9 oz.), the male being slightly larger than the
female). The plumage is brown-black, with the exception of the
undertail feathers and a white stripe on the sides. The beak and
frontal shield, (which is horny) are yellow and red; the legs are
green. The young are a uniform brown above, grayish beneath,
with a greenish beak.
Habitat Ponds, rivers and marshes with canebrakes and
bushes.
Distribution Europe, Africa, Asia, America.
Life and habits The nest is built near water, sometimes on it,
or in bushes. Built by both adults, it is a platform of plant matter
in which two or three clutches are reared annually, each of
which has 5–11 eggs (up to 21; but the largest clutches may
belong to two females). Both the adults incubate the eggs for
19–22 days. The nidifugous nestlings remain in the nest for
quite a few days, then make for the water and fly at 6–7 weeks,
still in the care of their parents. The young of the first clutch
may help to feed those in the later clutches. The Moorhen or
Common Gallinule feeds mainly on plants but also on aquatic
invertebrates and small fish.
Note: The drawing shows a chick.

180 GALLUS GALLUS
Red Junglefowl

Classification Order Galliformes, Family Phasianidae.
Characteristics This is the forebear of the domestic chicken,
with the male weighing up to 1,300 grams (3 lbs.). The male's
tarsal bones have a long spur. The tail has 14–16 rectrices.
The male's plumage is distinctive, showing reddish, green,
black and bluish. There is a crest on the head and wattles on
the sides of the beak. The female is brownish, smaller—up to
740 grams (26 oz.)—with no crest or wattles. Other species of
this genus include the Gray Junglefowl (*G. sonneratii*), the
Ceylon Junglefowl (*G. lafayettii*) and the Green Junglefowl (*G.
varius*).
Habitat Forests, woods, dry scrub.
Distribution Southeast Asia.
Life and habits As mentioned by Martin Luhmann, the Red
Junglefowl was reduced to the domestic state a long time ago
in its country of origin. In the fourteenth and fifteenth centuries
B.C., domestic fowl were taken from India to China. Three
groups of these birds are indicated as the forebears of the various domestic breeds currently living: the ground-dwelling fowl,
the wild fowl of Cochin China, and the fighting cock. It nests on
the ground, and the 5–6 eggs (maximum of 9) are incubated by
the female. The Red Junglefowl lives in groups, except during
the reproductive period. In the spring each male mates with
3–5 females, fighting for his own private territory.

181 GARRULUS GLANDARIUS
Eurasian Jay

Classification Order Passeriformes, Family Corvidae.
Characteristics It measures 32 cm. long (12.5″) and weighs about 170 grams (6 oz.). The body plumage is pinkish brown with the exception of the black tail, white rump and a crest of white and black feathers on the head. The wings have blue coverts with black bars and a large white marking. The young and females are more or less the same as the male.
Habitat Broadleaf and coniferous woods.
Distribution Asia, Europe, northwestern Africa.
Life and habits The cup-shaped nest consists of dry twigs, is lined with horsehair and small roots, and is built in a tree. Each year there is one clutch of 3–10 eggs (most commonly 5, 6, or 7), which are incubated by both parents for 16–17 days. The nidicolous nestlings are reared and fed by both adults and fly at 19 or 20 days. The Eurasian Jay's diet consists mainly of seeds, berries, nuts and acorns (the latter may account for up to 50 percent of the diet) and quite a large percentage of large insects, invertebrates and sometimes the eggs and chicks of passeriforms, snatched from nests. Before the mating season the Eurasian Jay tends to gather in groups and play collective games, pursuing each other in the air and adopting strange postures, with the wings held open to display the bright coloration.

182 GAVIA ARCTICA
Arctic or Black-throated Loon

Classification Order Gaviiformes, Family Gaviidae.
Characteristics It measures 58–67 cm. in length (23–27″), has a wing span of 120 cm. (48″) and weighs 2–2.7 kg. (4.4–6 lbs.). The nuptial plumage is black uppermost with white markings, gray on the neck, black on the throat, with thin white stripes, and white lower down. The beak is black. Adults in winter and the young have gray upper and white lower parts.
Habitat Freshwater lakes, coastal waters.
Distribution North America, northern Asia and northern Europe.
Life and habits It nests on lakes, in open terrain (tundra) or wooded areas (taiga), building its nest near water. In a hollow in the ground it heaps up vegetable matter and lays two eggs, the only annual clutch. These are incubated by both adults for 28 or 29 days. The nidifugous nestlings head for the nearest water and are fed by the parents. They fly at 2 months, when they can already feed themselves. The Black-throated Loon feeds by making long dives underwater, to a depth of 20 meters and more (65 feet), using its legs to propel itself. This is how it catches its prey, mainly small fish, crustaceans and mollusks. Migratory by nature, this species often winters on large lakes and at sea.

183 GAVIA IMMER
Great Northern Diver or Common Loon

Classification   Order Gaviiformes, Family Gaviidae.
Characteristics   This species is 80 cm. long (31"), with a wing span of 130 cm. (51"), and weighs up to 4.2 kg. (9.2 lbs.)—the males being larger than the females—the nuptial plumage of adults has a black and white-marked back, black head, black neck with a collar of white stripes, and white lower parts. The long, sharp beak is also black. The young, and the adults in winter, have gray upper and white lower parts.
Habitat   Freshwater lakes and coastal waters.
Distribution   Northern regions of America.
Life and habits   The nest is made usually on a small island, near the water, or amid reeds, and consists in the first case of a thinly lined hollow, and in the second of a wide platform made of plant matter. The single annual clutch has 1–3 eggs (most commonly 2), which are incubated for 29–30 days by both sexes. The parents look after the chicks together; these are nidifugous and fly at 12 weeks, but can feed themselves by 6 weeks. The diet consists of fish, crustaceans and mollusks (including cephalopods—cuttlefish, octopus, etc.) caught during underwater dives, which last on average 40–60 seconds. Like the Black-throated Loon (*G. arctica*), this species also has to run across the surface of the water before becoming airborne.

184 GELOCHELIDON NILOTICA
Gull-billed Tern

Classification   Order Charadriiformes, Family Laridae.
Characteristics   About 39 cm. long (15"). Its upper plumage is pale gray, and white lower down. The short, strong beak is entirely black, as are the top of the head and the upper sides of the head. In winter the head is white, shaded with gray, and may have a few black stripes. The tail is slightly forked. When on the ground, it shows its tarsal bones longer than those of, for example, the Sandwich Tern (*Sterna sandvicensis*). In young individuals the top of the head and upper parts have tawny shades with a few brown markings on the back.
Habitat   Marshlands, lagoons, salt works, sandy coasts, lakes, inland waters.
Distribution   Europe, eastern Asia, Australia, America.
Life and habits   It nests in colonies on the ground, preferably on sandy beaches. The nest is dug out of sand or earth and is covered with plant matter. It lays one clutch with 2–5 eggs (most often just 3), which are incubated by both parents for 22 or 23 days, once the last egg has been laid. The somewhat nidifugous nestlings are reared by both parents and fly at about 4 or 5 weeks. The Gull-billed Tern feeds on fish, small mammals, eggs, small birds, lizards, frogs, tadpoles, and invertebrates.

185 GEOCOCCYX CALIFORNIANUS
Greater Roadrunner

Classification Order Cuculiformes, Family Cuculidae.
Characteristics About 60 cm. long (24″), it has a stream-lined appearance, with strong legs and a very long tail. The plumage is dark uppermost with white markings, off-white lower down, with black stripes. A crest of black feathers adorns the head. The legs and beak are blue. The sexes are similar.
Habitat Arid regions and deserts that have shrubs and cacti.
Distribution Western North America.
Life and habits It is a ground-dwelling bird with short wings, for making short flights; the long tail is used as a rudder for changing direction when the bird runs fast over the ground, reaching up to 24 kph. (15 mph.). The nest is made in a bush or cactus. The female lays 2–8 eggs (usually 3, 4 or 5), and incubates them for 17–18 days. We do not know the exact age at which the young can fly, but they can run at 3 weeks and find their own food. The diet consists of animals caught on the ground—insects, lizards, snakes (including poisonous ones), scorpions, small rodents and birds. To catch snakes it uses a special technique, keeping a close watch on the reptile's movements and waiting for the precise instant to grab the snake just behind the jaws with its beak.

186 GERONTICUS EREMITA
Northern Bald Ibis

Classification Order Ciconiiformes, Family Threskiornithidae
Characteristics About 72 cm. long (28″), it has dark plumage with metallic green and purple highlights. On the nape, a few long feathers form a distinctive tuft. The head and throat are bare and dark red, the top of the head is blue, the beak is long and slightly curved, and the legs are dark red. The sexes are similar; the young have a more bronze over-all coloration.
Habitat Arid areas and mountainous regions, often near villages.
Distribution In about 1600 this bird also existed in southern Europe as far as Switzerland. Now a very rare and threatened species, it exists in localized colonies in Asia Minor and north-western Africa.
Life and habits It nests in colonies in rocks (in the village of Birecik, Turkey, in nests on rocky ledges between houses). It lays 3 or 4 eggs (more rarely 5 or 6), which are incubated from the laying of the first one for 27 or 28 days. The nestlings remain in the nest for 46–51 days. The Bald Ibis feeds on insects, but also on small birds, mammals and reptiles. It is an extremely rare species (many of the colonies once known have vanished); poaching, environmental changes and insecticides are among the causes responsible for its progressive disappearance. It is presently the object of a World Wildlife Fund conservation scheme.

187 GLAREOLA PRATINCOLA
Eurasian Pratincole

Classification   Order Charadriiformes, Family Glareolidae.
Characteristics   About 22 cm. long (8.7"), with long, thin wings and a forked tail. The upper parts are olive brown, and the lower parts are tawny with a cream-colored patch on the throat and breast. The base of the tail is white, the legs and tail black. The young have a wide pectoral band with dark stripes. Similar species include the Black-winged Pratincole (*G. nordmanni*), which has black lower-wing surfaces (not chestnut); it is found in eastern Europe and Asia (western Siberia).
Habitat   Brackish marshes, lowlands and mud flats.
Distribution   Southern Europe, North Africa, western Asia.
Life and habits   It nests in colonies, making its nest in a shallow hollow in the ground, possibly surrounded by vegetation. There is a single annual clutch of 2–4 eggs (commonly 3), which are incubated by both sexes for 17 or 18 days. The somewhat nidifugous young are first fed by the parents; then, at 8–10 days, they feed themselves; they fly at 22 days. This species, which is very nimble in flight, feeds in the air on medium-sized insects—orthopterans (grasshoppers, etc.), odonata (dragonflies) and coleopterans (beetles).

---

188 GOURA CRISTATA
Blue Crowned Pigeon

Classification   Order Columbiformes, Family Columbidae.
Characteristics   The crowned pigeons belong to the Subfamily Gourinae. These birds are often found in zoos and parks because of their ornamental value. They have a grayish-blue plumage and a tuft, or crown, which is fan shaped, on the head. The males are 78–85 cm. long (31–34") and weigh about 1.3 kg. (nearly 3 lbs.). The Blue Crowned Pigeon has bluish, ash-gray plumage. The crown and tip of the tail are pale blue-gray. Around the eyes is a black rim and on the wings a white marking, while on the middle of the back is a chestnut-colored band. The legs are grayish and the feet reddish; the beak is gray. There are two other known species: Victoria Crowned Pigeon (*G. victoria*) and Maroon-breasted Crowned Pigeon (*G. scheepmakeri*).
Habitat   Forest.
Distribution   Western New Guinea and nearby islands.
Life and habits   These birds feed mainly on fruit, berries and also seeds. They are solitary or live in small groups, feeding on the ground. They nest in trees and lay two eggs. Hunting has reduced the numbers of these birds, although they are currently protected.

189 GRACULA RELIGIOSA
Hill Myna

Classification   Order Passeriformes, Family Sturnidae.
Characteristics   The Sturnidae family, which includes 6 genera and 12 species, ranges in over-all length from 24 to 37 cm. (9.5–14.5"). The Hill Myna is about 25 cm. long (10"). It is a very well known bird, unfortunately the subject of a considerable trade, because of its ability in captivity to copy the human voice. Its plumage is black; its beak is strong and yellow, with variously shaped fleshy yellow lobes, the shape depending on the subspecies (many ornithologists recognize 11 subspecies of the Hill Myna, according to H. Bruns). The wings are black with a white edge. Among the other species are the Ceylon Myna (*G. ptilogenys*) and the Celebes Myna (*Streptocitta albicollis*), found only in the Celebes.
Habitat   Forests, woods, near water.
Distribution   Southeast Asia.
Life and habits   It is a gregarious bird and usually lives in large groups. It feeds mainly on fruit, but also on invertebrates. Its voice has a great range, and young birds, after their first year of life, are brilliant mimics of the human voice. It usually lays 2–4 eggs. The nidicolous nestlings leave the nest after about four weeks, becoming independent at 6–8 weeks.

190 GRUS GRUS
Eurasian Crane

Classification   Order Gruiformes, Family Gruidae.
Characteristics   About 112 cm. long (44"). Its plumage is gray with a white stripe at the sides of the head and neck; the face and throat are black. The top of the head is red, and the secondary remiges are long and form a sort of drooping blackish tail. Immature birds have a browner head and upper parts and a thinner tail. In flight they show a long outstretched neck and the black base of the remiges.
Habitat   Marshlands, fields, steppes.
Distribution   Europe, Asia, North Africa.
Life and habits   It makes strong, guttural sounds (for example: *kr-rooh* and *kr-r-r*). It generally migrates in a V formation and is gregarious by nature, except in the breeding season. It nests on the ground amid vegetation. It lays a single clutch of 1–3 eggs (ordinarily 2), which are incubated by both parents, but mainly the female, for 28–30 days. The nidifugous nestlings are reared by both parents and are independent in about 10 weeks.

191 GRUS LEUCOGERANUS
Siberian White Crane

Classification   Order Gruiformes, Family Gruidae.
Characteristics   About 137 cm. long (54″), it has white plumage with black primary remiges. The beak and bare parts of the head and legs are red. Young birds have a whitish plumage uppermost, tending to be rust colored; the head is feathered and the lower parts are white with brownish markings. A similar species is the Manchurian Crane (*G. japonensis*), with a differently colored beak and bare parts and a different series of black markings on the wings.
Habitat   Tundra, lakes with vegetation, cultivated fields, watercourses.
Distribution   Northern Asia, wintering in the southern portions.
Life and habits   It builds a nest made of dry twigs and reeds amid the vegetation near water. It lays a single clutch with generally two eggs, which are incubated by both adults. The young are reared by both parents. The Siberian White Crane feeds both on animals (fish, lizards and frogs) and on vegetable matter.

192 GYPAETUS BARBATUS
Bearded Vulture (Lammergeier)

Classification   Order Falconiformes, Family Accipitridae.
Characteristics   About 108 cm. long (43″). Its back, wings and tail are blackish gray, with the middle of the feathers white; the lower parts are pinkish or off-white. The black, stiff feathers around the eye are distinctive and extend beyond the beak, forming a kind of goatee. Immature birds have a uniform brown coloring.
Habitat   High mountainous regions, vagrant to lowlands.
Distribution   An increasingly rare species, it exists in some parts of North Africa, as well as in the eastern and southern areas of that continent, and in some parts of central Asia. The European population has decreased alarmingly—40–50 pairs nesting and very localized in Spain and Greece, with a very few individuals or isolated pairs still surviving in Corsica, Crete, Rhodes and Sardinia.
Life and habits   It nests among rocky cliffs, in well-protected hollows and cracks. It lays one egg, and sometimes two. Incubation is the task of the female and lasts about 53 days. The nestling is fed by both parents. It makes its first flight at 107–117 days. The Bearded Vulture feeds mainly on carrion and organic waste, with a preference for large bones, which it often drops from a great height in order to shatter them and remove the marrow (its tongue is specially suited to this operation).

195 HAGEDASHIA HAGEDASH
Hadada Ibis

Classification Order Ciconiiformes, Family Threskiornithidae.

Characteristics This ibis has greenish-brown plumage with bronze-colored highlights; the beak is curved downward. The scientific name of the species comes from the cry that this bird makes.

Habitat Marshland, woods up to 2,000 m. (6,500 ft.).

Distribution Africa.

Life and habits It nests in trees 2–7 meters above the ground (6–23 feet). It usually lays 3 or 4 eggs, which are incubated by both parents. Incubation lasts for about 26 days. The nidicolous nestlings are reared by both parents and leave the nest at about 35 days. When the mating period is over and the young have left the nest, these birds gather in small groups of up to 30 individuals.

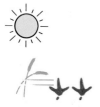

196 HALIAEETUS ALBICILLA
White-tailed Eagle

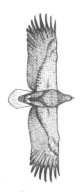

Classification Order Falconiformes, Family Accipitridae.

Characteristics About 77 cm. long (30″). The female is usually larger than the male. In appearance it is squat and bulky. The plumage is brownish, darker in the upper parts, with a lighter head and completely white wedge-shaped tail in the adult (in the young it is dark). It has a broad yellow beak, and yellow and blackish legs. The tarsal bones have no feathers. In flight it looks like a large and majestic bird of prey, with large wings with flat tips. A similar species is Pallas's Fish Eagle (*H. leucoryphus*), which is smaller and darker in color, and has a white tail with a black bar at the tip.

Habitat Coasts and reefs, islands and inland lakes near marshes, estuaries.

Distribution Europe and Asia.

Life and habits It nests in trees, but also on the ground and on rocks in large, crude nests. It lays 1–4 eggs (usually 2, and rarely 4), which are incubated for 35–45 days, mainly by the female. The nestlings are reared by both parents and fly at about 70 days, although they stay near the nest for a further 35–40 days. The White-tailed Eagle feeds mainly on fish, mammals, carrion and birds.

197 HALIAEETUS LEUCOCEPHALUS
Bald Eagle

Classification   Order Falconiformes, Family Accipitridae.
Characteristics   About 85–105 cm. long (33–42"), it is a very strong-looking bird, with a wing span of 2.45 m. (96") in more developed individuals. The adult is completely dark brown, except for the head and tail, which are white. The immature bird (which starts to adopt the adult plumage after its third year) has a brown head and tail, like the rest of the body. The female is larger than the male, the former weighing up to 6.3 kg. (14 lbs.), the latter not exceeding 4.6 kg. (10 lbs.).
Habitat   Rocky and wooded seacoasts, lakesides and riverbanks.
Distribution   North America.
Life and habits   This is usually a solitary bird of prey, but in winter it may gather in groups in the same area when there is abundant food available. The nest, which is a huge collection of branches, is built in trees, and sometimes among rocks. It lays 1–3 eggs (usually 2), which are incubated by both sexes for about 35 days. The nestlings leave the nest at 10–11 weeks. The diet consists of fish, and to a lesser degree, birds and medium-sized mammals, with some carrion. In recent years a series of factors, including poisoning through DDT accumulation, has caused the numbers of this species to drop dramatically.

198 HALIAEETUS VOCIFER
African Fish Eagle

Classification   Order Falconiformes, Family Accipitridae.
Characteristics   About 70–80 cm. long (28–32"). The upper parts are hazel-brown, and the lower hazel colored. The tail, head and neck are white in the adult and striped with brown in immature birds. The female is larger than the male. The wing span of almost 2 meters (80") is a distinctive feature (it reaches 2.3 meters (90") in the female). The male's weight reaches 2.5 kg. (5.5 lbs.); the female's reaches 3.6 kg. (8 lbs.). A similar species is the Madagascar Fish Eagle (*H. vociferoides*).
Habitat   Wooded and rocky lakesides and watercourses.
Distribution   Central southern Africa.
Life and habits   It nests from sea level to about 2,000 meters (6,500 ft.), always near lake districts or marshland. The nest is a large mound of branches, usually in trees; when there are no trees it nests on the ground, in bushes or on rocks. The clutch has 1–3 eggs (usually 2) laid at intervals of 3 days, at the start of the dry season. The female incubates them for 44–45 days, with occasional help from the male. The young (in many cases only the largest survives) make their first flight at 65–75 days. This species feeds mainly on fish (90 percent of the diet) caught in swift swoops, and, to a lesser degree, birds and carrion.

199 HALIASTUR INDUS
Brahminy Kite

Classification Order Falconiformes, Family Accipitridae.
Characteristics Of medium dimensions, about 43–50 cm. long (17–20″). The coloring of the body is a uniform reddish brown, except for the head and breast, which are white. Immature birds are a uniform brown with lighter stripes.
Habitat Coastal zones, paddy fields, watercourses and marshes.
Distribution India, Ceylon (Sri Lanka), tropical Asia and southern China to northern Australia.
Life and habits It nests up to 2,500 meters (8,200 ft.), always near some kind of water, and even appears in coastal towns and cities and ports in search of food. Where it is very common—as in India—it becomes gregarious. The nest is built in a lone tree, or sometimes a building. It consists of dry branches and green leaves with pieces of wool, paper and fish bones. It lays 1–4 eggs (usually 2), which are incubated by the female, who is fed by her mate. Incubation seems to last 26 or 27 days, but precise data are not available. The young leave the nest after 50–55 days in Australia (probably earlier in India). The diet is varied and consists of frogs, crabs, fish, insects and all kinds of waste (carrion).

200 HIERAAETUS FASCIATUS
Bonelli's Eagle

Classification Order Falconiformes, Family Accipitridae.
Characteristics About 69 cm. long (27″), slender in appearance, with dark upper parts and pale lower parts, the latter with long dark markings. Immature birds have tawny lower parts. The female is larger than the male. In flight the adults have a dark lower-wing surface with a more accentuated band and a pale belly. A similar species is the Booted Eagle (*H. pennatus*), which is about 52 cm. long (20.5″) and has a fairly varied coloring, with two commoner phases—one dark and one light.
Habitat Wooded regions, some sparsely wooded areas, scrub.
Distribution Southern Europe, central and southern Asia, Africa.
Life and habits It nests among rocks, more rarely in trees. It lays 2 eggs (sometimes 1, rarely 3), which are incubated by both parents for 42–44 days. The nestlings fly at about 65 days, but remain with their parents for a further 8 weeks or more. Bonelli's Eagle feeds on wild rabbits, hares, other small mammals, birds (such as partridges) and lizards; it hunts by swooping, or following its victim along rocky cliffs or through scrub.

201 HIMANTOPUS HIMANTOPUS
Black-winged Stilt

Classification   Order Charadriiformes, Family Recurvirostridae.

Characteristics   An unmistakable bird, about 38 cm. long (15″), with a long black beak. It has black upper and white lower plumage; the legs are long and red. In flight the legs jut out beyond the tail. In winter, males and females both have white heads and tails, whereas in spring and summer the rear of the male's head is black. The young are more brownish, with a pale edge to the feathers on the back and wings.

Habitat   Marshes, ponds, lagoons, lakes, marshlands in general.

Distribution   Central-southern Europe, Asia, Africa, America and Australia.

Life and habits   The Black-winged Stilt builds a nest made of mud, plant matter, shells, various bits and pieces, in shallow water or amid bog plants. It lays a single clutch, usually with 3 eggs (but also 4 or 5), which are incubated by both sexes for 25 or 26 days. The nidifugous young are reared by both parents and become independent at about 4 weeks. This extremely elegant mud-dwelling bird feeds on insects, various invertebrates and vegetable matter, found between the bottom mud and the water's surface. It is gregarious and nests in colonies. It makes a distinctive call, which may sound like a very shrill *kyik-kyik-kyik*.

---

202 HIPPOLAIS POLYGLOTTA
Melodious Warbler

Classification   Order Passeriformes, Family Sylviidae.

Characteristics   This warbler is about 13 cm. long (5″) and weighs about 11 grams (0.4 oz.). The upper parts are olive green, the lower bright yellow, and there is a brightly colored eyebrow over the eye. The legs are pink. The young more or less resemble the adults. The beak is long and thin, designed for an insectivorous diet. Among similar species is the Icterine Warbler (*H. icterina*), which has very similar plumage (except for the legs, which are gray) and lives in Asia and central-northern Europe.

Habitat   Woods, cultivated land, gardens.

Distribution   North Africa, southern Europe.

Life and habits   The nest is built in hedgerows in cultivated land and in undergrowth often near clearings and water. It is cup-shaped and made of grass, cobwebs, horsehair and feathers, by the female. Each year there is a single clutch (sometimes two), which consists of 4 eggs incubated solely by the female for 12 or 13 days. The nidicolous nestlings are reared by both members of the pair and fly at 12 days. The diet consists of insects and other small invertebrates, sometimes caught in mid-air. The Melodious Warbler's song consists of a first part, which is an imitation of the song of other birds (sparrows, swallows, blackbirds), and a second part, which consists of a warbling sound. It is a migratory species and winters in Africa.

203 HIRUNDO RUSTICA
Barn Swallow

Classification   Order Passeriformes, Family Hirundinidae.
Characteristics   About 19 cm. long (7.5″), it is easily recognizable by its forked tail with long rectrices; the upper parts of the plumage are metallic dark blue, the lower whitish with cream-colored shades; the forehead and throat are reddish, and there is a dark blue band on the upper breast. Young birds have a generally duller plumage, and the outer rectrices are shorter. A similar species is the Red-rumped Swallow (*H. daurica*), which has a reddish rump and tawny throat and lower parts.
Habitat   Country areas, cultivated land near water, rural buildings.
Distribution   Europe, Asia, Africa and North America.
Life and habits   A gregarious bird, except for the reproductive period. It nests in various environments, generally near water and in open countryside. The nest may be made in hollows, eaves, et cetera. It is built by both sexes, and is cup-shaped and made of mud and plant matter. Barn Swallows lay 2 or 3 clutches with 3–8 eggs (usually 4 or 5), incubated mainly by the female, for 17–24 days. The nidicolous nestlings are reared by both parents and leave the nest at 17–24 days. The Barn Swallow's diet consists typically of insects caught in midair.

204 HYDRANASSA TRICOLOR
Tricolored Heron

Classification   Order Ciconiiformes, Family Ardeidae.
Characteristics   About 60–70 cm. long (24–28″), it has a long neck and very pointed beak. The plumage is reddish brown on the back, white on the lower parts, gray on the neck and wings. In immature birds the neck is reddish brown.
Habitat   Coastal wetlands, fresh and brackish water, marshes.
Distribution   North America and South America.
Life and habits   Generally nonmigratory, it may be migratory in the extreme areas of its distribution. Gregarious by nature, it nests in colonies in trees near water. In the nest, made of dry branches, it usually lays 3 or 4 eggs (sometimes 5, 6 or 7), which are incubated by both adults for about 21 days; both parents look after the young. We do not know precisely the rate of growth of the young, but they do remain in the nest for about 3 or 4 weeks. The diet consists of aquatic animals and small fish (especially saltwater species) as well as grasshoppers and other insects caught on shores and banks. It uses a specific fishing technique, moving through the water with its wings unfolded, thus inviting fish to take refuge in the shadow cast on the water's surface. It then catches them with its very sharp beak, which it wields like a harpoon.

205 HYDROBATES PELAGICUS
European Storm Petrel

Classification   Order Procellariiformes, Family Hydrobatidae.

Characteristics   About 15 cm. long (6"). The general coloring is dark, with a white rump, square tail and long wings. The lower parts are also dark. Young birds are very much like adults. It has slender legs, with the front toes webbed.

Habitat   Open sea, islands and rocky coasts.

Distribution   Atlantic coast of Europe and western Mediterranean.

Life and habits   It flies skimming low over the sea, often following ships. It nests in colonies and frequents its nesting place particularly by twilight and at night. The nest is a sort of burrow or tunnel, dug by the pair, which ends in a larger chamber. It lays a single clutch of one white egg, which is incubated by both sexes for about 38–40 days. The nidicolous nestling is fed with regurgitated food by both parents, preferably at night, at intervals of 2 or 3 days. It leaves the nest at 56–64 days. The European Storm Petrel feeds on plankton and animal substances found on the sea's surface.

206 HYDROPHASIANUS CHIRURGUS
Pheasant-tailed Jacana

Classification   Order Charadriiformes, Family Jacanidae.

Characteristics   The Jacanidae have a distant resemblance to the Rallidae (rails). The Pheasant-tailed Jacana is an unmistakable bird—the plumage is blackish brown, with white head and neck. There is also white on the wings. The tail is very long, hence the name "pheasant-tailed." On the nape of the neck there is a yellow mark. As in other Jacanidae, the legs have very long toes. Among other species is the African Jacana (*Actophilornis africana*), which is found in Africa south of the Sahara.

Habitat   Wetlands, riverbanks.

Distribution   Southern Asia.

Life and habits   In the Jacanidae the sexes have a similar coloration, but the females are usually larger than the males. The behavior and reproduction of the Pheasant-tailed Jacana have been studied by ornithologist Alfred Hoffmann. It nests near water, laying 4 eggs, which are incubated almost solely by the male. The female may mate with 2, 3 or 4 males. The nidicolous nestlings swim and are good at diving.

207 HYDROPROGNE CASPIA (STERNA CASPIA)
Caspian Tern

Classification Order Charadriiformes, Family Laridae.
Characteristics This tern is about 52 cm. long (21″). The upper parts are pale gray; the rump, forked tail and lower parts are white. The primaries are dark brown toward the tip. The legs are black, as are the top and sides of the head in summer; they turn white striped with black in winter. The large strong beak is red. Young birds are brownish on the top of the head, the upper parts are speckled with brown, and the beak is lighter. A similar species is the Royal Tern (*S. maxima*), which does not have the blackish marking on the remiges. Its beak is more orange and its tail is more forked.
Habitat Seacoasts, sandy and stony islands, lakes, large rivers.
Distribution Europe, Asia, North America, Australia.
Life and habits It nests in hollows on the ground, preferably in sand. It lays a single clutch, with usually 2 or 3 eggs (sometimes only 1), which are incubated by both sexes for 20–22 days. The seminidifugous nestlings are reared by both parents, leaving the nest after a few days and flying at 25–30 days. The Caspian Tern feeds mainly on fish.

208 ICTERUS GALBULA
Baltimore Oriole

Classification Order Passeriformes, Family Icteridae.
Characteristics This species is about 17.5–20 cm. long (7–8″), the front of the male's body plumage, wings and tail are black, with the exception of a white bar on the shoulders. The remaining lower parts and two stripes on the upper parts of the wings are orange. The female is olive gray uppermost, pale yellow lower down, and it has two pale bars on the wings. In winter the coloring of the plumage of both sexes becomes duller.
Habitat Forests with clearings, cultivated land, city parks.
Distribution North and Central America.
Life and habits This bird has a melodious song, and has also adapted to living in city parks and suburbs. It nests in tallish trees and makes a cup-shaped nest of vegetable fibers, wool and horsehair, suspended from two small branches. It lays 4–6 eggs (usually 4). Hatching takes 12–14 days, and incubation is the female's job alone. The nestlings can fly at 14 days. This is a migratory species and it spends the coldest months in the hotter parts of Central America. It feeds on insects, spiders and other small invertebrates, completing its insectivorous diet with berries, fruit and other plant matter.

209 ICTERUS ICTERUS
Troupial

Classification   Order Passeriformes, Family Icteridae.
Characteristics   The Icteridae are common in the Americas, and they are called "American orioles." They range in size from 15 to 55 cm. (6–22"). The beak is conical and varies in length; it is pointed and, in some species (such as the genus *Cacicus*), large with a conspicuous *scutum* (shield) or frontal casque. The wings have nine primaries. The plumage is quite variable. It is usually black with bright brown, red or yellow markings, sometimes with stripes. There are 87–93 species in this family, depending on the classification; among them is the Bobolink (*Dolichonyx oryzivorus*), which makes the longest migration. The Troupial is about 30–35 cm. long (12–14"), with a mainly reddish-yellow color, and black wings and tail (there are broad white markings on the wings), and a black head.
Habitat   Forests.
Distribution   South America.
Life and habits   These birds are omnivorous; their diet being made up of invertebrates, seeds and fruit. A few are polygamous and some species, including the cowbirds, are parasitic. They normally lay 2 eggs (sometimes as many as 4, 5 or 6). Incubation lasts 10–14 days, and the nidicolous nestlings remain in the nest for 19–30 days.

---

210 INDICATOR INDICATOR
Black-throated Honeyguide

Classification   Order Piciformes, Family Indicatoridae.
Characteristics   The family Indicatoridae includes species whose length ranges from 10 to 20 cm. (4–8"), with 9 primaries, and rather dull plumage (with yellow or white markings in a few species). These are for the most part parasitic birds like cuckoos. The Black-throated Honeyguide has brownish-gray plumage, darker uppermost with a pale mark tending to pale yellow at the back of the eye. Other species in the family include the Scale-throated Honeyguide (*I. variegatus*), the Lesser Honeyguide (*I. minor*) and the Least Honeyguide (*I. exilis*).
Habitat   Scrub and savanna.
Distribution   Africa south of the Sahara.
Life and habits   The family name *Indicatoridae* probably derives from the habit of its member species the Black-throated Honeyguide and, to a lesser extent, *I. variegatus*, of guiding the Ratel (genus *Mellivora*) and natives to the hives of wild honeybees. The Ratel and man use the actual comb and leave the remains for the honeyguides, which feed particularly on the wax contained in the comb. It has been proved that at least 6 species of honeyguides are parasitic. The nestlings remain in the nest for about a month.
Note: The photo shows a female.

211 IXOBRYCHUS MINUTUS
Little Bittern

Classification Order Ciconiiformes, Family Ardeidae.
Characteristics About 36 cm. long (14″), the male has a black nape, top of the head, scapulars, back and rump, with greenish highlights; the throat and breast are tawny and lighter at the sides; the tail and wings are black with cream-colored wing coverts. The tough beak is long and yellow, and is streaked with green. The female has brownish upper parts and lighter, striped lower parts. Young birds are speckled and spotted.
Habitat Lakes, ponds, rivers, marshlands.,
Distribution Europe, Asia, Africa and Australia.
Life and habits It builds a nest made of vegetable matter, preferably amid reeds. It lays a single clutch (sometimes 2) with 4–10 eggs (most often 5 or 6), which are incubated by both adults for a period of 16–19 days. The nidicolous young are fed by both parents; they stay in the nest for 7–9 days and can fly at about 30 days. The Little Bittern feeds mainly on insects and other invertebrates. It has a distinctive mimetic position amid reeds or canes.

---

212 JACANA SPINOSA
American Jacana

Classification Order Charadriiformes, Family Jacanidae.
Characteristics The Jacanidae are birds with very long toes, particularly the hind ones. One species—*Irediparra gallinacea*—has a claw of 7 cm. (2.75″). With such feet the Jacanidae are designed for running over the floating leaves of aquatic plants. The American Jacana is 20 cm. long (8″) and weighs about 100 grams (3.5 ounces); it has brown plumage, a yellow or red frontal shield, and a pointed spur at the angle of the wing. The head, breast and back are all black, and there is yellow on the wings, which is even more visible when the bird is flying. The legs are greenish.
Habitat Wetlands, riverbanks.
Distribution Mexico to South America.
Life and habits The name comes from the popular native name given to this bird by the Tupi Indians, *jassana*. Like the other species of Jacanidae, the American Jacana builds a nest of vegetable matter supported in or floating on the water. Here it lays usually 4 eggs, which are incubated for 22–25 days. The female hardly takes part in the task of incubation and mates with several males.

213 JUNCO OREGANUS
Oregon Junco

Classification   Order Passeriformes, Family Fringillidae.
Characteristics   About 13–15 cm. long (5–6″). The head
and neck are dark gray and the wings are pale ocher; the tail is
brown and the sides are pink. The young have a brown-striped
plumage. But there are considerable variations, geographically
speaking, in the plumage coloring.   A similar species is the
Slate-colored Junco (*J. hyemalis*).
Habitat   Coniferous forests and mixed coniferous and broadleaf woods.
Distribution   North America.
Life and habits   It nests in the northernmost parts from which
it migrates in autumn toward more temperate regions. The nest
is a cup of grass, bits of bark and horsehair and is made on the
ground among the roots of trees, or among rocks. Sometimes
there are two clutches a year, and 4–6 eggs are laid in each;
these are incubated for 11 or 12 days by both sexes. The nestlings leave the nest after about 14 days. The diet consists of
seeds and insects in equal parts in summer, and only of seeds
in winter. The nestlings are fed almost solely with insects and
larvae.

214 JYNX TORQUILLA
Wryneck

Classification   Order Piciformes, Family Picidae.
Characteristics   About 16 cm. long (6.5″), it looks more like
a passeriform than a woodpecker. The coloring of the plumage
is extremely mimetic; the upper parts are tawny gray-brown,
and the lower parts more tawny with closely set brown barring.
As in other woodpeckers, the feet have two front toes and two
hind ones. The feathers on top of the head are erectile.
Habitat   Woods, forests, parks, and areas with scattered
trees.
Distribution   Europe, Asia and Africa.
Life and habits   It makes a *kyee-kyee-kyee* sound, strong
and nasal and repetitive. It feeds on the ground and climbs up
tree trunks like other woodpeckers. It nests in hollows in trees
and in brickwork. It lays a single clutch (sometimes two) consisting generally of 7–10 eggs (sometimes 5–14). These are
incubated by both sexes for 12–14 days. The nidicolous nestlings are fed by both parents and leave the nest at about 19–21
days.

215 KAKATOE GALERITA (CACATUA GA-LERITA)
Great Sulphur-crested Cockatoo

Classification Order Psittaciformes, Family Psittacidae.
Characteristics The individual species of parrots in the genus *Kakatoe* range from 32 to 50 cm. in length (13–20″). They have light plumage, with a tuft of feathers on the head and markings on the cheeks. This species, with others, belongs to the subfamily Cacatuinae, typical of the Indo-Australian zone. Some of these birds, like the Palm Cockatoo (*Probosciger aterrimus*), reach a length of 80 cm. (31″). The Great Sulphur-crested Cockatoo is about 50 cm. long (20″) and has white plumage, a blackish beak and a yellow crest on the head. Among other species in the genus *Cacatua*, the Pink Cockatoo (*C. leadbeateri*) is about 38 cm. long (15″), and the Galah, or Rose-breasted Cockatoo (*C. roseicapilla*) is about 37 cm. long (14.5″).
Habitat Scrub and forests.
Distribution Australia and New Guinea.
Life and habits It nests in hollows in trees and usually lays 2 eggs. Incubation is the task of the female, mainly, and lasts about 30 days. The nidicolous nestlings leave the nest after about 10 weeks. The Rose-breasted Cockatoo is the commonest species in Australia and has to compete with the Common Starling (introduced by man) for its nesting holes.

216 KETUPA ZEYLONENSIS
Brown Fish Owl

Classification Order Strigiformes, Family Strigidae.
Characteristics About 48–51 cm. long (19–20″). It has dark brown plumage on the upper parts, and lighter lower parts, with long black markings. The eyes are yellow. Two long tufts of dark feathers are present on the head. The wing span of the largest individuals reaches 190 cm. (75″).
Habitat Forests along watercourses, marshes and mangrove swamps.
Distribution Tropical Asia and the Middle East (recently became extinct in southern Turkey).
Life and habits An essential factor for this nocturnal and twilight predator is the presence of fresh- or saltwater areas for food and dense forest for nesting. Little is known about how it reproduces. The nest is built in a hollow in a tree or in the abandoned nest of a bird of prey. The clutch has 1–3 eggs. No other details are known, except that the young acquire a plumage resembling that of the adult in their first year. It feeds mainly on fish (to a lesser extent on birds, reptiles and mammals) which it sometimes catches by walking carefully in water, and at others by swooping from a perch. The toes on the feet have sharp scales with which it grips slippery fish.

217 LAGOPUS MUTUS
Rock Ptarmigan

Classification Order Galliformes, Family Tetraonidae.
Characteristics About 35 cm. long (14″), weighing 425–600 grams (15–21 oz). Its legs and toes are covered with feathers, which enable it to walk on snow without sinking in. Over the eye there is a caruncle of red skin. In the summer plumage the upper parts are gray (male) or brown (female), and the wings and belly are white. In winter the plumage is completely white, except for the black rectrices. There is a transitional plumage in spring and autumn. Among similar species is the Willow Ptarmigan (*L. lagopus*), which lives mainly in bushy birch trees, willows and heather in the northern parts of Europe, Asia and America.
Habitat Mountainous regions with herbaceous vegetation.
Distribution Europe, Asia and North America.
Life and habits This species is found in mountainous regions above the tree and shrub lines. The nest is made in a hollow in the ground, sometimes sheltered by rocks or clumps of grass, and lined with grass and feathers. There is a single annual clutch of 3–12 eggs (normally between 5 and 10), laid at intervals of 1 or 2 days and incubated by the female for 24–26 days. The nidifugous nestlings can make their first flight at 10 days. The diet consists of seeds, buds and, to a lesser extent, small invertebrates found on the ground.

218 LANIUS COLLURIO
Red-backed Shrike

Classification Order Passeriformes, Family Laniidae.
Characteristics About 17 cm. long (6–7″) and weighs on average 30 grams (1 oz.). The upper parts of the male are chestnut colored, the rump and head are gray with a black stripe crossing the eye. The lower parts are white, while the tail is black with white sides. The female is brown uppermost, and tawny beneath, with dark markings. The young resemble the female.
Habitat Cultivated land.
Distribution Europe, western Asia, Africa.
Life and habits The nest is built in a bush or small tree. There is one clutch a year of 5 or 6 eggs incubated by the female (with occasional help from the male) for 14–16 days. The nidicolous nestlings are fed by both adults and fly at 12–16 days. The prey is sighted from a perch and caught either in mid-air or on the ground and often "impaled" on thorns and spikes on branches to be eaten later. The diet consists of insects, other invertebrates, small mammals, reptiles and amphibians. In his nuptial display the male shows off the bright coloration of his plumage by posing with his wings dangling and vibrating, beak pointed to the sky. He then offers the female prey, by inviting her to visit the bush chosen for building the nest.

219 LANIUS EXCUBITOR
Northern or Great Gray Shrike

Classification Order Passeriformes, Family Laniidae.
Characteristics About 26 cm. long (10″) and weighs about 65 grams (2.3 oz.). The upper plumage is gray, except for a stripe across the eye and the wings, which are black. The lower parts are white. The female has dark bars on her breast; the young are gray-brown, barred on the lower parts. Among similar species is the Lesser Gray Shrike (*L. minor*), whose coloration is almost the same, and which is found in Asia, Europe and, in winter, Africa.
Habitat Cultivated land, clearings in woods, open terrain.
Distribution North America, Europe, Asia, North Africa.
Life and habits The cup-shaped nest, made of grass, small branches and wool, is built in bushes or trees. The single annual clutch of 5–9 eggs (normally not more than 7), is incubated mainly by the female for about 15 days. The nidicolous nestlings are fed by both parents and fly at 19 or 20 days, becoming independent at about 35 days. The hunting technique used by the Great Gray Shrike is the same as that of the Red-backed Shrike (*L. collurio*), but the diet consists mainly of large insects—coleopterans and orthopterans (beetles and grasshoppers), small mammals, reptiles and small birds.

---

220 LANIUS SENATOR
Woodchat Shrike

Classification Order Passeriformes, Family Laniidae.
Characteristics About 17 cm. long (7″) and weighs on average 40 grams (1.4 oz.). The head and nape of the neck are reddish. The upper parts are brown-black except for two white bands on the wings; the rump is white, as are the lower parts. The brown-gray young have barring and traces of white on the wings.
Habitat Mediterranean scrub (*maquis*), wooded country.
Distribution Western Asia, North Africa, central and southern Europe.
Life and habits The cup-shaped nest is built in trees (sometimes in bushes) and consists of grass and roots, lined with wool, feathers, et cetera. There is usually one annual clutch (occasionally two) of 5 or 6 eggs incubated mainly by the female for 16 days. The nidicolous nestlings are fed by both parents and fly at 19 or 20 days. Like the other shrikes, this species swoops down upon its prey from a perch. The diet consists mainly of insects (coleopterans, orthopterans and lepidopterans), but also of lizards, young birds and small mammals. In the nuptial display the male stands in front of the female, lowers his head with his red and black feathers puffed out and offers her food with his beak.

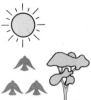

221 LARUS ARGENTATUS
Herring Gull

Classification Order Charadriiformes, Family Laridae.
Characteristics About 56 cm. long (22″). Its plumage is gray uppermost and light lower down; the head is white, the tough beak is yellowish with a red marking toward the tip. The coloring of the legs may vary, depending on the subspecies, from reddish to yellowish. Immature individuals have a dark brown coloring speckled with brown, with dark primary remiges, a darker beak, and brown legs. Before assuming their adult plumage, which happens after about 3 years, the young are grayish with brown markings.
Habitat Coasts, estuaries, lakes, rivers and even inland areas.
Distribution Europe, Asia, North America, North Africa.
Life and habits It nests in colonies on the ground, laying usually 2 or 3 eggs (at intervals, of 2 or 3 days), these are incubated by both adults (mainly by the female) for 25–33 days. The nestlings, reared by both parents, fly at about 6 weeks. The Herring Gull feeds on fish, mollusks, refuse, various invertebrates, small mammals and birds and vegetable matter.

222 LARUS MELANOCEPHALUS
Mediterranean Gull

Classification Order Charadriiformes, Family Laridae.
Characteristics About 38.5 cm. long (15″), it has gray upper and light lower parts. The beak is red with a black mark and quite strong. In the nuptial plumage the head is entirely black. Adults in flight are easily identifiable, because there is no black on the wings. Young individuals have dark secondary and blackish primary remiges.
Habitat Seas, coasts, freshwater and marshland.
Distribution Localized on the coasts of the Aegean and Black Sea; in other parts of the Mediterranean and in Asia Minor.
Life and habits It nests on the ground amid vegetation. It lays a single clutch usually of 3 eggs (sometimes 2). We do not have much data about its reproductive biology. The ornithologist Paul Isenmann has followed the nesting pattern in Greece and observed that it feeds on fish, mollusks, annelids and other invertebrates (he even found a small rodent in the droppings of this species). Paul Geroudet mentions that the Mediterranean Gull has nested in Hungary; Voucher and Roux report it in Switzerland; Johnson and Isenmann tell of it in the Camargue, and it is becoming more and more frequent in other parts of the Mediterranean.

223 LARUS RIDIBUNDUS
Black-headed Gull

Classification   Order Charadriiformes, Family Laridae.
Characteristics   About 37 cm. long (14.5″). The upper plumage is grayish and the lower is paler. The legs are red—yellowish red in the young. The beak is thin and reddish; in summer it has a dark brown hood. In winter the head is white with a dark marking on the sides. In flight it shows a white front edge.
Habitat   Coastal zones and inland areas.
Distribution   Europe and Asia.
Life and habits   It nests in colonies on the ground, rarely in trees. It lays a single clutch of 2–6 eggs (normally 3), which are incubated by both parents, once the first egg is laid, for 21–27 days. The nestlings are reared by both parents and can fly at 5 or 6 weeks. The Black-headed Gull feeds on vegetable matter, invertebrates and other small animals.

224 LEIPOA OCELLATA
Mallee Fowl

Classification   Order Galliformes, Family Megapodiidae.
Characteristics   The Mallee Fowl has an over-all grayish coloring and a browner back, and the front of the neck and breast have a central line of dark feathers. Very strong, grayish legs.
Habitat   Arid, bush-covered terrain.
Distribution   Australia.
Life and habits   The family Megapodiidae is known throughout the world of birds for the procedures it adopts for incubation. Some species make direct use of the sun's heat, laying their eggs on a beach in the sunniest spots; others dig deep tunnels up to a meter (3 ft.) deep, in places heated by volcanic heat; still others build huge mounds of leaves and loam up to 5 meters high and 12 meters in diameter (16 ft. and 40 ft.), where the heat necessary for incubation is produced by the sun and the decomposition of leaves. The male Mallee Fowl digs a trench 2 meters wide (80″) and 1.2 meters deep (48″), which he covers with dry branches and leaves. These, once soaked by rain, are covered with sand, making a small hillock up to 1.5 meters (60″) high. After 4 months the female lays up to 35 eggs in this nest at intervals of 4–8 days, with the male checking that the temperature is 88–92 degrees F. (27–37 degrees C.) at each laying, by covering or uncovering the mound as necessary.

225 LEPTOPTILOS CRUMENIFERUS
Marabou Stork

Classification Order Ciconiiformes, Family Ciconiidae.
Characteristics The species in the genus *Leptoptilos* are large Ciconiidae (storks) reaching an over-all length of 1.4 meters (55″), with a wing span of 3 meters (10 feet) and a weight of 5 kg. (11 lbs.). Two of the three known species have a large sac of connective tissue on the neck. The Marabou Stork has grayish wings, back and tail with green highlights, white primary coverts at the tip and white lower parts. In flight the head is held tucked in. Some ornithologists merge this species in a subspecies with the Asian Greater Adjutant (*L. dubius*). The third species, also Asian, is the Lesser Adjutant (*L. javanicus*), which does not have the sac on the throat; its wing span can reach 3.2 meters (126″) (the largest of all terrestrial birds).
Habitat Lowlands, savanna, marshlands, lakes, watercourses.
Distribution Africa.

Life and habits It nests in trees or rocks, sometimes in colonies. At the end of the rainy season it lays 2 or 3 eggs, which are incubated for about 30 days. The nestlings can fly at about 116 days, and they leave the nest at about 130 days—in effect, at the start of the next rainy season. It feeds mainly on carrion.

---

226 LIMOSA LIMOSA
Black-tailed Godwit

Classification Order Charadriiformes, Family Scolopacidae.
Characteristics About 41 cm. long (16″). In summer it is chestnut colored on the head and upper part of the breast, with dark stripes, while the lower breast and sides are white, with blackish bars. The upper parts are dark brown. In winter the plumage is gray-brown uppermost, with paler lower parts. The beak is long, pink, tinted with black.
Habitat Grassland and wetlands, marshes, lagoons, swamps, coastal areas and beaches.
Distribution Europe and Asia.
Life and habits It nests on the ground in grassy fields and marshy meadows. It lays a single annual clutch with 3–5 eggs, but usually 4, laid at intervals of 1 or 2 days. Incubation, the task of both parents, starts with the laying of the third or fourth egg and lasts 22–24 days. The nidicolous nestlings are reared by both parents. They fly at about 4 weeks. The Black-tailed Godwit feeds on invertebrates (insects, crustaceans, mollusks, worms), fish, tadpoles and vegetable matter.

227 LOPHAETUS OCCIPITALIS
Long-crested Eagle

Classification Order Falconiformes, Family Accipitridae.
Characteristics About 50–55 cm. long (20–22''), it has a sturdy body and very dark plumage. The upper and lower parts are uniformly brown, almost black, with the exception of the white marking on the carpus and at the base of the tail. The iris is golden yellow, and on the head is a long tuft of black feathers. The male, weighing 0.9–1.3 kg. (2–3 lbs.) is sometimes smaller than the female, which weighs 1.3–1.5 kg. (3–3.3 lbs.).
Habitat Woods, forests (tropical) and cultivated land.
Distribution Central and southern Africa.
Life and habits It spends a lot of time perched at the top of a tree or stake, keeping an eye on the area roundabout in search of possible prey. The nest is built between 7 and 20 meters (23–65 feet) above the ground in a very leafy tree (often a eucalyptus) situated more often than not in a river valley. It usually lays 2 eggs (sometimes only 1) in the latter half of the dry season, at the start of the rainy season. Only the female has been observed sitting on the eggs, and we do not know the length of incubation. The nestlings fly at about 55 days, and often only the tougher of a clutch of two will survive. It feeds on small and medium-sized animals caught on the ground—small mammals, lizards, snakes and insects.

228 LOPHORTYX GAMBELII
Gambel's Quail

Classification Order Galliformes, Family Phasianidae.
Characteristics About 25–28 cm. long (10–11.5''), it is squat-looking with strong legs that enable it to run fast on the ground. The male's plumage is brown uppermost, with various bars and markings; it is ocher on the breast, with a large black patch, and reddish on the sides. It is further characterized by a long plume on the head, which curves forward. The female and young are of a more uniform color, tending to brown. A similar species is the California Quail (*L. californicus*), which has a barred breast with no black marking.
Habitat Desert regions with bushes.
Distribution North America (southwestern U.S.).
Life and habits Environmental characteristics of areas frequented by this bird are large arid expanses with bushy vegetation and small water sources. The nest is made in a hollow in the ground amid sage plants and grasses. There are 9–14 eggs (most commonly 10–12), and they are incubated by the female for 21–24 days. The nestlings can fly at 10 days, but leave the nest shortly after hatching. The diet consists mainly of seeds, buds, and fruits, with a small percentage of insects.

229 LOXIA CURVIROSTRA
Red Crossbill

Classification   Order Passeriformes, Family Fringillidae.
Characteristics   About 16 cm. in length (6.5″) and weighs around 35 grams (1.25 ounces), the males being slightly larger than the females. The male has a purplish-red head, lower parts and rump; the wings and tail are brown. Uppermost the female is gray-green, lower down yellow-green. The young resemble the female, but have whitish lower parts with black markings. The beak is distinctive, with the points of the mandibles crossed.
Habitat   Coniferous woods.
Distribution   North America, North Africa, Europe and northern Asia.
Life and habits   This species frequents mainly fir woods, but also pine and larch woods. The nest—a cup-shaped structure of coniferous twigs, moss and lichens—is built in trees. The single annual clutch of 3 or 4 eggs is often laid in midwinter, when the conifers bear their fruit. The eggs, laid at intervals of one day, are incubated by the female for 13–16 days. The nestlings, fed by both parents, fly at 17–22 days. The Red Crossbill's diet consists of insects and berries, as well as the seeds of conifers, which it extracts from the kernels with its specifically designed beak.

230 LUNDA CIRRHATA
Tufted Puffin

Classification   Order Charadriiformes, Family Alcidae.
Characteristics   The body is squat, with narrow, short wings; it is about 37 cm. long (14.5″). The plumage is completely black, except for the white face. A tuft of yellow feathers runs from the head down the back. The fairly wide and high-set beak is red, as are the legs and webbed feet. In the winter plumage and in that of immature birds, the black parts become brown.
Habitat   Rocky crags, open sea.
Distribution   Arctic Ocean (from the Bering Sea to northern Japan).
Life and habits   This generally nonmigratory species is found in very large colonies on high and rocky coasts. It makes its nest in hollows in the ground and sometimes in cracks in rocks. A single egg is laid and incubated by both parents for a still-undetermined length of time. The nestling, fed by both adults, flies at about 45 days. Once reproduction is over, both adults and young head out to sea, to areas with more abundant fish. In fact these birds feed on fish caught in the sea, diving beneath the surface, sometimes to considerable depths, with the help of their broad webbed feet and wings.

231 LUSCINIA MEGARHYNCHOS
Nightingale

Classification   Order Passeriformes, Family Turdidae.
Characteristics   This species is 16 cm. long (6.5″) and weighs on average 23 grams (0.8 ounces). Its upper plumage is brown, with reddish shades on the tail and rump; the lower parts are white, with tawny shades. The young are speckled with brown and white. Among similar species is the Thrush Nightingale (*L. luscinia*), with similar coloration (although the lower parts are spotted with gray); it is found in central-eastern Europe and western Asia.
Habitat   Broadleaf woods, wooded country with bushes.
Distribution   Northwestern Africa, Europe and western Asia.
Life and habits   The nest is a cup-shaped structure of dry leaves and grass, made by the female amid thick vegetation, often near water. A single annual clutch contains 3–7 eggs (normally 4 or 5), which are incubated by the female for 13 or 14 days. Both parents rear the nidicolous young, which fly at 11–12 days. The Nightingale feeds mainly on insects, larvae and small invertebrates, and to a lesser extent on berries. The male delimits his territory and attracts the female with his song, often sung at night; he also performs a display in front of his mate, beating his wings and wagging his head and tail.

232 LUSCINIA SVECICA
Bluethroat

Classification   Order Passeriformes, Family Turdidae.
Characteristics   This species is about 13.5 cm. long (5.3″) and weighs about 18 grams (0.6 oz.). Its beak is thin. The male has brown upper parts except for the chestnut base of the tail and the white lower parts. The throat and breast are blue, with a mark in the middle that is reddish in the Scandinavian subspecies (*L. s. svecica*) and white in the western subspecies (*L. s. cyanecula*). The female and young are without the blue marking and have dark stripes.
Habitat   Willow and birch stands, often near water.
Distribution   Central-northern Europe, northern Asia.
Life and habits   The nest is made by the female on the ground, at the bottom of a bush or among the roots of a tree. Each year there is 1 clutch (sometimes 2) of 5–7 eggs (occasionally as many as 9), which are incubated by the female for 14 or 15 days. The nidicolous nestlings are fed by both parents and fly at about 15 days of age. The Bluethroat feeds on insects and their larvae, on small invertebrates, and on certain berries in autumn. The male sings a nuptial song in the air, dropping to the ground with his wings and tail extended. In this display he stands opposite the female with his tail open like a fan, wings hanging, and nods his head repeatedly to the left and right.

233 LYBIUS BIDENTATUS
Double-toothed Barbet

Classification   Order Piciformes, Family Capitonidae.
Characteristics   The Capitonidae are birds with brightly colored plumage; the head is sturdy, the beak is quite large, and is surrounded at the base by stiff bristles. The size of the species varies from 9 to 32 cm. (3.5–12.5″). The African barbets have adapted to the most varied of environments, from virgin forest to open and steppelike terrain. The species in the genus *Lybius* have a distinctive beak, on the edges of which there are tooth-like protuberances. The Double-toothed Barbet, about 23 cm. long (9″), is one of the largest barbets, with blackish coloration on the upper parts, dark red on the throat, breast and belly, and a yellow stripe around the eye. A similar species is the Black-collared Barbet (*L. torquatus*) which is about 20 cm. long (8″), with bright coloring and a red head and throat, yellow belly and a black stripe running across the breast and the nape of the neck.
Habitat   Open areas with bushes.
Distribution   Eastern Africa.
Life and habits   These birds are usually solitary or live in pairs, and have arboreal habits. They nest in holes made in old trees or in the ground. They lay 2–5 eggs, which are incubated by both parents. The nidicolous nestlings stay in the nest for more than a week and are reared by both parents. They feed on fruit, seeds and invertebrates.

234 LYRURUS TETRIX
Black Grouse

Classification   Order Galliformes, Family Tetraonidae.
Characteristics   The male is about 61.5 cm. long (24″) and unmistakable because of the bluish-black coloration of the plumage, and the distinctive lyre-shaped tail. On the wings there is a white wing bar, and the lower tail coverts are white. The female, which is about 42 cm. long (16.5″), is brown with black bars; the undertail and underwing are white, and the tail is slightly forked. Both the male and the female have a red caruncle above the eye; the beak and legs are blackish brown. Young birds resemble the female, but are smaller.
Habitat   Coniferous forests, clearings, wooded areas, rocky regions, places with low vegetation, marshy ground with vegetation.
Distribution   Central and northern Europe, central Asia.
Life and habits   It nests on the ground by digging a hollow. It lays usually one clutch with 6–10 eggs (sometimes 5–16), which are incubated by the female for 23–26 days. The nidifugous nestlings are reared by the female and fly at about a month. The Black Grouse has a mainly vegetarian diet.
Note: The drawing shows a male.

235 MACRONECTES GIGANTEUS
Southern Giant Fulmar

Classification   Order Procellariiformes, Family Procellarii-
dae.
Characteristics   The giant fulmars are large birds, up to 75
cm. long (30″), with a wing span that can reach 2 meters
(80″). In 1966 ornithologists Bourne and Warham subdivided
the genus *Macronectes* into two species: the Southern Giant
Fulmar (*M. giganteus*), which has grayish-brownish plumage,
with various shading depending on the bird, and the Northern
Giant Fulmar (*M. halli*), which has no shadings in the plumage
and has a white face. The general features tally with those of
the fulmars, because, according to the distinction proposed for
the family Procellariidae in 1965 by W. B. Alexander and other
ornithologists, the giant fulmars belong to the subfamily Ful-
mariinae.
Habitat   Coasts, open sea.
Distribution   Antarctic and subantarctic waters.
Life and habits   The giant fulmars feed mainly on dead animals and young seabirds, and they frequently steal the eggs
and young from penguin colonies. The two species reproduce
together in the Macquarie Islands. *M. halli* lays its eggs in August, and *M. giganteus* later. They make long migrations, particularly when young, reaching the coasts of Chile, Southern
Africa, and Australia.

236 MEGACERYLE MAXIMA (CERYLE MAXIMA)
Giant Kingfisher

Classification   Order Coraciiformes, Family Alcedinidae.
Characteristics   About 40 cm. long (16″), it has a grayish
coloring, with two stripes and black and white markings. The
head is blackish with a tuft of dark feathers at the top. The
breast and sides of the neck are brown, and parts on the lower
areas of the body are reddish brown; in females this area extends to the abdomen. The beak is strong and blackish. Other,
similar species are the Belted Kingfisher (*Ceryle alcyon*), up to
33 cm. long (13″), found in North America, and the Amazon
Kingfisher (*Chloroceryle amazona*), up to 28 cm. long (11″),
found in tropical America.
Habitat   Along rivers, lakes.
Distribution   Africa.
Life and habits   This species frequents forest areas along
watercourses and expanses of water in Africa south of the Sahara. It perches in trees and bushes and plunges down to the
water to catch its prey (fishes and amphibians). It often nests
with several pairs together, like a small colony. It may lay 2
clutches a year.

237 MELANOCORYPHA CALANDRA
Calandra Lark

Classification   Order Passeriformes, Family Alaudidae.
Characteristics   About 19 cm. long (7.5"), weighing on average 65 grams (2.3 oz.). The body is fairly squat, and the beak is short and tough. The upper parts are brown, with dark and tawny stripes; the lower parts are tawny, with brown stripes. Beside the neck there is a clearly visible black marking. Distinctive features in the air include the white sides of the tail and the rear edges of the wings. The female and young are like the male.
Habitat   Cultivated land, steppe, semidesert.
Distribution   Southern Europe, North Africa and western Asia.
Life and habits   The nest is made in a shallow hole in the ground, often protected by grass or a bush, and is a cup-shaped structure of dry grass stalks. Every year two clutches are reared, each of which is made up of 4 or 5 eggs (sometimes as many as 7), which are incubated for about 16 days solely by the female. The nidicolous young are looked after by both adults and stay in the nest for about 10 days. The diet of the Calandra Lark consists mainly of graminaceous seeds and to a lesser degree of insects (which are essential to the diet of the young). The males of this species sing nuptial songs while flying about 10 meters (35 feet) above the ground.

238 MELEAGRIS GALLOPAVO
Wild Turkey

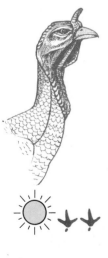

Classification   Order Galliformes, Family Phasianidae.
Characteristics   This is a large galliform, with the males reaching a length of 100–125 cm. (40–50") and a weight of 18 kg. (40 lbs.), although the wild forms rarely exceed 11 kg. (24 lbs.). The females are smaller and have a duller plumage; the coloring of the plumage is dark with greenish, yellowish and bronze highlights. The skin of the head and neck is rough and reddish with blue shades. On the forehead there is a fleshy appendage that swells when the animal is courting. There may also be wattles hanging from the front of the neck, while a beard of coarse bristles protrudes from the breast. A similar species is the Ocellated Turkey (*Agriocharis ocellata*), which is smaller and lighter in color.
Habitat   Woods with clearings and fields.
Distribution   North America.
Life and habits   These are ground-dwelling birds, which will fly, if pressed, for a kilometer (half a mile) or more; they feed on vegetable matter (acorns, cherries, strawberries, grapes, nuts and maize). Turkeys may be either polygamous or monogamous. In wild males sexual maturity is reached after 2 years. Nesting occurs on the ground, with as many as 15–20 eggs being laid. Nests with more eggs than this belong to more than one female. The female incubates the eggs for 28 days.

239 MELOPSITTACUS UNDULATUS
Budgerigar

Classification   Order Psittaciformes, Family Psittacidae.
Characteristics   About 18 cm. long (7″), this is the smallest
species in the subfamily Psittacinae, tribe Platycercinae. In the
natural form the coloring is mainly light green and pale yellow,
with darker wings and a blackish-blue tail. In captivity (this
being the most widely reared and undoubtedly the most commonly caged small parrot) various forms have emerged: dark
green with tawny shading, albino, blue, yellow, gray, and so
on.
Habitat   Open terrain, scrub.
Distribution   Australia.
Life and habits   This species was described for the first time
by the scholar Shaw in 1794. The first Budgerigars were
brought to Europe by the well-known English ornithologist
John Gould in 1840. From then on the species has been widely
reared in captivity and lives throughout the world in those familiar sad little cages. It usually lays 4–8 eggs. The nidicolous
nestlings open their eyes at about 8 days and leave the nest at
about 4 weeks. They can reproduce at the age of 3 months.
This is a sociable little bird, which lives in small groups, feeding
on seeds and leaves.

240 MENURA NOVAEHOLLANDIAE
Superb Lyrebird

Classification   Order Passeriformes, Family Menuridae.
Characteristics   Up to 100 cm. long (40″), this is an unmistakable bird. In the male the tail consists of a pair of very slender feathers, six pairs of fringed feathers and a pair of very
long, but strong and curved, outer rectrices. These two "lyre"
feathers, which reach a length of about 75 cm. (30″) and a
width of almost 4 cm (1.5″), are violet, with silvery shades in
the lower parts, and are patterned with half-moon designs; they
are brown-yellow. A similar species is Albert's Lyrebird (*M. al-
berti*), which is about 75 cm. long (30″) and has black lyre
feathers.
Habitat   Forests.
Distribution   Eastern Australia.
Life and habits   It nests on the ground among rocks or in
forks in trees. The female lays a single egg, which she incubates for about 6 weeks. The nidicolous nestling stays in the
nest for six weeks after hatching. In his courtship display, the
male bends his tail forward, covering his body with it. This species feeds mainly on invertebrates. Recent research by C. G.
Sibley concerning the protein of egg white (albumen) shows a
phylogenetic relationship among the Menuridae, the birds of
paradise, and the bowerbirds.

241 MERGUS MERGANSER
Goosander or Common Merganser

Classification   Order Anseriformes, Family Anatidae.
Characteristics   The male, which is about 75.5 cm. long, (30″) has a dark green head, white breast and sides, but sometimes with pink shades, and black upper parts; the rump and tail are gray. In flight the wings and tail look white, and the head and primaries black. The female, which is about 57.5 cm. long (23″), has a brownish head with a conspicuous crest and a white mark on the throat; the back and sides are grayish, the breast and lower parts pinkish white. In flight it shows a large wing marking. The distinctive legs and beak of the genus *Mergus* are red, the latter with serrated edges. Young birds resemble the females, but have a shorter crest, browner upper parts and grayish breast and throat.
Habitat   Lakes, rivers, marshlands.
Distribution   Europe, Asia, North America.
Life and habits   It generally nests in hollows in trees 7–8 meters (approximately 25 ft.) above the ground, in a sheltered spot. It lays one clutch of 7–14 eggs (rarely 15), which are incubated by the female for 32–35 days. The nidifugous nestlings are reared by the female and are independent after about 5 weeks. The Goosander feeds mainly on animals (fish, amphibians, crustaceans and worms.)

242 MEROPS APIASTER
Eurasian Bee-eater

Classification   Order Coraciiformes, Family Meropidae.
Characteristics   About 27 cm. long (11″), weighing on average 55 grams (2 oz.). The beak is long and thin; the central rectrices of the tail jut out beyond the others in adults. The upper parts are brown and yellow, while the tail and wings are blue-green. The lower parts are blue, except for the throat, which is yellow. The iris is purplish red.
Habitat   Cultivated land, open and arid terrain.
Distribution   Southern Europe, Africa, and Asia.
Life and habits   It nests in colonies and builds its nest at the end of a tunnel between 70 and 250 cm. long (28–100″), dug with the beak and legs by both members of the pair. The tunnel is dug usually in a downward slope, sometimes on the ground, horizontally. The end chamber may be lined with the remains of eaten insects. The single annual clutch has 4–7 eggs (sometimes up to 10) incubated by both sexes for 24 days. The nidicolous nestlings are fed by both parents and can fly at about 24 days. Bee-eaters feed on insects caught in flight, especially Hymenoptera (bees, wasps, etc.), to whose poison it is immune, dragonflies, Coleoptera, et cetera. The undigested remains of the prey are ejected from the beak in the form of small pellets.
Note: The drawing shows a bee-eater in an aggressive posture.

243 MILVUS MILVUS
Red Kite

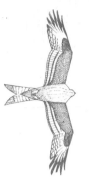

Classification Order Falconiformes, Family Accipitridae
Characteristics This species is about 62 cm. long (24″). It has dark brown upper plumage, with light-edged feathers, and rust-reddish lower parts with dark stripes. Young birds have a paler coloring; the head is browner. In flight the Red Kite has a long tail, which is forked and pale, long, angular wings, and light coloring on the undertail. A similar species is the Black Kite (*M. migrans*), which is 57 cm. long (22″) and darker, with a less forked tail.
Habitat Wooded zones, lowlands, cultivated areas with trees.
Distribution Europe, Asia Minor, northwestern Africa. The Black Kite is found in Europe, Asia, Africa and Australia.
Life and habits Nests in trees, often using the old nest of another bird of prey or member of the Corvidae. It lays 2–3 eggs (sometimes 4, rarely 1 or 5) which are mainly or solely incubated by the female for 28–30 days. The eggs are laid at intervals of 3 days, and incubation starts when the first egg is laid. The nestlings make their first flight at 45–50 days but stay by the nest for a further two weeks. The Red Kite feeds on small mammals and birds, carrion, amphibians, fish and insects.

244 MIMUS POLYGLOTTOS
Northern Mockingbird

Classification Order Passeriformes, Family Mimidae.
Characteristics About 22–27 cm. long (9–11″), it is slender in appearance with quite a long tail. The plumage is dark gray on the upper parts, light gray on the lower. When in the air it shows two wing bars and a large white mark at the tip of the wings. The fairly slender beak is black. The song consists of various musical notes, often copied from other birds.
Habitat Cultivated land, woods with clearings, city parks.
Distribution North America.
Life and habits This species is often found in areas where man is prevalent, and it nests near buildings. The nest is built in a bush or small tree. This mockingbird lays 3–6 eggs (usually 4 or 5), which are incubated for 12 days by just the female. Both adults feed and rear the nestlings, which can fly at 10–12 days. It is a mainly nonmigratory species, although in autumn the northernmost populations may migrate south. The diet consists of vegetable matter (berries, seeds, wild fruit) gathered on the ground or from the branches of plants, and animals (insects, spiders, small invertebrates and sometimes small vertebrates). The nestlings are fed with an animal diet.

245 MNIOTILTA VARIA
Black and White Warbler

Classification   Order Passeriformes, Family Parulidae.
Characteristics   A small bird, about 12 cm. long (4.5″), it has a long, slender beak and a slightly forked tail. The male's plumage is black uppermost, with broad white stripes on the back and head, and white lower down with black markings. The female has white lower parts with gray markings on just the sides and breast.
Habitat   Broadleaf woods, especially ones with clearings.
Distribution   North America, migrating south to northern South America.
Life and habits   This is a migratory species, which arrives in its nesting areas in North America after spending the winter in Central and South America. The nest is a woven cup of leaves, grass and horsehair, built on the ground at the bottom of trees or in the foliage of a bush. The clutch of 4–5 eggs (usually 5) is incubated for 10 days, or slightly more, by just the female. The nestlings can fly at 8–12 days, but follow their parents around for a while more, and are fed by them outside the nest. The diet is almost entirely made up of insects, caught in flight or taken from the bark of trees.

246 MOLOTHRUS ATER
Brown-headed Cowbird

Classification   Order Passeriformes, Family Icteridae.
Characteristics   About 18–20 cm. long (7–8″). The male is brown on the head and breast, black with green highlights on the rest of his body. The female and young are dark brown on the upper parts, gray on the lower, with a dark mark on the breast. The beak is short and conical. A similar species is the Bay-winged Cowbird (*M. badius*).
Habitat   Cultivated land, hedgerows and woods along rivers.
Distribution   North America.
Life and habits   In the northernmost zones of its distribution, this species is migratory and spends the winter farther south. It is a parasitic bird; it lays its eggs in the nests of other species (206 different hosts have been recorded), especially warblers and sparrows. The female, each season, lays up to 5 eggs, each one in a different nest. Incubation lasts 10–12 days, much shorter than in many host species. The nestlings can fly at 10 days and cohabit with the legitimate young in the nest. The diet consists mainly of seeds, fruit and berries, and to a lesser extent, insects and other invertebrates. But the nestlings are almost always reared on an insectivorous diet by the adoptive parents.

247 MOLOTHRUS BONARIENSIS
Glossy Cowbird

Classification   Order Passeriformes, Family Icteridae.
Characteristics   The Glossy Cowbird has a uniform bluish-black plumage with greenish highlights on the wings. It has strong legs and a conical, strong beak, both dark. The family to which it belongs—Icteridae—is typical of the New World and has a considerable variety of species. In the view of various scholars, these birds originate from South America, probably from the Pliocene epoch (upper Tertiary period, between one and eleven million years ago), after the closure of the Central American isthmus; they also migrated to North America, where they evolved into various forms. Many species in the family have yellow plumage; hence the family name (from the Greek *ikteros,* "oriole").
Habitat   Woods, open terrain.
Distribution   South America.

Life and habits   Like other species of Icteridae, the Glossy Cowbird is parasitic. As stressed by ornithologist H. Friedmann, parasitism is a behavioral aspect that was acquired quite late in the course of the phylogeny of the Icteridae. The females of this species may lay eggs that differ greatly in shape and coloration from those of the host. The nidicolous nestling "outmaneuvers" the young of the adopted species and stays in the nest for 10–15 days.

248 MONTICOLA SAXATILIS
Rock Thrush

Classification   Order Passeriformes, Family Turdidae.
Characteristics   This species is about 19 cm. long (7.5") and weighs about 65 grams (2 oz.); the male is slightly larger than the female. The male in his nuptial plumage has a blue-gray head and back, a white rump and brick-red lower parts. The female and young have brown upper parts and white lower parts, with dark markings.
Habitat   Grassy terrain and rocky areas in hills and mountains.
Distribution   Northwestern Africa, southern Europe.
Life and habits   The Rock Thrush extends to considerable altitudes, in some places more than 3,000 meters (10,000 ft.). The cup-shaped nest, of moss and grass, is built in hollows in rocks or on the ground. Each year there is one clutch of 4 or 5 eggs (sometimes 6), incubated solely by the female for 14 or 15 days. The nidicolous nestlings are reared by both parents and fly at 14–16 days. The prey are caught on the ground and sometimes in the air. It feeds on insects (coleopterans, orthopterans, lepidopterans) various invertebrates, small lizards, amphibians, and also berries. In the nuptial flight the male flies up from the ground and, slowly flapping his wings, starts to sing and make circles in the air.

249 MONTICOLA SOLITARIUS
Blue Rock Thrush

Classification   Order Passeriformes, Family Turdidae.
Characteristics   About 20 cm. long (8″), weighing on average 65 grams (2 oz.). The male is completely blue-gray, becoming blackish in winter. The female is gray-brown with lighter bars and resembles the young. The beak is long and thin, appropriate for a mainly insectivorous diet, and the tail is short.
Habitat   Rocky regions, rocky seacoasts, Mediterranean *maquis.*
Distribution   North Africa, southern Europe, Asia.
Life and habits   It does not usually frequent very high mountains, but has been observed in the Himalayas at more than 4,000 meters (13,000 ft.). The nest is a cup of moss and grass built in a hole in rocks, or on a cliff or on a building, by the female. Each year there is usually one clutch (sometimes 2), of 3–6 eggs (ordinarily 4 or 5), incubated solely by the female for 12 or 13 days. The nidicolous nestlings are fed by both adults and fly at about 17 days. The diet consists mainly of insects and arachnids (spiders), but also of lizards and berries in autumn. This species is nonmigratory and even though solitary and shy by nature will not hesitate to colonize on monuments and among ruins in the most bustling of cities.

250 MONTIFRINGILLA NIVALIS
Snow Finch

Classification   Order Passeriformes, Family Ploceidae.
Characteristics   About 17 cm. long (7″), weighing about 40 grams (1.4 oz.). The upper parts are dark brown, the lower white. The wings are black and white, while the head is gray and the throat black. The female and the young have a paler coloring that is less well defined. The adult beak is black in summer and yellow in winter.
Habitat   Mountain peaks up to 2,000 meters (6,500 ft.).
Distribution   Europe, western Asia.
Life and habits   This species lives above the timber line in regions with glaciers, scree and rocky cliffs. The ornithologist P. Geroudet quotes as an altitude record for the Alps a pair nesting at 3,476 meters (11,404 ft.). Placed in a hole in rocks or in the burrow or lair of a mammal, the nest is a cup of grass, moss and feathers. Each year there is one clutch (sometimes two) of 4 or 5 eggs incubated for 13 or 14 days by both sexes. The adults rear the nidicolous young together, the latter flying at 21 days. The diet consists mainly of seeds and berries, but also of insects and other small invertebrates. The male Snow Finch sings during his nuptial flight, in which, after making various circular flights, he glides down to the ground. In winter this is a markedly gregarious species.

251 MOTACILLA ALBA
Pied or White Wagtail

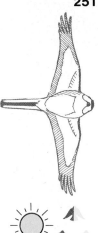

Classification Order Passeriformes, Family Motacillidae.
Characteristics About 17.5 cm. long (7″), including the tail, which is nearly 9 cm. (3.5″). It weighs on average 23 grams (0.8 oz.). The beak is long and thin, and the legs too are quite long. The upper parts are gray in the continental subspecies (*M. a. alba*), black in the English subspecies (*M. a. yarrellii*). The lower parts are white, while the head and breast have a distinctive black and white design which is less marked in females and young birds. The edges of the tail are white.
Habitat Cultivated land, fields and meadows near water.
Distribution Europe, Asia, northwest Africa.
Life and habits The nest is made in a hole in rocks, in a tree or on a building, often near water; it is a cup of grass, moss, feathers and so on, and it is built by the female. Each year there are two clutches or, in northern regions, just one, of 3–7 eggs (usually 5 or 6), incubated almost solely by the female for 12–14 days. The nidicolous young are reared by both parents and fly at 13–16 days. The Pied Wagtail feeds on the ground, where it moves briskly wagging its tail. The diet consists of insects (mainly dipterans), small worms and mollusks.

252 MOTACILLA CINEREA
Gray Wagtail

Classification Order Passeriformes, Family Motacillidae.
Characteristics About 18 cm. long (7″). In summer the male has olive-gray upper parts, a yellow-green rump, a white eyebrow, gray sides of the head with a white stripe, and yellow lower parts with whitish under the wings. There is also black on the chin and throat (this coloration is absent in the winter plumage). The female's chin and throat are whitish or speckled with black; her lower parts are paler.
Habitat Near watercourses in mountainous and hilly regions, lowlands, cultivated areas.
Distribution Europe, Asia, North Africa.
Life and habits It nests up to 1,800 meters (5,900 ft.). The nest is cup-shaped, built by both sexes with twigs, stalks, moss and dry leaves. It lays one clutch (sometimes 2) of usually 4–6 eggs (more rarely 3 or 7). Incubation is the task of the female and lasts 11–14 days. The nidicolous nestlings leave the nest at 11–13 days and can fly at about 17 days. The Gray Wagtail feeds mainly on invertebrates (insects and larvae).

253 MOTACILLA FLAVA
Yellow Wagtail

Classification   Order Passeriformes, Family Motacillidae.
Characteristics   About 16.5 cm. long (6.5″). The coloring of the plumage, especially about the head, varies greatly among the several subspecies. The head of the adult male in his nuptial plumage is bluish gray, with a white eyebrow; the upper parts are olive green, the lower parts yellow, and the remiges brown. The female has a whitish eyebrow, brown upper parts and yellow lower parts.
Habitat   Wetlands, marshlands, cultivated areas near water.
Distribution   Varies according to the subspecies, but includes Europe, Asia, Africa, and Alaska.
Life and habits   It nests on the ground in hollows, often amid vegetation. The nest is a small cup. The Yellow Wagtail lays one or two clutches of usually 5 or 6 eggs (rarely 7), which are incubated mainly by the female for 12–14 days. The nidicolous nestlings are reared by both parents, and they leave the nest at 10–13 days and fly at about 17 days. This species has a very wide distribution, with marked genetic variability; in some subspecies the rhythm and moment of sexual maturity differ, as well as the departure times toward the nesting areas.

---

254 MUSCICAPA STRIATA
Spotted Flycatcher

Classification   Order Passeriformes, Family Muscicapidae.
Characteristics   About 13 or 14 cm. long (5.5″). The upper parts are grayish brown with brown stripes on the head; the lower parts are grayish white, with brown lines at the sides of the throat and breast and on the flanks. The sexes are similar. The young have brown upper parts, with light yellowish markings; the lower parts are yellowish white with blackish stripes at the sides and on the breast.
Habitat   Woods, gardens and parks.
Distribution   Europe, Africa, Asia Minor, Iran and India.
Life and habits   It nests on anything prominent, in the fork of a branch or where a branch has been snapped off, thus creating a jutting surface, in walls covered with creepers or in shrubs, where it builds a nest made of moss, small roots, horsehair, feathers and down. It lays 4 or 5 eggs (more rarely 2, 6 or 7); these are incubated mainly by the female, who is fed by the male, for 11–15 days. The nidicolous nestlings leave the nest on average after 12–15 days and are fed by the parents for a further 20 days. The Spotted Flycatcher feeds on insects (especially dipterans, hymenopterans, coleopterans and dragonflies), as well as on worms and berries.

255 MYZOMELA NIGRA (CERTHIONIX NIGER)
Black Honeyeater

Classification   Order Passeriformes, Family Meliphagidae.
Characteristics   The Meliphagidae include species that vary
in size from 10 to 45 cm. (4–18″). They have a long tongue
that is tubular and covered with bristles, in many species with a
division near the tip. The sides of the tongue roll up to form a
kind of tube through which nectar and nectar-eating insects
are conveyed to the throat. The beak is quite long and curved.
As a rule the plumage of Meliphagidae is of "ordinary" coloration, although in some species there are patches of bare skin,
fleshy growths, and tufts of colored feathers beside the head.
The Black Honeyeater is about 10 cm. long (4″), has a blackish coloring on the upper parts and blackish white on the lower.
The female has duller coloring, brownish with white eyebrows.
Habitat   Forests.
Distribution   Australia.
Life and habits   The Black Honeyeater builds a cup-shaped
nest of grass, twigs and cobwebs, in which it usually lays two
eggs. Incubation is mainly the task of the female (who also
builds the nest) and lasts about 18 days. The nidicolous nestlings stay in the nest for a further 18 days, being reared by both
parents.

256 NANNOPTERUM HARRISI
Galapagos or Flightless Cormorant

Classification   Order Pelecaniformes, Family Phalacrocoracidae
Characteristics   About 96 cm. long (38″), this is the only
living species of cormorant that cannot fly, and also the rarest.
The very small wings are about 25 cm. (10″) long. It weighs
about 2 kg. (4.5 lbs.). The plumage is brown with purplish
highlights on the wing feathers. The head and neck are covered with long hairlike feathers.
Habitat   Rocky seacoast.
Distribution   Isabela Island in the Galapagos Archipelago.
Life and habits   The Galapagos Cormorant nests on rocks
close to the sea, where it builds a nest of seaweed and twigs. In
it it lays 1 or 2 eggs, which are incubated for 23–25 days. This
flightless species feeds on fish and mollusks, mainly octopus. It
is protected by law, and at the present time, according to esti-
mates made by the International Union for the Conservation of
Nature, there are no more than 1,000 individuals surviving in
all. It has been easy to hunt because of its inability to fly.

257 NECTARINIA FAMOSA
Malachite Sunbird

Classification   Order Passeriformes, Family Nectariniidae.
Characteristics   The Family Nectariniidae includes 8 genera with 108 species. These birds vary in length from 9 to 25 cm. (3.5–10″), and are considered the Old World counterpart of the American hummingbirds. Their similarities with the hummingbirds, however, are superficial. The beak is long and slender, generally bent downward. The tongue is long and extendable, designed for sucking in the nectar from flowers and catching insects. The tarsal bones are long and usually thin, with curved claws. In the wings are 10 primaries and in the tail 12 rectrices. The coloring of the plumage is usually bright. The male Malachite Sunbird has a greenish plumage with bronze shades. On the sides there are bright yellow feathers. The female has a more yellowish-olive colored plumage.
Habitat   Forests, lowland plains.
Distribution   Eastern and southern Africa.
Life and habits   It builds a nest like a small bag hanging from a branch, with an aperture. It is built with various materials, above all cobwebs. It lays two eggs. Sunbirds exist in various environments from forests to the edge of the desert, to mountains. As a rule they live alone or in pairs, sometimes gathering in small groups.

258 NEOPHRON PERCNOPTERUS
Egyptian Vulture

Classification   Order Falconiformes, Family Accipitridae.
Characteristics   About 61 cm. long (24.5″). It has white plumage with black wing tips. The beak is thin, with a blackish tip. The skin of the face and featherless neck is yellowish. The young are blackish brown and, through the different moltings, become paler and paler in color, taking on the full adult plumage at the age of 5 or 6. The skin on the face and throat is darker.
Habitat   Mountainous rocky regions, hills, lowlands and desert.
Distribution   Southern Europe, southwestern Asia, and Africa.
Life and habits   It nests at various altitudes (from places almost at sea level up to 3,600 meters (11,800 ft.) in the Caucasus. Its crude nest, made of a few small branches and covered with rubbish, is made in holes, in nooks in rocks, and rarely in trees. It lays 1 or 2 eggs (rarely 3) at intervals of 3 or 4 days; the eggs are incubated by both sexes for 42 days. The young are reared by both parents and fly at about 90 days. The Egyptian Vulture feeds on carrion, rubbish, rotten fruit and even dung. It rarely catches live prey, such as lizards or tortoises; it is well-known for its habit of using stones to break open Ostrich eggs.

259 NESTOR NOTABILIS
Kea

Classification   Order Psittaciformes, Family Psittacidae.
Characteristics   The parrots in the subfamily Nestorinae
reach an over-all length of 50 cm. (20″) and have a rather dull
plumage. The Kea has brown coloring with a reddish back and
greenish wings and tail. A similar species is the Kaka (*N.
meridionalis*), the precise numbers of which are not known, but
it is a species in danger of becoming extinct.
Habitat   Mountains up to 1,300 meters (4,300 feet); it moves
lower down in winter.
Distribution   New Zealand.
Life and habits   The coloring of the plumage, strong, compact body and beak give the Nestorinae a passing resemblance to birds of prey. Although they are vegetarian (eating
seeds, fruit and buds) these parrots also eat carrion, the pla-
centas of sheep, et cetera. They nest in holes in trees, laying 2
or 3 eggs (rarely 4). Incubation and rearing the young are undertaken by both parents. Incubation lasts up to 29 days. The
young stay in the nest for about 13 weeks. For some time
sheep farmers have asserted that keas attack and kill their
livestock. Ornithologist Jackson of Christchurch, New Zealand, considers that this may have happened, but only occasionally.

---

260 NOTHOGRAX URUMUTUM
Nocturnal Curassow

Classification   Order Galliformes, Family Cracidae.
Characteristics   Ornithologist Alexander Skutch identifies
two tribes in the family Cracidae: the Cracinae and the Penelo-
pinae. The Cracinae includes species most of which have an
erectile tuft on the top of the head and fleshy protuberances at
the base of the beak. The Nocturnal Curassow has its upper
parts and tail streaked with black and brown; the tail and lower
parts are reddish orange, the beak and legs are red, and there
is a yellowish area around the eye.
Habitat   Forests, scrub, lowlands.
Distribution   South America.
Life and habits   The smaller species of Cracidae (curassows
and guans) lead a mainly arboreal life, while the larger species
are ground-dwelling. Both feed mainly on vegetable matter
(fruit, seeds, leaves and shoots) as well as occasional invertebrates and small vertebrates. They usually nest in trees or
bushes, building a nest made of branches, leaves and other
plant matter. As a rule they lay 2 eggs, which are incubated by
the female for a period that ranges from 26 to 30 days—in the
species the Helmeted Curassow (*Pauxi pauxi*) for 33–34 days.
The nestlings are nidifugous. A basic work on the Cracidae has
been published by ornithologists Jean Delacour and Dean
Amadon (*Curassows and Related Birds*).

261 NUCIFRAGA CARYOCATACTES
Eurasian Nutcracker

Classification   Order Passeriformes, Family Corvidae.
Characteristics   About 32 cm. long (12.5″), it has dark
brown plumage with numerous white markings; the sides of the
tail and undertail are white. The beak is tough and pointed. In
flight it shows close pale speckling.
Habitat   Coniferous and mixed forests.
Distribution   Europe and Asia.
Life and habits   It nests in trees and lays a single clutch of
usually 3–4 eggs (sometimes 2 or 5), which are incubated by
the female for 17–19 days. The nidicolous young are reared by
both parents; they leave the nest at 21–28 days and remain
dependent on the parents for about 2 or 3 more months. The
Eurasian Nutcracker feeds mainly on the seeds of conifers,
plus berries, invertebrates and even small birds. This species
buries coniferous seeds in the ground; somehow it manages to
find and exhume its buried larders when the ground is covered
with snow.

262 NUMENIUS ARQUATA
Eurasian Curlew

Classification   Order Charadriiformes, Family Scolopacidae.
Characteristics   About 57 cm. long (22″), it has a distinctive
downward-curving beak of considerable length. The plumage
is quite uniform, striped brown, and darker uppermost. The
legs are greenish gray. Similar species are the Whimbrel (*N.
phaeopus*), which is about 39 cm. long (15.5″), with a shorter
beak and dark stripes on the top of the head, and the Slender-
billed Curlew (*N. tenuirostris*), also about 39 cm. long, with
dark markings on its lower parts.
Habitat   Heathland, wetlands, marshlands, tundra, coasts
and estuaries.
Distribution   Europe, Asia and Africa.
Life and habits   It nests on the ground in wet and grassy
places. It lays a single clutch, of usually 4 eggs (occasionally 3
or 5), which are incubated by both sexes, mainly by the female,
for 26–30 days. The nidifugous nestlings are reared by both
parents and fly at approximately 5 or 6 weeks. Its typical song
is a *cour-li*. It feeds on invertebrates and vegetable matter
(berries, seeds, grain).

263 NUMIDA MELEAGRIS
Helmeted Guineafowl

Classification   Order Galliformes, Family Phasianidae.
Characteristics   On the top of the head there is a short helmet; the neck and head are almost bare of feathers and bluish; there are a few wattles near the beak; the plumage is brown with whitish speckling. There is also the Vulturine Guineafowl (*Acryllium vulturinum*), which has no helmet but a distinctive collar of lanceolate blue-black feathers with a white stripe.
Habitat   Open terrain, lowlands, savannah, scrub.
Distribution   Africa.
Life and habits   It nests on the ground amid vegetation. It probably lays a single clutch, with usually 8–12 eggs (sometimes up to 20; but these clutches can be attributed to two females). Incubation is the task of mainly the female and lasts 24 or 25 days. The nidifugous nestlings are reared by the female. They may stay together and form small groups. The Helmeted Guineafowl is the forebear of our domestic Guineafowl.

264 NYCTEA SCANDIACA
Snowy Owl

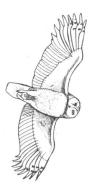

Classification   Order Strigiformes, Family Strigidae.
Characteristics   About 52–65 cm. long (21–26″), it has white plumage with a certain amount of brown barring. The female is larger and generally more barred than the male. Immature birds are darker in color.
Habitat   Tundra and hills in the Arctic region. It makes winter migrations during which it may be found in marshland, on lake shores and by the sea.
Distribution   The Arctic circle. It may sometimes move to more southerly areas; during longer migrations these may amount to nothing less than invasions, and it may occur in even more southerly regions.
Life and habits   The Snowy Owl perches conspicuously on rocks or in trees. In hunting, it kills its prey in flight. It feeds on small mammals (rabbits, mice, lemmings), birds (geese, ducks and gulls) and invertebrates. It nests on the ground in hollows, laying a single clutch of 4–10 eggs (up to 15 in some cases) which the female incubates for about 32–37 days. The nidicolous young leave the nest at 3 or 4 weeks and fly at about 8 or 9 weeks. In some years, when food is scarce, the Snowy Owl may not rest at all.

265 NYCTICORAX NYCTICORAX
Black-crowned Night Heron

Classification   Order Ciconiiformes, Family Ardeidae.
Characteristics   About 60 cm. long (24″), it is squat-looking with short legs. The coloring of the upper parts is black and gray; it has three long white feathers on the nape of its neck, which is black; the lower parts are white. The young have dark brown coloring uppermost, speckled and striped with tawny white; lower down they are grayish brown with dark stripes. In flight they show their squat, compact shape with rounded tail and wings.
Habitat   Wooded marshlands, riverbanks and lake shores.
Distribution   Central and southern Europe, southern Asia, some parts of Africa and America.
Life and habits   Except for the reproductive period, the Black-crowned Night Heron is most active at twilight; it nests in mixed colonies with other species of Ardeidae, in trees or bushes near water. It lays 3 or 4 eggs (sometimes 5), which are incubated by both adults for about 21 days. The nestlings may leave the nest after about 4 weeks; they become independent in 7 or 8 weeks. They feed on fish, amphibians and other aquatic creatures. The sound they make is like a raucous *kaak-kuak*.

---

266 OCEANITES OCEANICUS
Wilson's Storm Petrel

Classification   Order Procellariiformes, Family Hydrobatidae.
Characteristics   About 18 cm. long (7″). Its upper parts are dark, the rump white and the tail square-shaped. The legs are quite long and end with two yellow webbed feet that jut out beyond the tail in flight. In flight it also shows a pale wing bar, the extent of which varies from bird to bird. It often appears to be walking on water, with its wings extended and held either raised or horizontal, its tail opened like a fan, making a series of glides with its legs dangling.
Habitat   Open sea, rocky islands.
Distribution   Islands in the South Atlantic, it migrates to and winters in the North Atlantic.
Life and habits   It nests in December and January in crevices in rocks or in specially made passages dug by both adults. It lays a single clutch with one white egg, which is incubated for 39–48 days. The nidicolous young bird is reared by both parents and fed with regurgitated food. This species feeds on the fat and oil of cetaceans (whales), as well as marine invertebrates (like crustaceans). During courtship it makes harsh and repeated notes and the two partners stand together preening each other's head feathers with their beaks.

267 OCEANODROMA LEUCORHOA
Leach's Storm Petrel

Classification Order Procellariiformes, Family Hydrobatidae.

Characteristics About 20.5 cm. long (8"). Its plumage is dark with a white rump crossed by a dark gray bar; the tail is forked. It is larger, with longer wings and darker plumage than Wilson's Storm Petrel (*Oceanites oceanicus*) and the European Storm Petrel (*Hydrobates pelagicus*). Other species of the same genus include the Band-rumped Storm Petrel (*Oceanodroma castro*), which is about 19 cm. long (7.5"), with a slightly forked tail, a white band across the rump and an overall dark plumage.

Habitat Open sea, rocky and wooded islands.

Distribution Breeds locally in the northern hemisphere and migrates further south.

Life and habits It nests in colonies in a hollow dug in the ground, where it lays a single white egg. Incubation falls to both parents and lasts about 41 or 42 days. The nidicolous nestling is fed at irregular intervals by one parent. It opens its eyes at about 15 days. After 40 days it is quite well developed, but does not leave the nest for the sea until 63–70 days after hatching. It feeds on plankton, the remains of whales and seals, mollusks and small fish. During courtship the males enter the passages of the nests making sounds to attract the female.

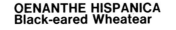

268 OENANTHE HISPANICA
Black-eared Wheatear

Classification Order Passeriformes, Family Turdidae.

Characteristics About 14.5 cm. long (5.7"). The male has pale golden-tawny plumage uppermost, with a black marking on the eyes and cheeks, and either a whitish throat or a black throat and face. The tail is white, the outer rectrices are pale with a central spot, and the central ones are dark. The female is duller and without the black marking on the face. The wings are black. There are two recognized subspecies, *O. h. hispanica*, with a more western distribution, and *O. h. melanoleuca,* with a more eastern distribution.

Habitat Arid areas with rocks, meadows and cultivated land.

Distribution Southern Europe, Africa, Asia Minor and the Near East.

Life and habits It generally nests on the ground amid low vegetation in a cup-shaped nest made of plant matter. It lays two clutches of 4 or 5 eggs. The female incubates them for about 15 days. The nidicolous nestlings are reared by both parents. The Black-eared Wheatear's diet consists mainly of invertebrates (insects, etc.). It is migratory and winters south of the Sahara.

269 OENANTHE OENANTHE
Northern Wheatear

Classification   Order Passeriformes, Family Turdidae.
Characteristics   About 14.5 cm. long (5.7″). The male's upper parts are gray-brown and the wings dark; a black band crosses the eye, and the lower parts are white. The female is more brownish. Male and female have a white rump and white sides on the tail, while the terminal band and central tail feathers are black. The beak and legs are also black. Young birds are speckled.
Habitat   Meadows, stony areas, heathland, bushy areas.
Distribution   Europe, Asia, northwestern Africa, and northern North America (Alaska, Greenland).
Life and habits   It nests in holes or hollows in the ground, or in rabbit warrens. It lays one or two clutches, with 3–8 eggs (usually 5 or 6), which are incubated by both sexes, but mainly by the female, for about 14 days. The nidicolous nestlings are reared by both parents and remain in the nest for about 15 days. The Northern Wheatear's diet consists mainly of invertebrates.

270 OPISTHOCOMUS HOATZIN
Hoatzin

Classification   Order Galliformes, Family Opisthocomidae.
Characteristics   About 60 cm. long (24″), weighing about 800 grams (28.5 oz.). The tarsal bones are very strong and have four toes. It has 10 primaries. The plumage is dark brown uppermost and pale lower down; on the head there is a tuft of feathers and a bluish area around the eye. The tail is long. In young birds there is a first and second toe on the wing, ending with strong claws, but they atrophy with time. These claws help them to move in trees.
Habitat   Forests.
Distribution   South America.
Life and habits   Hoatzins live in small groups of about a dozen individuals. Young Hoatzins can swim if they fall into water. The diet is mainly leaves. The crop is huge (50 times larger than the stomach, which accounts, as mentioned by Gunther Niethammer, for 13 percent of the bird's total weight) and is situated at the front of the atrophied carina, which is why the Hoatzin's ability to fly is very reduced. It sometimes nests in small colonies in branches near water, laying 2–5 eggs, which are incubated by both sexes for about 28 days. The down-covered young stay in the nest for about 14 days.

271 ORIOLUS ORIOLUS
Golden Oriole

Classification   Order Passeriformes, Family Oriolidae.
Characteristics   About 24 cm. long (10″). The male has an unmistakable coloring—bright yellow, with yellow-flecked black wings and tail. The female and young are yellowish green, with darker wings and tail and the lower parts with dark stripes.
Habitat   Woods, forests, parks and gardens.
Distribution   Europe, western Asia and northwestern Africa.
Life and habits   The nest, which is made almost entirely by the female, is very distinctive—a cup of dry twigs, grass, well-arranged vegetable matter, built in the fork of two horizontal branches. In it the Golden Oriole usually lays 3 or 4 eggs (rarely 6), which are incubated by both parents for 14 or 15 days. The nestlings are reared by both parents and leave the nest after 14 or 15 days. As a rule the Golden Oriole lays a single clutch, but sometimes may lay two. Its diet is decidedly insectivorous in spring, and fruit-based in autumn. The male has a characteristic song like a *weela-weeo*.

272 OTIS TARDA
Great Bustard

Classification   Order Gruiformes, Family Otididae.
Characteristics   The male is about 102 cm. long (41″) and the female about 80 cm. (31.5″). It is a large bird with brownish coloration and dark barring uppermost, and white lower down. The head is grayish, the breast and bottom of the neck chestnut, with black edges; the male has whitish feathers under his chin, which are swept backward. In flight it shows a very long white band on the wings and the outer half of the remiges is black. Seen from beneath, it looks predominantly white.
Habitat   Steppe, grassy regions, cultivated land.
Distribution   Some regions of Europe (Iberian peninsula, East Germany and eastern Europe), central Asia.
Life and habits   It nests on the ground amid vegetation. It lays a single clutch, usually with 2 or 3 eggs (occasionally 4), which are incubated by the female for 25–28 days. The nidifugous nestlings are reared by the female. They fly at about 4 weeks and are independent by about 5. The Great Bustard feeds mainly on plant matter.

273 OTIS TETRAX
Little Bustard

Classification   Order Gruiformes, Family Otididae.
Characteristics   About 43 cm. long (17"), it resembles the
Great Bustard, but is much smaller. The upper parts and top of
the head are streaked and sand-colored; lower down the coloring is white. In spring the male has a bright black and white
collar, the face is bluish gray, and the legs are dark yellow. The
young females and males (the latter in winter) are brownish
with no collar or facial coloring.
Habitat   Cultivated land, grassy areas, meadows, dry areas
with sparse vegetation.
Distribution   Southern Europe, Asia, northwestern Africa.
Life and habits   It nests in hollows on the ground. Incubation
is the task of the female, who lays usually one clutch, but
sometimes two. The male tends to the female during incubation, which lasts for about 20 or 21 days. The nidifugous nestlings are reared by the female, until they can feed themselves
and become independent. The Little Bustard feeds on invertebrates (mollusks, insects and worms) and plant matter.

274 OTUS SCOPS
Common Scops Owl

Classification   Order Strigiformes, Family Strigidae.
Characteristics   About 19 cm. long (7.5"), it has grayish-
brown plumage with pale streaking. It has distinctive tufts at
the ears. As a rule, individuals have two phases of coloration—one grayer and one browner.
Habitat   Woods, parks and gardens.
Distribution   Central-southern Europe, Africa and Asia.
Life and habits   It has a distinctive song, which sounds like a
melancholy and insistently repeated *pew*, and is made mainly
at night. It nests in holes in trees, in walls, in old buildings, or in
the old nest of another bird. It lays one clutch, with usually 4 or
5 eggs (sometimes 3 or 6), which are incubated only by the female for 24 or 25 days. The nidicolous nestlings are fed by the
female with food brought by the male, and they leave the nest
at 3 weeks; they start to be independent at about 7 weeks. The
Common Scops Owl's diet consists mainly of invertebrates (insects).

275 PADDA ORYZIVORA
Java Finch

Classification   Order Passeriformes, Family Estrildidae.
Characteristics   The Java Finch is about 14 cm. long (5.5″), the largest species in the family. Its plumage has a distinctive coloring. The tough beak is pinkish, the head is black with a large white marking on each side. The rest of the plumage is gray uppermost; lower down, from the bottom of the breast downward, it becomes suffused with pink. The tail is dark. Among other species of Estrildidae are the Cut-throat Finch (*Amadina fasciata*), which has a brown and gray mimetic plumage with lighter areas and a red throat; and the Red-breasted Parrotfinch (*Erythura psittacea*), which is red and green. Both species are well known because they are often kept in captivity for ornamental reasons.
Habitat   Forests.
Distribution   Java and Bali.
Life and habits   This species has been introduced into many parts of Southeast Asia, Hawaii, St. Helena, Zanzibar, and the coast of East Africa. The first attempts to rear it in captivity were made in China and Japan, where a white-plumaged form was introduced.

---

276 PAGODROMA NIVEA
Snow Petrel

Classification   Order Procellariiformes, Family Procellariidae.
Characteristics   About 35 cm. long (14″), it is unmistakable for its snow-white plumage, the black marking in front of the eyes and the black beak. Another species, the Antarctic Petrel (*Thalassoica antarctica*), is about 45 cm. long (18″).
Habitat   Coasts, sea.
Distribution   Antarctic coasts; also, as mentioned by B. Stonehouse, farther north at altitudes of 2,000 meters (6,500 ft.); inland more than 300 km. (200 miles) from the coast; and in a more northerly belt, up to the southern coast of South Georgia and Bouvet Island.
Life and habits   It feeds on fish, mollusks, crustaceans and other marine invertebrates that it catches flying over the surface of the sea in areas near the pack ice. The eggs are laid in late November or early December; the young leave the nest in March. In his book *Birds of the Ocean* the ornithologist W. B. Alexander considers that of all the birds in the world the Snow Petrel lives at the southernmost latitude.

277 PANDION HALIAEETUS
Osprey

Classification Order Falconiformes, Family Pandionidae.
Characteristics About 55 cm. long (22"). The upper parts are dark brown, the lower whitish, with a dark bar across the eye. In flight the wings appear angular, and there are two dark markings in the carpal area.
Habitat In places near water, lakes and rivers near woods, rocky crags, sandy coasts.
Distribution Worldwide, except the polar regions and South America.
Life and habits It nests in trees, on rocky or sandy coasts, using for many consecutive years a crude nest made of dry twigs and branches and plant matter that are accumulated year after year. It lays 2–5 eggs (usually 3), which are incubated by both adults, but mainly by the female, for 35–38 days. The newborn young stay in the nest for 51–63 days (from the birth of the firstborn). The Osprey feeds almost exclusively on fish, which it catches by diving into the water and grabbing the prey with its feet (which has 2 front and 2 hind toes to help the bird to grasp).

---

278 PANURUS BIARMICUS
Bearded Reedling

Classification Order Passeriformes, Family Timaliidae.
Characteristics This species is about 16 cm. long (6.5"). The upper plumage is tawny, the lower gray-pink; the tail is long and tawny. The male has an ash-gray head with a black marking that starts from the eye and extends down the sides of the neck; the lower tail coverts are also black. There is white on the wings. The female is paler, with no black.
Habitat Areas with water and vegetation, marshland, cane-brakes.
Distribution Europe, central and western Asia.
Life and habits The Bearded Reedling builds a cup-shaped nest amid the reeds, with vegetable matter (both birds do the building). It lays two, and sometimes three, clutches, with usually 5–7 eggs (sometimes up to 12). The eggs are incubated by both parents for 12 or 13 days. The nidicolous young are reared by both parents and stay in the nest for 9–12 days.

279 PARADISEA APODA
Greater Bird of Paradise

Classification Order Passeriformes, Family Paradiseidae.
Characteristics Among the stunning birds of paradise, the species range in length from 63 to 100 cm. (25–40″), including the rectrices. On their sides the males have a swept-back tuft of very fine feathers that can be erected by means of special muscles. It has brown plumage, darker on the breast, with a yellow head, green throat and a black marking around the beak. At the sides there is a tuft of yellow feathers, and the central rectrices are long and threadlike. As a rule the females have an over-all brown plumage. Ornithologists recognize two subspecies of Greater Birds of Paradise. Among other species are the Lesser Bird of Paradise (*P. minor*), the Blue Bird of Paradise (*P. rudolphi*), and the Emperor of Germany's Bird of Paradise (*P. gulielmi*).
Habitat Forest.
Distribution New Guinea.
Life and habits The feathers of this species were those most frequently exported to Europe. The nuptial display includes the spreading of wings, with erect ornamental feathers and the head facing downward. The males perform their displays collectively, sometimes even on the same tree. This species nests in trees, making a cup-shaped nest, and laying 1 or 2 eggs.

280 PARUS ATER
Coal Tit

Classification Order Passeriformes, Family Paridae.
Characteristics About 11 cm. long (4.5″). The top of the head is black, with a white patch on the nape, and white cheeks; the throat and upper breast are black. The upper parts are greenish gray, with a white double wing band. The lower parts are white, with slightly brownish sides. The beak is black, and the legs are bluish gray. Young birds have yellowish cheeks, lower parts and nape.
Habitat Coniferous and mixed wood, parks.
Distribution Europe, Asia, northwestern Africa.
Life and habits It nests in holes in trees and walls, rarely on the ground. It lays two clutches of 7–9 eggs (sometimes 12); these are incubated by the female, which is fed by the male, for 14–18 days. The nidicolous young, which open their eyes 7 or 8 days after they are hatched; are reared by both parents and leave the nest at about 16–19 days. They become independent two weeks later. The Coal Tit feeds on cereals, on the seeds of conifers and other trees, and on invertebrates.

281 PARUS CAERULEUS
Blue Tit

Classification Order Passeriformes, Family Paridae.
Characteristics About 11.5 cm. long (4.5″). The top of the head, tail and wings are all blue; the lower parts are yellow, the cheeks are white, and there is a black stripe running across the nape of the neck; the eyes and throat are also black. The upper parts are greenish, but yellowish on the rump. The beak is black with a brownish tip, the legs are bluish. The female is less brightly colored. Young birds have brown-green upper parts and yellowish checks.
Habitat Mixed woodland, parks and gardens.
Distribution Europe, Asia Minor, central-western Asia, and northwestern Africa.
Life and habits It nests in holes in trees or in walls, laying usually one clutch (sometimes 2) of 5–16 eggs (normally 7–12); these are incubated by the female, which is fed by the male, for 12–16 days. The nidicolous young are reared by both parents, and they stay in the nest for about 15–23 days. The Blue Tit feeds on invertebrates (insects and their larvae and eggs), various seeds, and sometimes berries.

282 PARUS CRISTATUS
Crested Tit

Classification Order Passeriformes, Family Paridae.
Characteristics About 11–12 cm. long (4.5″), it is easily identified by the crest on the top of the head and the black and white speckling. The face is white with a black stripe that runs from behind the eye to the cheeks; the throat has a black collar. The upper parts are brownish gray, the lower whitish, with slightly tawny sides. The beak is black, the legs are bluish. The female has a shorter crest and a narrower collar. Young birds have an even shorter crest, a not very marked collar, darker upper parts and whitish lower parts.
Habitat Coniferous and mixed woods, parks.
Distribution Europe.
Life and habits It nests in holes in old trees and elsewhere. It usually lays a single clutch (sometimes 2) of 4–11 eggs (usually 4–8); these are incubated by the female, which is fed by the male, for 13–18 days. The nidicolous nestlings are reared by both parents and spend 17–21 days in the nest. The Crested Tit feeds mainly on invertebrates and seeds (particularly coniferous seeds).

283 PARUS MAJOR
Great Tit

Classification Order Passeriformes, Family Paridae.
Characteristics About 14 cm. long (5.5"). It has a black head and throat, white cheeks, and yellow lower parts, with a central black stripe. The back is yellowish green uppermost and grayish on the rump. The remiges are black with two outer primary feathers edged with bluish; the inner secondaries are grayish. The tail is bluish brown, the outer rectrices white. The beak is black, and the legs are grayish. The young have a paler coloration, less distinct, with a less marked central stripe.
Habitat Woods, parks and gardens.
Distribution Europe, Asia and northwestern Africa.
Life and habits It nests in holes in trees and walls; like other tits and other species that nest in holes, it readily occupies artificial nesting boxes. It lays one clutch (sometimes two) of usually 7–15 eggs (normally 8–13). These are incubated for 13 or 14 days by the female, who is fed by the male. The nidicolous nestlings are reared by both parents; they leave the nest at 16–22 days and are independent in 2–4 weeks. The Great Tit feeds on invertebrates, seeds, berries and cereals.

284 PASSER DOMESTICUS
House Sparrow

Classification Order Passeriformes, Family Ploceidae.
Characteristics About 14.5 cm. long (5.7"). The top of the male's head is dark (in the Italian subspecies *P. d. italiae*, which some scholars consider a separate species, the head of the male is chestnut-colored), with a chestnut nape, black throat and whitish cheeks. The upper plumage is brownish gray, with more chestnut coloring and some whitish on the wings; on the sides there is some reddish and grayish shading. The beak is black in summer, yellowish brown in winter, and the legs are pale brown. The female has no black on her throat and the plumage is usually more uniform and brownish.
Habitat Cultivated land, buildings, urban areas.
Distribution Europe, Asia, northwestern Africa. Introduced to the Americas, southern Africa, Australia, New Zealand and certain oceanic islands.
Life and habits The House Sparrow makes its roundish nest of plant matter, usually in holes or in trees. It lays three clutches, usually with 3–5 eggs (more rarely up to 8), which are incubated by the female, as soon as laying is over, for 11–14 days. The nidicolous young are fed by the parents mainly with insects, and they stay in the nest for about 15 days.

285 PASSER MONTANUS
Eurasian Tree Sparrow

Classification   Order Passeriformes, Family Ploceidae.
Characteristics   About 14 cm. long (5.5″). The top of the head and nape are light brownish, the upper parts of the plumage are brownish with some black areas. The sides of the head and neck are white with a distinctive black mark at the ear. The chin and throat are black. The lower parts are white with grayish shading. The beak is black in summer, brown in winter with the base yellowish; the legs are pale brown. Young birds resemble the adults; but the throat and ear markings are blackish gray.
Habitat   In more rural areas than the House Sparrow; in hilly or untilled land.
Distribution   Europe, Asia. Introduced to some parts of southeast Asia, North America and Australia.
Life and habits   It nests in holes in trees and walls, where it builds a crude, round nest of plant matter. In it it lays 2 or 3 clutches of usually 4–6 eggs (more rarely 2–9), which are incubated by both sexes for 11–14 days, roughly. The nidicolous nestlings are reared by both parents and stay in the nest for 12–14 days. The diet consists of seeds, grain, and various invertebrates (insects and spiders).

286 PASSERINA CIRIS
Painted Bunting

Classification   Order Passeriformes, Family Fringillidae.
Characteristics   About 13 cm. long (5″). It has a short, strong beak designed for breaking seeds. The male has very bright plumage—violet on the head, green on the back, and scarlet on the remaining parts. The female is yellow-green on the upper parts, and yellow on the lower, like young individuals.
Habitat   Fields with bushes, hedgerows, woodland clearings.
Distribution   North America (southern United States and Mexico), and Central America.
Life and habits   When this species has spent the winter in Central America, it migrates in spring to its nesting areas farther north. Despite its very bright coloration, the male is a hard bird to spot, because it is a shy creature. The nest is cup-shaped and is made of grass, roots and vegetable fibers hidden among foliage in bushes. It lays 3–4 eggs, which are incubated for 12 days by the female. We do not know the exact age at which the young are able to fly, but it is probably about 12 days. They are fed and reared by both parents. The diet consists of seeds and insects, which are the main ingredient of the summer diet of adults and nestlings.

287 PASTOR ROSEUS (STURNUS ROSEUS)
Rose-colored Starling

Classification Order Passeriformes, Family Sturnidae.
Characteristics About 21.5 cm. long (8.5″). The coloring is unmistakable—the body is pink with a black head, tail and wings; on the head there is a very slight crest; the legs are pinkish; the beak is orange-yellow in summer and brown in winter. Young birds are brownish with dark wings.
Habitat Steppe, grasslands, rocky terrain, cultivated areas.
Distribution Southeast Europe, Asia Minor and central Asia, accidental in other areas.
Life and habits It generally nests in colonies, which change their nesting area every year. The nesting period varies, depending on the availability of food. It lays a single clutch of usually 5–6 eggs (more rarely 3–9) laid at intervals of a day. They are incubated by the female for about 11–14 days. The nidicolous nestlings are fed by both parents and stay in the nest for 14–19 days. Ornithologist Kai Curry-Lindahl points out that the Rose-colored Starling, when nesting on the Russian and Hungarian steppes, makes an autumn flight of 2,000 miles southeastward to India. Its diet consists mainly of insects (orthopterans, coleopterans) and also fruit.

288 PATAGONA GIGAS
Giant Hummingbird

Classification Order Trochiliformes, Family Trochilidae.
Characteristics The hummingbirds vary in size from 6 to 22 cm. in length (2.4–9″) over-all, and in weight from 2 to 20 grams (0.07–0.7 oz.). The beak is usually long—from 6 to 110 mm. (0.2–4.3 inches) and slender, with a long, forked tongue. The Giant Hummingbird is the largest species of Trochilidae, being the size of a large swift, with rather dull plumage compared with most hummingbirds. It is brown uppermost with greenish highlights on the back and violet on the wings; the beak is long and straight and the tail is slightly forked.
Habitat Arid temperate zone.
Distribution South America.
Life and habits Ornithologists J. Berlioz and H. O. Wagner record 321 species of Trochiliformes; J. Peters and his successors and D. Poley 327 species. To maintain homoiothermy hummingbirds need to spend a great deal of energy. They usually lay 2 eggs (rarely 1 or 3) which are incubated for 14–21 days; the young leave the nest at 22 or 23 days, depending on the species.

293 PERISOREUS INFAUSTUS
Siberian Jay

Classification Order Passeriformes, Family Corvidae.
Characteristics About 30 cm. long (12″). The males are slightly larger than the females. The plumage is brownish gray, with a darker head. The primary coverts and base of the primaries are slightly reddish, as are the outer rectrices, while the inner ones are grayish. The beak and legs are dark. In flight it shows reddish-orange coloring on the wings, rump and tail.
Habitat Coniferous and birch forests.
Distribution Northern regions of eastern Europe and Asia.
Life and habits It nests in trees, laying a single clutch of usually 4 eggs (rarely 3 or 5); these are incubated by the female, who is fed by the male, for 18–20 days. The nidicolous young are reared by both parents and open their eyes at 7 or 8 days. They leave the nest at 21–24 days, then stay in family groups through the winter. The Siberian Jay feeds on berries and fruit in winter, and on invertebrates in spring and summer, sometimes eating the eggs of other species of birds.

294 PERNIS APIVORUS
Honey Buzzard

Classification Order Falconiformes, Family Accipitridae.
Characteristics About 55 cm. long (22″). Its coloring is quite variable with different phases (lighter, darker and intermediate). The upper parts tend to dark brown, the lower light with dark barring and marks. The beak is black with a gray base, the cere is yellow and blackish, the legs are yellowish. In flight it resembles the Old World Buzzard, but has a smaller head, longer neck, narrower and longer wings, and a longer tail with a dark terminal band and two thinner bands toward the base.
Habitat Woods, clearings, *maquis*.
Distribution Europe, Asia and Africa.
Life and habits It nests in trees, often using the old nest of another large bird. It lays a single clutch of 1–3 eggs, which are incubated by both sexes for about 30–35 days. The nestlings are reared by both parents, and make their first flight at about 40–44 days, but return to the nest, even if only occasionally, for 2–8 further weeks. The Honey Buzzard's diet consists mainly of wasps and their larvae, honey, and other large insects. It also feeds on small mammals, eggs and small birds, lizards, frogs, and sometimes on berries and fruit.

295 PETRONIA PETRONIA
Rock Sparrow

Classification   Order Passeriformes, Family Ploceidae.
Characteristics   About 15 cm. long (6″), it looks roughly like a female House Sparrow: the plumage is usually light brown with a pale eyebrow over which there is a dark stripe. The top of the head is light-colored. There are roundish markings on the tips of the rectrices. There is also a distinctive yellowish mark on the breast, but this is not easy to spot in the wild. The upper parts are dark and striped.
Habitat   Open countryside, hilly and mountainous regions, villages and ruins.
Distribution   Southern Europe, northwestern Africa, Asia.
Life and habits   It nests in holes in rocks and in trees, laying one (sometimes 2) clutch of 4–8 eggs (usually 5 or 6), which are incubated for about a fortnight. The nidicolous young stay in the nest about 21 days and are reared by both parents. The song is a characteristic *"pey-i."* The Rock Sparrow's diet consists of seeds, grain and invertebrates.

296 PHAETHON AETHEREUS
Red-billed Tropicbird

Classification   Order Pelecaniformes, Family Pelecanidae.
Characteristics   It is very streamlined in appearance, with long, narrow wings and the two central tail rectrices longer and thread-shaped. It is about 90–105 cm. long (35–42″), excluding the central rectrices. It is a uniform white color with barring on the back and a black ring around the eye. The beak is bright red. In flight it shows two black marks at the wing tips. The young are striped with black and do not have the longer rectrices.
Habitat   Open sea and coasts during breeding.
Distribution   Tropical parts of the Pacific, Atlantic and Indian oceans.
Life and habits   Not very gregarious by nature, it flies long distances at sea, sometimes landing on the water and swimming for short stretches. It approaches coasts in the nesting period to lay a single egg on the bare sand or among rocks or reefs. The parents take turns at incubating the egg for 41–45 days. The nestling can fly after 70–100 days and follows its parents around for a long time. The diet of tropicbirds consists of fish and cephalopods (squid), which they catch as they fly over the surface of the sea and, from a certain height, dive like terns.

297 PHAINOPEPLA NITENS
Phainopepla

Classification Order Passeriformes, Family Bombycillidae.
Characteristics About 18 cm. long (7″) the male is entirely black, except for a large white marking at the wing tip, easily visible in flight. The plumage is silklike, and the head is capped by a prominent crest of feathers. The female and the young are grayer, with less well-defined wing markings. The wings are wide and short, the beak long and thin.
Habitat Areas covered with bushes, arid woods and parks.
Distribution Southwestern North America.
Life and habits It frequents arid areas with sparse vegetation. It is partly migratory. Although gregarious, pairs nest on their own. The tree nest is made with plant matter by the male alone. Both sexes incubate the eggs, 2–4 in number (more commonly 2 or 3), for 14–16 days. The nestlings fly at 19 days. The predatory technique of these birds includes darting from a perch on the branches of trees and catching their prey in mid-air. The diet consists essentially of flying insects (dipterans, lepidopterans) and a high proportion of numerous types of wild berries.

---

298 PHALACROCORAX AFRICANUS
Long-tailed Cormorant

Classification Order Pelecaniformes, Family Phalacrocoracidae.
Characteristics About 58 cm. long (23″), it differs from the Great Cormorant (*P. carbo*) by being smaller, with the general coloration of the plumage black, and a slight crest and white feathers behind the eye; the tail is quite long. Immature individuals have whitish-brown lower parts. Among other species of cormorant are the Double-crested Cormorant (*P. auritus*), found in North America; the Little Pied Cormorant (*P. melanoleucus*), found in the island belt between Java, the Solomon Islands, New Zealand and Australia; and the Pygmy Cormorant (*P. pygmaeus*) of southeastern Europe and southwestern Asia.
Habitat Shores of lakes and banks of watercourses, coastal waters, marshland.
Distribution Africa.
Life and habits Its habits are like those of the other cormorants. As mentioned by G. F. van Tets, the species of Phalacrocoracidae can be distinguished on the basis of their ecological and ethological features, forming four groups: lesser cormorants, greater cormorants, crested cormorants, and guano-producing cormorants. *P. africanus* belongs to the lesser cormorants, and feeds on fish and marine invertebrates.

299 PHALACROCORAX ARISTOTELIS
European Shag

Classification   Order Pelecaniformes, Family Phalacrocoracidae.

Characteristics   About 76 cm. long (30″), much smaller in size than the Great Cormorant, and differing from it by having a thin, short neck, a narrower head and a proportionately longer beak. The plumage is blackish green. In the breeding period this species has a short crest on its head. The young are usually browner and paler lower down. It swims both on the surface and underwater.

Habitat   Rocky coasts, cliffs.

Distribution   Europe, northwestern Africa and Asia Minor.

Life and habits   It nests in colonies, in crude nests made of seaweed, leaves and twigs, by both adults. It usually lays 3 eggs (sometimes 2, 4 or 5, more rarely 6), which are incubated by both parents, once the first egg is laid, for about 30 days. The young leave the nest at about 55 days and become independent after about three more weeks. The European Shag feeds on fish, marine invertebrates and plant matter.

300 PHALACROCORAX BOUGAINVILLEI
Guanay Cormorant

Classification   Order Pelecaniformes, Family Phalacrocoracidae.

Characteristics   About 68 cm. long (27″). It has a crest of feathers on the top of the head, dark upper parts, light lower parts, eyes surrounded by greenish bare skin, and red legs. Of all the various species of cormorant it leads the most aerial life and has the strongest and longest wings.

Habitat   Coasts, islands.

Distribution   South America (Pacific coast).

Life and habits   This cormorant is one of the greatest producers of guano—that is, the droppings that accumulate in the breeding colonies and constitute a much-sought-after fertilizer, because of its high nitrogen content. In some coastal islands the density of these cormorants is remarkable, as described by ornithologist Jean Dorst: on every square meter (11 sq. ft.) there may be on average 3 pairs of Guanay Cormorants (and because each pair rears on average two young, this makes 12 birds per square meter). Unlike the other cormorants, the Guanay feeds mainly on fish, which it catches by plunging from the air into the water.

301 PHALACROCORAX CARBO
Great Cormorant

Classification Order Pelecaniformes, Family Phalacrocoracidae.

Characteristics About 92 cm. long (36″), with a distinctive shape, dark coloration, a long neck, and a long beak with a hooked tip. The chin and sides of the face are white (in the subspecies *P. c. sinensis,* and only in the nuptial plumage, the white on the head is more extensive); in the breeding period there are two white markings on the flanks. Immature birds are brownish with pale lower parts.

Habitat Coasts, lagoons, estuaries, often also lakes and rivers.

Distribution Various parts of Europe, central and southern Asia, Africa, Australia and eastern North America.

Life and habits It nests on rocky coasts and also in trees, building a crude mound of twigs, grass, seaweed and various other plant matter. It lays 3 or 4 eggs (sometimes up to 6) which are incubated by both sexes for 28 or 29 days. The young are nidicolous, open their eyes at 4 or 5 days, and are reared and looked after by their parents. They fly at about 50–60 days, but do not become independent for another 11–12 weeks. The Great Cormorant dives through the water catching fish and crustaceans (it also eats vegetable matter). In its typical posture it stands with its wings half-opened, drying its plumage in the sun.

302 PHALAROPUS LOBATUS
Red-necked Phalarope

Classification Order Charadriiformes, Family Phalaropodidae.

Characteristics About 16.5 cm. long (6.5″). In summer its plumage is dark uppermost, the throat and lower parts are white, and there is an orange marking down the sides of the neck. The beak is long, black and thin. In winter the plumage is dull and grayish. In flight it shows a white wing bar. The phalaropes have slightly webbed toes at the base with lobate edges, and they are good swimmers.

Habitat Marshlands, grassy wetlands, tundra, coasts.

Distribution Europe, Asia, Africa and North America.

Life and habits The phalaropes are among the birds that show a reversal of sex roles: it is the female who is more brightly colored than the male, who takes the initiative in courtship, and who, after laying the eggs, leaves the male to rear the young. The Red-necked Phalarope nests on the ground, in a hollow amid vegetation, laying a single clutch of usually 4 eggs (sometimes 3) which are incubated by the male for 18–20 days. The nidifugous nestlings are reared by the male for 18–22 days. Phalaropes feed on invertebrates and also on plant matter.

303 PHAROMACHRUS MOCINNO
Quetzal

Classification   Order Trogoniformes, Family Trogonidae.
Characteristics   The Trogonidae are brightly colored, with long wedge-shaped tails, and short, tough and slightly hooked beaks. The Quetzal is a magnificent bird, the male having green and red plumage with a yellow beak and upper tail coverts that are green and very long indeed, reaching up to 105 cm. in length (42″). The female has a duller coloration—green and brown, dark beak and no long upper tail coverts. The full length of the tail coverts, in the male, is reached at the age of three.
Habitat   Forests.
Distribution   From southern Mexico to Panama.
Life and habits   Worshiped by the Mayas and the Aztecs, the Quetzal is the emblem of Guatemala (and the currency of this country takes the name of this bird). It is mainly gregarious, except for the breeding period. Ornithologist Alexander F. Skutch has studied its nesting habits: it lays 1 or 2 clutches a year in holes in trees, especially in rotting trunks. There are usually 2 eggs, incubated by both sexes for 17 or 18 days. The nestlings stay in the nest for some 30 days. The Quetzal feeds mainly on plant matter and invertebrates, frogs and lizards.

304 PHASIANUS COLCHICUS
Common Pheasant

Classification   Order Galliformes, Family Phasianidae.
Characteristics   The male is about 79 cm. long (31″), some 30 cm. (12″) of which are accounted for by the long tail; the female is about 60 cm. long (24″), with a shorter tail—only 20–25 cm. (8–10). The male is very brightly colored and varies greatly, depending on the subspecies. As a rule the head and neck are dark green with metallic highlights, with scarlet caruncles surrounding the eye. In addition it has tufts above the ears. The plumage of the rest of the body is brownish, with tawny markings and black stripes on the tail. A black variety has very dark lower parts. The female is less showy in appearance and is mainly brown.
Habitat   Wooded areas, cultivated land, fields and hilly regions.
Distribution   Originally from palaearctic western Asia, it has been introduced virtually throughout Europe, also in North America.
Life and habits   It generally nests on the ground, laying a single clutch of 7–15 eggs, laid on consecutive days. These are incubated by the female when laying is over for about 23–27 days. The nidifugous nestlings are reared by the female and can fly at 12–14 days. The male is polygamous. The varied diet includes acorns, hazel nuts, berries, seeds, leaves, cereals and vegetables, as well as various invertebrates.

305 PHILETARIUS SOCIUS
Sociable Weaver

Classification   Order Passeriformes, Family Ploceidae.
Characteristics   The Sociable Weaver is about 14 cm. long
(5.5") and has a dull, uniform coloration, with grayish-brown
upper parts that look like scales because of the light-edged
feathers on the back. The throat is blackish; the lower parts are
lighter colored and dull, though there are some black feathers
edged with lighter coloring at the sides. It belongs to the subfamily of Plocepasserinae, which, according to ornithologist
H. E. Wolters, includes 8 species.
Habitat   Savanna, scrub.
Distribution   Southern Africa.
Life and habits   The Sociable Weaver builds communal nests
of large proportions called *Familievoel* by people of southern
Africa. On strong branches or telegraph poles several pairs
using plant matter make a huge and extensive nest with various
small chambers for the individual pairs, with the opening
downward. The pairs are monogamous. These nests are used
for several years consecutively, with new materials being
added. Ornithologists N. E. and E. C. Collias observed a 100-
year-old colony consisting of four communal nests, the largest
of which was 4.8 m. long and 3.6 m. wide (15.7 × 11.8 ft.), and
had 125 apertures.

306 PHILOMACHUS PUGNAX
Ruff

Classification   Order Charadriiformes, Family Scolopacidae.
Characteristics   The male is about 25.5 cm. long (10"); the
female (called the Reeve) about 23.5 cm. (9"). In his nuptial
plumage the male is unmistakable: he has two erectile tufts
above the ears, and a wide collar of very variably colored feathers (a combination of black, chestnut, cream and white),
though this is present only for a short period. The upper parts
are dark brownish, the breast is tawny, the belly white. The autumn-winter plumage is brownish, with paler lower parts. The
young resemble the female, with more speckled upper parts. In
flying it clearly shows its dark tail with oval white markings on
the sides.
Habitat   Tundra, grass and wetlands, marshes and bogs.
Distribution   Europe, Asia and Africa.
Life and habits   In their magnificent nuptial plumage the
males vie for the females in special "arenas." Each male mates
with several females. The female lays usually 4 eggs (more
rarely 3) in a hole in the ground; these are incubated for 20 or
21 days. The nidifugous nestlings are reared by the female,
who looks after them for several days. The Ruff is a mainly insectivorous bird.

307 PHOENICOPTERUS RUBER
Greater Flamingo

Classification Order Phoenicopteriformes, Family Phoeni-copteridae.

Characteristics An unmistakable bird—up to 127 cm. long (50″), it has extremely long legs and neck and the distinctive "bent" beak that enables it to feed in a very specific manner by foraging through the bottom mud of marshlands. The young are smaller, with a whitish-brown coloration.

Habitat Lagoons, lakes, estuaries, marshlands in general.

Distribution Africa, southwestern Asia, Central America, and southern Europe.

Life and habits Generally gregarious, it nests in large colo-nies, building characteristic conical nests of mud and sand. Here it lays 1 or 2 eggs, which are incubated by both parents for about 28–32 days. The young leave their nest after about 4 days and follow their parents around. They will fly at about 78 days. The Greater Flamingo has two subspecies—*P. r. roseus* of Asia, Africa and southern Europe, and *P. r. ruber* of Central America. The other species of flamingo are the Chilean Fla-mingo (*P. chilensis*) of South America, the Lesser Flamingo (*Phoeniconaias minor*) of Africa and Asia and the two species of flamingo found in the lakes of the Andean upland plateaus in South America, James's Flamingo (*Phoenicoparrus jamesi*) and the Andean Flamingo (*P. andinus*).

308 PHOENICURUS OCHRURUS
Black Redstart

Classification Order Passeriformes, Family Turdidae.

Characteristics About 14 cm. long (5.5″). It has dark color-ing; the male has soot-black plumage with black breast and tail and a whitish wing marking. The plumage looks lighter in au-tumn. The female has a paler coloration, brownish, and brighter uppermost; the legs and beak are dark, the tail and rump reddish.

Habitat Rocky areas, old buildings, ruins, eaves.

Distribution Europe, central Asia and Africa.

Life and habits It nests in holes in rocks and walls, laying 2 clutches (sometimes 3) of usually 4–6 eggs, which are incu-bated by the female for a period of 12–16 days. The nidicolous nestlings are reared by both parents; they remain in the nest between 12 and 19 days. The diet consists mainly of inverte-brates (insects, etc.).

309 PHOENICURUS PHOENICURUS
Old World Redstart

Classification Order Passeriformes, Family Turdidae.
Characteristics About 14 cm. long (5.5"). The male has a distinctive plumage: the face and throat are black, the breast, sides and rump reddish, the top of the head and back bluish; there is a white marking forming an eyebrow. In the female the upper parts are grayish brown, and the lower pale tawny. Young birds have a speckled breast. The tail is reddish, with darker central rectrices.
Habitat Woods, parks and gardens.
Distribution Europe, Africa and Asia.
Life and habits It nests in holes in trees and in walls, and on buildings, laying 2 clutches of 4–10 eggs (usually 6 or 7), which are incubated by the female for 11–14 days. The nidicolous nestlings stay in the nest for 14–20 days and are reared by both parents. The diet is made up of invertebrates.

310 PHYLLOSCOPUS COLLYBITA
Chiffchaff

Classification Order Passeriformes, Family Sylviidae.
Characteristics About 10.5 cm. long (4"). The brownish upper parts have olive-green shadings; the back looks more greenish. The lower parts are pale reddish white. A similar species is the Willow Warbler (*P. trochilis*), but the latter has blackish legs and shaded coloration.
Habitat Woods, parks, gardens and open land.
Distribution Europe, Africa and Asia.
Life and habits It nests on the ground or amid low vegetation in bushes and brambles, where the female makes a round nest of grass, moss, dead leaves, feathers, et cetera, with a side opening. She lays one clutch of usually 4–9 eggs (sometimes a second clutch of 4 or 5), laid at intervals of a day, which she incubates for 13 or 14 days. The nidicolous nestlings stay in the nest for about 12–15 days. It has a distinctive song which goes *"chiff-chiff-chiff-chaff-chaff."* The diet consists of invertebrates (insects and spiders, etc.).

311 PICA PICA
Black-billed Magpie

Classification   Order Passeriformes, Family Corvidae.
Characteristics   It is about 46 cm. long (18″), the tail being about half, or 23 cm. (9″), of that length. Its plumage is black and white, with greenish highlights. The tail is long and tapering, the beak and legs black. In flight it is very distinctive: from above it is black with white scapular feathers and the central part of the primaries also white; the belly and wing tips are white.
Habitat   Open terrain, tilled land, copses.
Distribution   Europe, Asia, North Africa, western North America.
Life and habits   It makes a crude nest of twigs and plant matter covered with a dome of twigs. Here it lays a single clutch of usually 5–8 eggs (rarely up to 10), which are incubated by the female for 17 or 18 days. The nidicolous young are reared by both parents and stay in the nest for about 22–28 days. The Black-billed Magpie feeds mainly on invertebrates (insects). It makes a sound like *chak-chak-chak-chak.*

312 PICATHARTES GYMNOCEPHALUS
Yellow-headed Rockfowl

Classification   Order Passeriformes, Family Timaliidae.
Characteristics   In the Family Timaliidae the strange Rockfowl form the tribe Picathartinae. There are two species—the Yellow-headed Rockfowl and the Red-headed Rockfowl (*P. oreas*). The plumage of these birds is blackish gray, the lower parts are white, and the legs are very long. The Yellow-headed Rockfowl has orange-yellow coloration on its bare head with a black marking at the side. The other species has a red head, with black and blue included. The beak is black and strong.
Habitat   Forests, watercourses.
Distribution   Central-western Africa (localized).
Life and habits   Rockfowl live on the ground in forests, and they feed on insects, amphibians and fruit. Ornithologist Faust has studied the breeding behavior of the Yellow-headed Rockfowl in the Frankfurt zoo. It makes a nest of mud, earth, stalks and leaves. Incubation lasts about 19 days, and the nestling stays in the nest for 19–25 days. The Red-headed Rockfowl nests in bowllike nests made of mud and plant matter, laying 2 eggs.

313 PICOIDES TRIDACTYLUS
Northern Three-toed Woodpecker

Classification   Order Piciformes, Family Picidae.
Characteristics   About 21 cm. long (8.5"). It is black with a broad white stripe from the nape of the neck to the rump. The cheeks are black. The top of the male's head is yellow in the middle, while the top of the female's head is black. The lower parts are white with pale black barring on the sides. The legs have three toes. A North American species is the Yellow-bellied Sapsucker (*Sphyrapicus varius*), which is about 24 cm. long (9.5"), has several color variations (it usually has red on the forehead and throat) and feeds on tree sap as well as on insects.
Habitat   Forests and mountains.
Distribution   Mountainous and boreal regions of Europe, Asia and North America.
Life and habits   It nests in holes in trees, where it lays a single clutch of 3–6 eggs (usually 4 or 5), which are incubated by both sexes for about 14 days. The diet of this woodpecker consists of invertebrates (insects) found in trees, as well as seeds and fruit.

314 PICUS VIRIDIS
Green Woodpecker

Classification   Order Piciformes, Family Picidae.
Characteristics   About 31 cm. long (12.5"). The plumage is green uppermost, paler lower down; the top of the head is red, the rump yellowish, the sides of the head are black with red "mustaches" edged with black. Young birds have a paler coloration, with various stripes and bars.
Habitat   Woods, parks, gardens, zones with scattered trees.
Distribution   Europe, Asia Minor, northwestern Africa.
Life and habits   It nests in holes in trees, where it lays a single clutch of usually 5, 6 or 7 eggs (sometimes 4–9; rarely up to 11). Incubation is undertaken by both parents, who feed the young with regurgitated food. The young leave the nest at 18–21 days. The Green Woodpecker is mainly solitary; it climbs up tree trunks, where it feeds on invertebrates in the bark. It also feeds on the ground, especially on ants, and will also take berries and other vegetable matter. It has a distinctive flight pattern, alternating 3–4 wingbeats with undulating flight with the wings closed.

315 PIRANGA RUBRA
Summer Tanager

Classification   Order Passeriformes, Family Thraupidae.

Characteristics   About 18 cm. long (7″), it has a broad, strong beak, and quite bright plumage in the male. The male is a uniform red, darker on the wings and tail. The female and young, conversely, are olive brown uppermost, and pale yellow lower down. Similar species are the Scarlet Tanager (*P. olivacea*) and the Western Tanager (*P. ludoviciana*).

Habitat   Broadleaf and coniferous woods.

Distribution   North and South America.

Life and habits   It spends the summer in woods along rivers and in more arid woodland with oak, hornbeam, hazel and pine in the northerly parts of its distribution area, and winters in South America. The nest is made on a horizontal branch of a tree, with grass and small bits of bark, and is lined with vegetable fiber. The 2–5 (almost always 2) eggs are incubated solely by the female for about 12 days. The nestlings are fed by both parents and leave the nest at about 10 days. The diet consists of insects (mainly wasps, bees and other hymenopterans), berries and wild fruit.

316 PITANGUS SULPHURATUS
Great Kiskadee

Classification   Order Passeriformes, Family Tyrannidae.

Characteristics   The Tyrannidae vary in size from 6.5 to 30 cm. (2.5–12″); they are insectivorous and very aggressive. Morphologically speaking, they resemble the Old World flycatchers (Muscicapidae) and have 10 primaries. At the sides of the beak there are bristles, which are used to trap insects in mid-air. But in some species these bristles are not very well developed, and these feed mainly on seeds and berries. The form of the beak varies a lot. The Great Kiskadee, about 20 cm. long (8″), has reddish-brown plumage uppermost, and a black head with a white stripe above the eyes. The lower parts are bright yellow.

Habitat   Open woods.

Distribution   The Americas, from southern Texas to Argentina.

Life and habits   The Tyrannidae build various types of nests depending on the species—open, dome-shaped, in forks in trees, suspended on a mud platform, in rocks, or in holes in the ground. They are mainly monogamous birds. Depending on the species they lay 2–6 eggs, which are incubated for 12–23 days. The nidicolous nestlings stay in the nest about 14–28 days. The Great Kiskadee makes a large nest with a roof on top in a tree, and catches not only insects but sometimes small fish in ponds and streams, and also small lizards.

317 PITTA GUAJANA
Banded Pitta

Classification Order Passeriformes, Family Pittidae.
Characteristics The species of the family Pittidae are very bright-colored birds. The size varies from 15 to 28 cm. (6–11″). In their general appearance the Pittidae have a roundish body, large head, long legs and a short, square tail. They are found in the Old World from Africa (where there are two species) to Japan, Australia and the Solomon Islands. The Banded Pitta has bright-colored plumage, brownish uppermost, with dark but white-edged wings, a blue tail, black and light yellow head, a blackish band on the upper part of the breast and brown-streaked lower parts.
Habitat Forests.
Distribution Southeast Asia.
Life and habits Pittas live on the ground or not far from it in forests, and they reach altitudes of 2,500 meters (8,200 ft.). In general they fly for only short stretches, but in the migratory period they will fly to the tropics, as mentioned by Rudolf Berndt and Wilhelm Meise. They feed mainly on invertebrates, and sometimes also on lizards. They lay 2–6 eggs, depending on the species. The young are nidicolous.

318 PLATALEA LEUCORODIA
Old World Spoonbill

Classification Order Ciconiiformes, Family Threskiornithidae.
Characteristics About 86 cm. long (34″) this is a fairly unmistakable bird. It has white plumage with a tawny area at the base of the neck in summer, a tuft of feathers on top of the head in adults in summer, black legs, and a distinctive, spatula-shaped long beak, which is black with a yellowish tip. Young birds have no crest or throat markings; the tip of the primary remiges is black, the beak is grayish pink and the legs are grayish yellow. In flight its neck is extended.
Habitat Marshlands, estuaries, lagoons.
Distribution Some parts of Europe, southern Asia and Africa.
Life and habits It nests in colonies, usually in canebrakes, where it makes a nest of sticks, reeds and plant matter. It lays a single clutch of usually 4 eggs (sometimes 3 or 5, more rarely 6), which are incubated by both sexes for about 21 days. The nidicolous nestlings are reared by both parents and leave the nest at about 4 weeks; they fly at about 7 weeks. The Old World Spoonbill feeds on small animals (small fish, mollusks, frogs, and insects) and vegetable matter.

319 PLECTROPHENAX NIVALIS
Snow Bunting

Classification Order Passeriformes, Family Emberizidae.
Characteristics About 16.5 cm. long (6.5″). In the male the upper parts, head and neck are white, the other upper areas being black; the primaries are black with a white base, the secondaries mainly white with black markings at the tips. The wing coverts are white. The beak and legs are black. After its complete molting, which usually occurs between August and September, the upper parts, head, breast and sides have reddish brown edges and the beak is yellow with a black tip. The female has blackish-gray upper parts, the lower being whitish with grayish markings on the sides of the breast.
Habitat Open terrain, stony ground, tundra, seacoasts and sometimes fields.
Distribution Northern parts of Europe, Asia and America.
Life and habits It nests on the ground, in holes in rocks or in old buildings. The male is sometimes polygamous. The female lays two clutches of usually 4–6 eggs (more rarely 7 or 8), which she incubates for 10–15 days. The nidicolous nestlings are fed at first by the female, then by both adults. They stay in the nest for about 10–14 days. This is one of the most northerly birds, feeding mainly on seeds, but also on invertebrates (insects, etc.).

---

320 PLEGADIS FALCINELLUS
Glossy Ibis

Classification Order Ciconiiformes, Family Threskiornithidae.
Characteristics About 56 cm. long (22″), it has a uniform blackish plumage with green and reddish shadings, tending more to purplish brown in spring and more to black in winter. The beak is long and arched, the legs grayish brown. Young birds have a more uniform coloring and are browner with pale lower parts. In flight the neck and legs are extended, and it looks hunched.
Habitat Marshlands and bogs, lagoons and seacoasts.
Distribution Southern Europe, southern Asia, East Africa, North America and Australia.
Life and habits Gregarious by nature, it nests in colonies with other species of marsh birds. The crude nest is made of sticks and branches amid reeds, in bushes or in trees. It lays 3 or 4 eggs (occasionally 5, rarely 6), which are incubated by both sexes, but mainly by the female, for 21–25 days. The young are reared by both parents and fed with regurgitated food; they can fly after about 6 weeks. The Glossy Ibis feeds on insects, mollusks, small amphibians and small fish.

321 PLOCEUS SPEKEI
Speke's Weaver

Classification Order Passeriformes, Family Ploceidae.
Characteristics The subfamily Ploceinae includes the species of weavers, with 68 species distributed among 15 genera, according to various ornithologists. Of these, as mentioned by H. Edmund Wolters, 5 species live in southern Africa, 2 in Madagascar, and all the rest elsewhere in Africa. Most of the species live in open savanna, others in forest. Speke's Weaver has yellowish plumage, with a greenish back and wings with black barring. The male has a black mark on the side of the face and below the beak on the throat. The beak is tough and slightly curved. The female is olive brown.
Habitat Open savanna.
Distribution Africa.
Life and habits In open savanna, where most of the Ploceinae live, they lead a communal life in impressive nesting colonies and are mainly polygamous. Some species, in the course of their evolution, moved to the forests and became monogamous and nonsocial, and also transformed the shape of the nest. The nest is built by weaving a ring attached to branches and then closing it in to form the "incubation chamber."

322 PLUVIALIS APRICARIA
Greater Golden Plover

Classification Order Charadriiformes, Family Charadriidae.
Characteristics About 28 cm. long (11″). The upper parts are dark brown with some golden yellow evident. The lower parts of the wings are white, the tail and rump are dark-colored; the face, throat, breast and belly are black in summer, while in the winter months the lower parts are whitish with black and yellow bars. A very similar species is the Lesser Golden Plover (*P. dominica*), which in summer, unlike the Greater Golden Plover, has smoky-gray rather than whitish axillary feathers and undertail.
Habitat Moors, tundra, estuaries, coasts and fields.
Distribution Europe and Asia.
Life and habits It nests on the ground amid vegetation, laying a single clutch of usually 4 eggs (sometimes 3), which are incubated by both sexes, mainly the female, for about 27 or 28 days. The nidifugous nestlings are reared by both parents and become independent at about one month. They feed mainly on invertebrates (insects, worms, mollusks, crustaceans and spiders), as well as vegetable matter.

323 PLUVIALIS SQUATAROLA
Gray or Black-bellied Plover

Classification Order Charadriiformes, Family Charadriidae.
Characteristics About 28 cm. long (11″). The spring and summer plumage is grayish uppermost, with silver-flecked feathers. The lower parts are black, starting from the cheeks and throat, but there is no black on the lower part of the belly and the undertail. In autumn and winter this plumage fades, and the upper parts are pale gray, with the lower parts whitish with black axillary feathers.
Habitat Tundra, marshlands, estuaries, seacoasts.
Distribution It nests chiefly above the Arctic Circle, and migrates south to Europe, Asia, Australia, and South America.
Life and habits It nests on the ground, laying a single clutch of usually 4 eggs (rarely 3), which are incubated by both sexes for about 23 days. The nidifugous nestlings are reared by both parents. It makes a sad call that sounds like a *tlee-u-ee*. The Gray Plover feeds on invertebrates (mollusks, crustaceans, insects) and also on vegetable matter.

324 PLUVIANUS AEGYPTIUS
Egyptian Plover or Crocodile Bird

Classification Order Charadriiformes, Family Glareolidae.
Characteristics This is a distinctive bird, with pale gray plumage uppermost and pale yellow and whitish lower down. There is black and white on the wings. The head is black with a white stripe across it. The black extends to the upper part of the back, and a black stripe runs across the lower parts to the lower breast. The legs are greenish gray.
Habitat Sandy riverbanks, marshlands.
Distribution Tropical Africa.
Life and habits It nests on the ground in hollows, in sandy areas along riverbanks and lake shores. It usually lays 3 eggs (sometimes 2 or 4), which are incubated for a period the precise length of which is not yet known. The nidifugous nestlings follow their parents around and are reared by them to start with. The Egyptian Plover buries its eggs—and sometimes even its young—in the sand. Legend has it that this species pecks scraps of food from the gaping jaws of crocodiles. This has come about because it is often seen with crocodiles or on its back (hence its alternate name). It is not a true plover, and is no longer found in Egypt.

325 PODARGUS STRIGOIDES
Tawny Frogmouth

Classification   Order Caprimulgiformes, Family Podargidae.
Characteristics   About 25 cm. long (10″), it is squat and strong looking, with a long, pointed tail, short, weak legs and a very wide, flat beak with a hooked tip. The eyes are set quite well forward to give good binocular vision. The plumage, which is similar in both sexes, is very mimetic, gray-brown and striped and speckled with white and brown.
Habitat   Tropical forest.
Distribution   Australia, Tasmania and New Guinea.
Life and habits   The frogmouths search for food mainly on the ground, ready to fly off at the slightest sign of danger into trees, where, because of their knack of staying stock-still, they merge remarkably well with the bark. The frogmouths have a large mouth; by being held agape and thus showing its bright internal coloring, like that of a flower, it seems to attract insects. The nest is made with small branches, down and lichens in trees; in it are laid 1 or 2 eggs incubated for 30 days by both sexes. The nestlings remain in the nest for quite a long time— the time still undetermined—and are reared and fed by both parents. The diet consists of animals caught on the ground amid foliage and in bushes—invertebrates, and even small amphibians and rodents.

326 PODICEPS CRISTATUS
Great Crested Grebe

Classification   Order Podicipediformes, Family Podicipedidae
Characteristics   About 47 cm. long (18.5″), weighing between 590 and 1,400 grams (21–50 ounces), it is the largest of the Old World grebes and is easily identifiable by the blackish ear crests and, in the breeding period, by chestnut and black plumes on the sides of the head. The young have a black and white striped head and neck. The chicks are light-colored with dark stripes.
Habitat   Ponds, marshes, bogs, marshland in general.
Distribution   Parts of Europe, Asia, Africa and Australia.
Life and habits   It builds a nest in marsh vegetation, anchoring the construction to it; at intervals of about 2 days the female lays 3–6 eggs (normally 4), which are incubated by both sexes and hatch after 25–29 days. The chicks are precocious and follow their parents about, and they feed themselves; they usually remain dependent on their parents for about 6 weeks (sometimes up to 12 weeks). There is an extremely distinctive courtship ceremony, which involves a preliminary phase between the two partners, a raising of the body on the water's surface and the so-called "penguin position," during which aquatic plants are offered.

327 PODICEPS GRISEGENA
Red-necked Grebe

Classification   Order Podicipediformes, Family Podicipedidae.

Characteristics   About 43 cm. long (17"). The summer plumage has gray-brown upper parts, with white lower down; the front of the neck and sides of the neck are chestnut, the base of the beak is yellow and the cheeks are whitish gray. The top of the head has small black tufts. In winter the plumage is like that of the Great Crested Grebe, but the Red-necked Grebe is smaller, with a black and yellow beak, a grayer neck, no white eyebrow, and on the top of the head a black mark that extends to the eyes.

Habitat   Marshland, lakes, slow-moving rivers, seacoasts, estuaries.

Distribution   Europe, Asia, North America.

Life and habits   It nests amid aquatic vegetation in a mound of sticks, canes and other vegetable matter, laying a single clutch of usually 4 or 5 eggs (more rarely 2–7) at intervals of a couple of days. Incubation is undertaken by both adults and lasts about 22–25 days. The nidifugous nestlings are reared by the parents and become independent within about 10 weeks. The Red-necked Grebe feeds on small fish, frogs and invertebrates (mollusks, insects).

328 PODICEPS RUFICOLLIS
Little Grebe

Classification   Order Podicipediformes, Family Podicipedidae.

Characteristics   About 27 cm. long (11"), it is certainly the commonest and smallest of the European grebes. In its summer plumage its coloring is dark brown with reddish cheeks, throat and forehead. The base of the beak is greenish yellow. In the winter plumage the coloration is lighter, brownish with a white throat. Young birds have a lighter-colored plumage with brown barring at the sides of the head.

Habitat   Marshlands, watercourses, lakes.

Distribution   Europe, Asia and Africa.

Life and habits   It nests amid aquatic vegetation, in a nest like that of other grebes—a floating heap anchored to the vegetation or to a spit of mud or land, made of sticks, canes and other vegetable matter. It lays two clutches (sometimes 3) of usually 4–6 eggs (occasionally 2, 3 or 7), which are incubated by both sexes for 19–25 days. The nidifugous nestlings (blackish brown, with reddish stripes) are reared by both parents; they become independent at 42 days and fly at 44–48 days. They are often carried about on their parents' backs. Grebes dive under water frequently. They make a *whit-whit* sound, loud and clipped. They feed on invertebrates, vegetable matter and small fish.

329 POEPHILA GOULDIAE (CHLOEBIA GOULDIAE)
Gouldian Finch

Classification   Order Passeriformes, Family Estrildidae.
Characteristics   About 11 cm. long (4.5"), it has threadlike central rectrices measuring a further 4 cm. (1.5"). It is a particularly bright-colored finch with upper parts green, a red head, black neck with a black stripe that extends to frame the red head, followed by a wider blue band at the sides, a violet-blue breast, and yellow lower parts with whitish shading, long black central tail recirices and a pale beak.
Habitat   Along watercourses, open terrain, savannah.
Distribution   Northern Australia.
Life and habits   This is a sociable bird; it does not make a nest, but breeds in holes in trees. It is particularly sensitive to cold and is best when the thermometer is at about 30° C (85° F). The Estrildidae make crude nests, almost spherical in shape with a diameter of 10–20 cm. (4–8"). They lay 4–6 eggs (rarely up to 9). Incubation lasts 12–16 days. The nidicolous young leave the nest after about 3 weeks.

330 POLEMAETUS BELLICOSUS
Martial Eagle

Classification   Order Falconiformes, Family Accipitridae.
Characteristics   A large bird, 72–90 cm. long (28–35"), its back, head and neck are gray-brown, as are the breast and wings. The lower parts are white with some black markings. The iris is yellow. A long crest of dark feathers tops the head. The female, which is slightly larger than the male, reaches a weight of 6.2 kg. (13.5 lbs.) and has a wing span of 2.5 meters (100").
Habitat   Savanna, bushy areas and semidesert.
Distribution   Central and southern Africa.
Life and habits   The nest or nests—because each pair has various nests used on a "rota-basis" each year—are made in tall trees. There is usually just the one egg, incubated solely by the female for about 45 days. The nestling makes its first flight at about 100 days. This species breeds irregularly and may not lay eggs every year. The diet consists mainly of birds (up to the size of a bustard) and medium and large mammals (hyrax, dik-dik) which it kills instantaneously with its remarkably strong talons. It uses two distinct hunting techniques: lying in wait, perched on a branch ready to swoop on the sighted prey, and "aerial reconnaissance," often from considerable heights.

331 POLYBORUS PLANCUS
Crested Caracara

Classification   Order Falconiformes, Family Falconidae.
Characteristics   About 50–65 cm. long (20–26″) this is a medium-sized bird of prey with a rather squat appearance. The upper parts are brown, darker on the head, where there is a short tuft of feathers, and on the upper breast. The throat and sides of the head are white, as are the remaining lower parts, which have dark bars. The iris is brown and the bare skin on the face red. Immature birds are less brightly colored. The wing span exceeds 1 meter (40″).
Habitat   Open terrain, both arid and marshy.
Distribution   Southern North America to South America.
Life and habits   This species nests from sea level up to 3,000 meters (10,000 ft.) in the Andes. The nest is built in trees, including palms and cacti, or on the ground where, as in the pampas, there are no trees. The clutch of 2 or 3 eggs (rarely 4) is incubated by the pair for about 28 days. Sometimes a second clutch is laid. The nestlings, fed by both parents, fly after 2–3 months. Thanks to its long legs, this bird of prey walks along the ground gathering food, which consists of all sorts of small creatures, carrion, and sometimes plant matter. It has been seen chasing other birds of prey to steal their food.

332 PORPHYRIO PORPHYRIO
Purple Swamphen

Classification   Order Gruiformes, Family Rallidae.
Characteristics   About 48 cm. long (19″), it is squat-looking, with handsome violet blue plumage, a white undertail, and a red shield on the front of the head; the legs have long red toes. The sexes are similar. Young birds are grayish brown uppermost and lighter lower down. The Purple Swamphen does not often fly; when it does, it shows long dangling legs.
Habitat   Canebrakes, marshes, bogs, lagoons with thick marsh vegetation.
Distribution   Southern Europe, Africa, central and southern Asia, Australia, Polynesia. In Europe it is localized in southern Spain and Sardinia.
Life and habits   The Purple Swamphen is fairly elusive by nature, hiding among thick reeds. It makes a nest of reeds and sticks and other vegetable matter in a marsh, and sometimes on open water. It usually lays 2–5 eggs (sometimes 7), which are incubated by both sexes but mainly by the female for 22–25 days. The nidifugous nestlings are reared by both parents. This species feeds on plant matter and aquatic creatures (from insects to frogs).

333 PROCELLARIA DIOMEDEA (PUFFINUS DIOMEDEA)
Cory's Shearwater

Classification Order Procellariiformes, Family Procellariidae.

Characteristics About 51 cm. long (20.5"). The upper parts are gray-brown, the lower white. The beak is large and yellow. The young resemble the adults. In flight it has a wing span of about 1 meter (40"). It appears grayish uppermost, with a sort of white V on the tail, which is darker; lower down it is white with dark wing and tail edges.

Habitat Open sea, rocky coasts.

Distribution Mediterranean waters and Atlantic ocean.

Life and habits It nests in colonies on pebbles and shingle and in cracks in rocks. The nest is crude, made of small branches, sticks and aquatic vegetation. It lays a single white egg, which is incubated by both sexes for a period of about 52–55 days. The nestling stays in the nest for an undetermined period (although about 5 months must elapse between incubation and emergence from the nest). Cory's Shearwater makes strange nocturnal *miaow*-ing noises; it feeds on marine invertebrates, fish eggs and plant matter.

334 PRUNELLA COLLARIS
Alpine Accentor

Classification Order Passeriformes, Family Prunellidae.

Characteristics About 17.5 cm. long (7"). The throat and chin are whitish speckled with black; the lower parts are bluish gray with reddish sides; the upper parts are striped gray-brown. The tail is dark brown, and light at the tip. In flight it shows white wing bars. Young birds do not have the speckling on the throat.

Habitat Mountains, rocky and stony areas, up to the perpetual snow line. In winter it descends to lower altitudes, even to lowland areas.

Distribution Europe, Asia, northwestern Africa.

Life and habits The cup-shaped nest is made with plant material by both adults, in holes in rocks or amid vegetation. It lays two clutches, usually of 3 or 4 eggs (rarely 5 or 6), which are incubated by both parents for 15 days. The nidicolous nestlings leave the nest after about 16 days. The Alpine Accentor feeds on invertebrates (insects and spiders) and vegetable matter (seeds and berries).

335 PRUNELLA MODULARIS
Dunnock or Hedge Accentor

Classification Order Passeriformes, Family Prunellidae.
Characteristics About 14.5 cm: long (5.7″). It has rather dull plumage; the upper parts are dark, striped with black; the breast, throat and head are gray, and the top of the head is brown. The lower parts are pale gray. Young birds have a less reddish coloration overall, with a browner head, and they are more speckled.
Habitat Parks, gardens, woods, bushes, hedgerows.
Distribution Europe and Asia Minor.
Life and habits The nest is made of plant matter (small branches, sticks, roots, dry leaves, moss, etc.) by the female, with occasional help from the male. It lays 2 clutches (sometimes 3) of usually 4 or 5 eggs (sometimes 3 or 6), which are incubated by the female for 12 or 13 days. The nidicolous nestlings are reared by both parents and stay in the nest for about 12 days. The Dunnock feeds on invertebrates but also on plant matter (seeds, etc.).

---

336 PSITTACUS ERITHACUS
African Gray Parrot

Classification Order Psittaciformes, Family Psittacidae
Characteristics About 40 cm. long (16″), this is a fairly unmistakable parrot, with overall grayish plumage, blackish remiges, a whitish face, paler gray lower parts, a whitish abdomen and a reddish tail. The African Gray Parrot is part of the tribe of Psittacinae, which are well known as good mimics of other birds and of human words. Among other species are the Greater Black Parrot (*Coracopsis vasa*), the Lesser Black Parrot (*C. nigra*), the Senegal Parrot (*Poicephalus senegalus*) and the Cape Parrot (*P. robustus*).
Habitat Forests, scrub, clearings and fields.
Distribution Central-western Africa.
Life and habits The African Gray Parrot is one of the best-known ''speaking'' parrots, showing a remarkable ability to link up words and sounds to given situations. It is often seen in groups, for example, when in search of food in cereal-crop fields. It usually lays 3 or 4 eggs at 3-day intervals. Incubation lasts about 30 days. The nidicolous nestlings stay in the nest for about 80 days. Once they have left the nest they follow their parents for about 4 months.

337 PTEROCLES ORIENTALIS
Black-bellied Sandgrouse

Classification Order Columbiformes, Family Pteroclidae.
Characteristics About 34 cm. long (13.5″). The male's upper parts are dark with various gray, reddish, blackish and yellow speckling. The head is grayish. The sides of the head are tawny. On the throat there is a black mark. The breast is gray with a black stripe, with the upper part of the belly pale and the rest black. In the tail the rectrices are slightly elongated. The female is more speckled and mimetic, with the breast spotted as far as the black stripe.
Habitat Arid regions, with stones, open terrain, semidesert and grassy steppe.
Distribution Spain, Portugal, Cyprus, Asia Minor and North Africa.
Life and habits It nests on the ground amid sparse vegetation, laying one or two clutches of usually 2 or 3 eggs, which are incubated by both sexes when the first egg is laid, for about 21 or 22 days. The nestlings are reared by both parents. The Black-bellied Sandgrouse is gregarious by nature and gathers in mixed flocks with the Pin-tailed Sandgrouse (*P. alchata*). It feeds on plant matter (berries, seeds and shoots).
Note: The drawing shows a male.

338 PTILONORHYNCHUS VIOLACEUS
Satin Bowerbird

Classification Order Passeriformes, Family Ptilonorhynchidae.
Characteristics The Ptilonorhynchidae is related to the birds of paradise, with a total length ranging from 23 to 38 cm. (9–15″). The Satin Bowerbird is about 32 cm. long (12.5″), with beautiful dark blue plumage that has metallic highlights. The female has a pale brown coloration, pale yellow lower down.
Habitat Forest.
Distribution Eastern Australia.
Life and habits The remarkable habits of bowerbirds were observed for the first time in 1839 by the ornithologist John Gould; in-depth studies of their behavior have since been made by ornithologists A. J. Marshall and E. T. Gilliard. Many species in this family make, out of branches, stalks and other plant materials, a kind of small hut, with an area in front of it where the male performs his display. These constructions are not used as nests but only as part of the male's courtship ritual.The Satin Bowerbird not only makes, out of sticks, its special platform with walls, but with its beak it also wields a small piece of bark, which it steeps in charcoal and fruit fragments mixed with saliva and then uses to "paint" its structures blue.

339 PUFFINUS PUFFINUS
Manx Shearwater

Classification Order Procellariiformes, Family Procellarii-dae.

Characteristics About 36 cm. long (14″). The upper plumage is very dark (almost black), with white lower parts. Seen in flight from below, it shows black wing edges (in the subspecies *P. p. puffinus*). The subspecies *P. p. mauretanicus* found in the western Mediterranean has brown upper parts and white lower areas, but with dark speckling; the subspecies *P. p. yelkouan* of the eastern Mediterranean has dark brown upper parts and very white lower parts.

Habitat Islands and rocky coasts, open sea.

Distribution Coastal regions and islands in the Atlantic, Mediterranean and Pacific areas.

Life and habits It lives in groups and is diurnal at sea, and crepuscular and nocturnal in its nesting area. It looks for food—fish and other marine animals—on the surface, diving occasionally. It nests in holes in the ground amid rocks and on grassy slopes—holes that are dug by both adults. It lays a single clutch of one egg, which is incubated by both parents for 52–54 days. The nidicolous nestling is reared for 59–62 days, after which the young bird stays in the nest burrow for about two more weeks before venturing forth.

---

340 PYGOSCELIS ADELIAE
Adelie Penguin

Classification Order Sphenisciformes, Family Spheniscidae.

Characteristics About 70 cm. long (27.5″), it weighs up to 5 kg. (11 lbs.). The feathers reach a length of 3.6 cm. (1.4″). The species in the genus *Pygoscelis* have quite a long tail, and no brightly colored areas in their plumage. The Adelie Penguin has black upper parts, white lower parts, and a black head with a white outline around the eye. The beak is short.

Habitat Coasts and seas.

Distribution Extreme southern coasts of Antarctica and nearby islands.

Life and habits It nests in colonies of mature nesting pairs (at least 4 years old) and immature birds who have to establish themselves and form pairs. The latter arrive later in the colony and nest in its "suburbs." In addition, and as confirmed by the in-depth studies made by ornithologist W. J. L. Sladen, there are also nonbreeding adults (usually 2 or 3 years old) and immature birds. The males build the nests, stealing materials from one another. The eggs are incubated for about 33–38 days by the male, with the female doing a shift after about 2 or 3 weeks. At four weeks the young start to fend for themselves a little, and at about five weeks they take to the water, helped by their parents.

341 PYRRHOCORAX GRACULUS
Yellow-billed or Alpine Chough

Classification   Order Passeriformes, Family Corvidae.
Characteristics   About 37 cm. long (14.5″). The plumage is black with greenish and bluish highlights. The not very long beak is yellow and the legs red. Young birds are brown with blackish legs. A similar bird is the Red-billed Chough (*P. pyrrhocorax* which has similar plumage with red legs (orange-red in young individuals) and a longer red beak (yellowish orange in the young).
Habitat   Mountainous areas; moves lower in winter.
Distribution   Mountains of southern Europe, central Asia and North Africa.
Life and habits   It nests in holes and cracks in mountainous regions, laying 3–6 eggs (most regularly 4); these are incubated by the female, who is fed by the male, for about 17–21 days. The nestlings remain in the nest for about 23–31 days. The Alpine Chough feeds mainly on invertebrates (insects and mollusks), vegetable matter (fruit and seeds), carrion and rubbish.

342 PYRRHULA PYRRHULA
Common Bullfinch

Classification   Order Passeriformes, Family Fringillidae.
Characteristics   About 14.5 cm. long (5.7″). The male's lower plumage is pink, the lower belly and undertail are white, and the upper parts bluish with a white rump. The head is bluish black. The female has a duller coloration, brownish lower down with white lower belly and undertail. The young resemble the female but have a brown head and yellowish-brown lowerparts.
Habitat   Woods, gardens and parks.
Distribution   Europe and Asia.
Life and habits   It nests in trees, building a cup-shaped nest of grass, moss, wool and twigs and lined with bark fragments and lichens. It lays 4–5 eggs (rarely 6 or 7), which are incubated mainly by the female for 12–14 days. The nidicolous nestlings stay in the nest 12–18 days. The Common Bullfinch lays a single clutch in its most northerly and easterly distribution areas, but two and even three elsewhere. It feeds on shoots, buds and seeds. It has a distinctive song which sounds like a plaintive *tioo-tioo.*

343 QUELEA QUELEA
Red-billed Quelea

Classification   Order Passeriformes, Family Ploceidae.
Characteristics   This bird is about 12 cm. long (5″), with a generally pinkish-brown coloration, darker uppermost with blackish speckling, and paler lower down, suffused with pink. The top of the head is pinkish, but scarcely so above the beak; the sides of the face are black, as is the neck. The large strong beak is red, the tail brown.
Habitat   Steppe and savanna.
Distribution   Africa.
Life and habits   This is a gregarious bird; outside the breeding period, it gathers in very large flocks, which often stay together forming colonies during the nesting period. Sometimes these colonies are extremely large and will cover several hundred acres and contain (as mentioned by ornithologists E. Thomas Gilliard and Hans Edmund Wolters) up to 10,000,000 nests. The nests are usually round and built in a tree. It is a monogamous bird. The nestlings stay in the nest for about 16 days, after an incubation period of about 13 days, and are reared by both parents. The Red-billed Quelea feeds mainly on seeds, often doing a great deal of damage to crops. Numerous ornithologists have studied this species, including H. J. Disney and A. J. Marshall.

---

344 RALLUS AQUATICUS
Water Rail

Classification   Order Gruiformes, Family Rallidae.
Characteristics   About 28 cm. long (11″). It has an olive brown plumage with black stripes uppermost, the sides are barred with black and white, the undertail is white, the sides of the head and the neck are grayish. The legs are brown or tending to greenish. The beak is long and red, the legs have long toes.
Habitat   Marshlands, ponds, rivers and lakes with plenty of aquatic vegetation.
Distribution   Europe, Asia, northwestern Africa.
Life and habits   It breeds amid aquatic vegetation in a nest built by both partners and made of leaves, grass, water plants, et cetera. The male begins the building of a nest several times before one projected nest is accepted by the female. She lays two clutches of 5–16 eggs (more commonly between 6 and 10). Incubation is undertaken by both adults, but mainly by the female, and lasts 19 or 20 days. The nidifugous nestlings are reared by their parents and become independent at about 7 or 8 weeks. The Water Rail has a distinctive call. It feeds on various invertebrates (insects, frogs, crustaceans, mollusks, annelids) as well as on small fish and vegetable matter (grasses, seeds, berries and fruit).

345 RAMPHASTOS SULPHURATUS
Keel-billed Toucan

Classification   Order Piciformes, Family Ramphastidae.
Characteristics   Toucans have diagonal serrations on the outer edges of their large bill. They have 10 rectrices, and strong legs with two front and two hind toes. Alexander Skutch identifies within the Ramphastidae 7 genera and 40 species. The Keel-billed Toucan is about 45–50 cm. long (18–20″), with black plumage and a broad yellowish band at the sides of the head, by the neck and on the upper breast, edged with red lower down. The beak is bright greenish yellow, red and blue with small black stripes. Its upper tail, like that of the Toco Toucan (*R. toco*), is white, and the undertail is reddish.
Habitat   Forest.
Distribution   Mexico to South America.
Life and habits   Toucans make a distinctive call. They nest in holes in trees; ornithologist L. Short mentions that they usually lay 3 eggs, which are incubated by both parents for about 16 days. The nidicolous nestlings open their eyes after 3 weeks and stay in the nest for about 44–50 days.

346 RAMPHASTOS TOCO
Toco Toucan

Classification   Order Piciformes, Family Ramphastidae.
Characteristics   The Ramphastidae, or toucans, have a distinctively large beak (or bill), often brightly colored, formed by a series of bony layers, which make it extremely tough, as well as light. The male Toco Toucan has a bill about 23 cm. long (9″), the female's being about 21.5 cm. (8.5″). The tongue is feather-shaped and in some species can be 15 cm. long (6″). The Toco Toucan is about 60 cm. long (24″), with black plumage and a large white marking at the sides of the head and on the neck. The bill is orange-yellow, with black at the base and on the tip of the upper jaw.
Habitat   Forest.
Distribution   South America.
Life and habits   It lives in flocks or family groups in trees, often pecking noisily against branches, or "clashing" bills together. It feeds mainly on fruit, but will also take invertebrates, and sometimes the eggs and young of other birds. It nests in holes in trees, often using nests abandoned by woodpeckers.

347 RECURVIROSTRA AVOSETTA
Pied Avocet

Classification Order Charadriiformes, Family Recurvirostridae.

Characteristics An unmistakable bird, about 43 cm. long (17″), it has a very distinctive plumage—white with black markings, a black head, and a long, black, upward-curving beak; the legs are grayish. The young have an irregularly white-marked coloration.

Habitat Marshes, lagoons, ponds.

Distribution Europe, Asia and Africa.

Life and habits It nests in colonies in marshlands or in a sandy spot; the nest is built on the sand or in a small hollow on the surface. In it the Pied Avocet lays a single clutch of 3–5 eggs (usually 4). The nidifugous young are reared by both parents and become independent at about 6 weeks. They feed mainly on insects and other invertebrates; these are caught by probing through marshy areas with the distinctive beak that is moved from side to side. It flies with its legs extended beyond the tail and, when resting, places its long beak between its shoulder blades.

348 REGULUS REGULUS
Goldcrest

Classification Order Passeriformes, Family Sylviidae.

Characteristics About 9 cm. long (3.5″). The upper parts of the plumage are grayish olive green, the lower parts are very pale olive gray. The brownish remiges have a greenish-white edging and a black central marking. The forehead is brown, the crest yellow with an orange center (yellowish in the female). Young individuals have a greenish olive-brown head with no crest. A similar species is the Firecrest (*R. ignicapillus*), whose crest is orange-red delimited by a black stripe.

Habitat Coniferous and mixed woods, parks.

Distribution Europe and Asia.

Life and habits It breeds in trees, in a round nest of plant material, leaves, and lichens, built by both sexes. It lays two clutches of usually 7–10 eggs (occasionally up to 13), which are incubated by the female for 14–17 days. The nidicolous nestlings are reared by both parents and stay in the nest for 16–21 days (opening their eyes at 7–8 days). The reproductive cycle is also similar for the Firecrest. It feeds on invertebrates (insects).

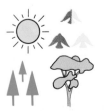

351 RHODOPECHYS GITHAGINEA
Trumpeter Finch

Classification   Order Passeriformes, Family Fringillidae.
Characteristics   About 14 cm. long (5.5″), it has a compact body and a stubby beak. The male is sandy grayish-brown, with pink shading on the rump, wings, face and lower parts. The beak, which is normally pale horn-yellow, becomes bright red in the breeding period. The female is duller and resembles the male in his winter plumage.
Habitat   Arid regions and steppes with sparse vegetation.
Distribution   North Africa, Asia Minor to Afghanistan, appears sometimes in certain parts of southern Europe (has nested in Spain and has been repeatedly observed in Malta and Sicily).
Life and habits   Quite gregarious by nature, in the breeding season it pairs off and isolates itself. It makes a crude nest on the ground, in cracks in rocks or walls. It lays 4–6 eggs, which are incubated for 13 or 14 days. The nestlings leave the nest after about 14 days and are independent about 11 days later. It feeds on seeds, young leaves and shoots. It has a distinctive song, like a nasal call, hence the name *Trumpeter*.

---

352 RHYNOCHETOS JUBATUS
Kagu

Classification   Order Gruiformes, Family Rhynchochetidae.
Characteristics   From afar it superficially resembles a Night Heron (*Nycticorax nycticorax*), the plumage being grayish white, and darker uppermost. Long, crestlike feathers top the head. The beak and legs are orange.
Habitat   Forests with plenty of undergrowth.
Distribution   New Caledonia.
Life and habits   It has crepuscular and nocturnal habits for the most part. At these times it moves about the forest in small groups in search of food. It breeds on the ground in a nest built by the female, who lays 3–4 eggs; these are incubated by both parents for about 35 days. The Kagu is a particularly rare species, and we have little knowledge of its numbers in the wild. Its progressive disappearance has been hastened considerably by the introduction of domestic predatory animals to the islands, by the destruction of forests, and by direct persecution from man. Thanks to the busy work of the New Caledonian Ornithological Society, the species is now under protection.

355 ROSTRHAMUS SOCIABILIS
Snail or Everglade Kite

Classification   Order Falconiformes, Family Accipitridae.
Characteristics   It has broad wings and a slightly forked tail, and is about 40–45 cm. long (16–18″). The male is slate-black, with the base of the tail white and the bare skin by the eye purple. The female and young are browner and have pale lower parts. The average weight of the nominal subspecies is 0.3 kg. for the male and 0.4 kg. for the female (0.7 and 0.9 lbs.). The beak is very curved and long. The wing span measures 110 cm. (44″). A similar species is the Slender-billed Kite (*R. hamatus*).
Habitat   Freshwater marshes and grassland.
Distribution   Tropical America.
Life and habits   It frequents marshy and very open places, in which it may gather in large flocks. It sometimes also nests in small colonies. The nest is a very light structure made amid grass and aquatic bushes. It lays 2–5 eggs (usually 2 or 3), which are incubated by both adults. The nestlings fly at about a month and follow their parents around for a longer period. The very specialized diet consists exclusively of water snails of the genus *Pomacea* which are removed from the shell with the curved beak. The subspecies *R. s. plumbeus* is extremely rare and confined to the Loxahatchee National Wildlife Refuge in southern Florida.

356 RUPICOLA RUPICOLA
Orange Cock of the Rock

Classification   Order Passeriformes, Family Cotingidae.
Characteristics   The family Cotingidae is a very interesting group of birds having fairly bright plumage with showy colorations, dilatable throat sacs, and bare or hanging wattles and caruncles. Species range in length from 7.5 to 50 cm. (3–20″). The Orange Cock of the Rock is a brightly colored bird. The male has orange plumage, with dark black and white wings and a dark tail bar. On the head is a round crest of erectile feathers, shaped like a helmet. On the forehead, back and wings there are fringed feathers. The female is brownish. A similar species is the Scarlet Cock of the Rock (*R. peruviana*), the male of which is scarlet and about 31 cm. long (12″), and the female of which is 26 cm. (10″).
Habitat   Forests.
Distribution   Northern South America.
Life and habits   Nesting takes place, often in small colonies, in the clefts of rocks. Generally, two eggs are laid. Noteworthy in the Orange Cock of the Rock is the male's mating display, a kind of dance which he executes by spreading his wings, turning his head and tail, hopping, and stepping around in an odd manner.

357 RYNCHOPS NIGRA
Black Skimmer

Classification   Order Charadriiformes, Family Rynchopidae.
Characteristics   The Black Skimmer is about 45 cm. long
(18″). It has long, pointed wings, webbed feet and a very odd
beak in which the lower mandible is much longer than the
upper. The upper parts are black, the lower white. The beak
and legs are red. In immature birds the upper parts are brown.
Habitat   Seacoasts, coastal lagoons and estuaries, marshes.
Distribution   America (Pacific and Atlantic coasts).
Life and habits   To find food this bird flies low over shallow
water with its beak held open and the lower jaw cutting through
the surface, funneling aquatic creatures into the mouth. Most
of its food is gathered at sunset or at night. Colonial by nature,
it establishes its nest in a bare hollow in the sand, laying in it
2–5 eggs (usually 4 or 5) which are incubated solely by the female. The nidifugous nestlings are fed by both parents. The
diet consists mainly of small surface fishes, crustaceans, and
plankton.

358 SARCORHAMPUS PAPA
King Vulture

Classification   Order Falconiformes, Family Cathartidae.
Characteristics   About 80 cm. long (31.5″). Its wings are
broad and quite short. The lower parts are white, as are the
upper, except for a small collar of feathers, the tail, and a broad
band on the rear edge of the wings, all of which are black. The
bare skin on the head and neck is orange and purplish blue;
immature birds are a uniform gray. It reaches a weight of 3.7
kg. (8 lbs.).
Habitat   Tropical forests and wooded lowlands.
Distribution   America, from Mexico to northern Argentina.
Life and habits   Although a very distinctive and quite common species, it has not been studied in depth. We know that it
builds its nest in trees (often very high up) and perhaps in rocky
places too. A single egg is laid and the incubation period lasts
56–58 days (data recorded in captivity). The nestling is fed by
both parents, who take turns to hatch the egg, and stays in the
nest for a long time. The female may lay a second egg, if the
first is taken from her, after about 6 weeks. The diet of this vulture consists solely of carrion of all sorts, which, with its very
strong beak, it manages to tear apart and eat before other vultures.

361 SCOLOPAX RUSTICOLA
Eurasian Woodcock

Classification   Order Charadriiformes, Family Scolopacidae.
Characteristics   About 34 cm. long (13.5″). Its plumage is very mimetic, with marbled brown, black and tawny upper parts, and light brown lower parts with fine dark brown barring. On the top of the head there is a series of transverse black bars. The beak is long, and the eyes are set well back on the round head. Young birds resemble the adults.
Habitat   Woods (oak, birch, larch and coniferous) with plenty of undergrowth, hilly regions, heathland.
Distribution   Europe and Asia.
Life and habits   The Eurasian Woodcock is active mainly at twilight; it flies swiftly with its beak held downward. It prefers being on the ground, and is not at ease perched in trees. It nests on the ground in hollows amid vegetation. It lays two clutches of 3–5 eggs (ordinarily 4; and in the second often only 3), which are incubated by the female for about 30–33 days. The nidifugous nestlings are reared by the female and can fly at about 10 days, becoming independent in about 5 or 6 weeks. It feeds mainly on invertebrates (worms, insects, larvae, mollusks and crustaceans) and vegetable matter (seeds, roots, grasses).

---

362 SCOPUS UMBRETTA
Hammerhead

Classification   Order Ciconiiformes, Family Scopidae.
Characteristics   About 50 cm. long (20″). The male and female are similar and brown in color; they have a distinctive head with a long, laterally squashed beak and a tuft of feathers at the back resembling a hammer overall. The young nestlings have orange eyes and yellowish green legs.
Habitat   Along watercourses, marshlands.
Distribution   Africa and Madagascar.
Life and habits   As a rule the Hammerhead lives alone or in pairs, though sometimes it may be found in groups of up to 7. Its flight is slow and undulating; its call harsh and raucous. Active mainly at twilight and at night, it feeds on aquatic animals. It makes a distinctive nest consisting of a huge mass of branches, sticks and other vegetable matter, with an outer diameter of up to 1.5 meters (60″). Inside there is a hole of about 30 cm. in diameter (12″). It lays 3–6 eggs, which are incubated for about 30 days. The nestlings remain in the nest for up to 50 days from birth.

363 SEIURUS AUROCAPILLUS
Ovenbird

Classification Order Passeriformes, Family Parulidae.
Characteristics About 15 cm. long (6″), this small bird has a long, thin beak well suited to its insectivorous diet. The upper parts are olive, the lower white with black markings. A golden stripe runs along the crown and is easily visible. The sexes have the same colored plumage.
Habitat Woods.
Distribution North America, wintering in the tropics.
Life and habits Migratory by nature, it spends the winter months in the tropical parts of Central America. It nests in broadleaf woods (oak, chestnut and maple) with thick undergrowth of grass and bushes. The nest is made with plant fibers, leaves and lichens and is built on the ground at the foot of a tree, hidden among grass and foliage. It lays 3–6 eggs (usually 3 or 4), which are incubated for 12–14 days by the female. The nestlings are fed by both parents and fly at 7–10 days. Every year there is just one clutch. The diet consists of insects, worms and other small invertebrates caught on the ground and in foliage, and to a lesser extent of seeds, berries and wild fruit.

364 SERICULUS CHRYSOCEPHALUS
Regent Bowerbird

Classification Order Passeriformes, Family Ptilonorhynchidae.
Characteristics Many ornithologists put the species of Ptilonorhynchidae, or bowerbirds, in a subfamily—the Ptilonorhynchinae—of the family Paradiseidae. The species of the genera *Ptilonorhynchus*, *Sericulus* and *Chlamydera* are included among the bowerbirds of the group that builds "bowers." The plumage of the Regent Bowerbird, which is about 30 cm. long (12″), is quite bright compared with the other species of bowerbird: it is black with yellowish top of the head and nape, and a yellowish marking on the wings.
Habitat Forest.
Distribution Eastern Australia.
Life and habits The ornithologist G. Evelyn Hutchinson, speaking of the behavior of bowerbirds, says that "in terms of variety and refinement there is no equal in the animal kingdom." The so-called "bower" builders use a platform—with a diameter of about 1.5 meters (60″)—of twigs and plant matter interwoven; in the middle they build two side walls with twigs and sticks inserted in the ground and crisscrossed together. In the middle the entrance to the bower and the sides of the walls are adorned with pebbles, berries, shells, glass chippings and bits of metal.

365 SERINUS CANARIA
Wild Canary

Classification   Order Passeriformes, Family Fringillidae.
Characteristics   About 10 cm. long (4″). Various ornithologists classify it as a subspecies of the Serin (*Serinus serinus*). The males have brownish-gray upper parts, a slightly yellowish rump, a yellow breast, and a pale yellow head with blackish markings. The female has a more uniform and brownish plumage. The Wild Canary is the forebear of all the different sorts of canary that now inhabit cages all over the world.
Habitat   Forest.
Distribution   In the wild—Canary Islands, Madeira and the Azores. Introduced into Bermuda.
Life and habits   In the wild it nests in trees or low vegetation, building a cup-shaped nest in which it lays usually 4 or 5 eggs (rarely 3), which are incubated solely by the female (who is fed by the male) for 13 or 14 days. The nidicolous nestlings are reared by both parents and stay in the nest for 18–21 days. In 1478, when the Spanish invaded the Canaries, they started to export these birds throughout Europe. There followed intensive rearing in captivity, giving rise to the remarkable varieties of forms with their great variety of plumage coloration.

---

366 SERINUS SERINUS
European Serin

Classification   Order Passeriformes, Family Fringillidae.
Characteristics   About 11.5 cm. long (4.5″). Its striped plumage is conspicuous: the upper parts are yellowish brown striped with brownish black; the back is yellow; the rump is greenish yellow; the lower parts are greenish yellow with brownish stripes and the belly is whitish. The remiges and rectrices are brownish black edged with greenish. The female is less yellow than the male, more striped on the breast and the head, with a paler rump.
Habitat   Woods, parks and gardens.
Distribution   Europe, Asia Minor, norhwestern Africa.
Life and habits   It nests in trees or amid vegetation in a cup-shaped nest of plant material, laying two clutches of 3–5 eggs (usually 4), which are incubated mainly by the female for about 13 days. The nidicolous nestlings are fed by both parents, leaving the nest at about 14 days, but depending on the parents for a further 6–7 days. The European Serin feeds on vegetable matter (seeds).

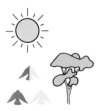

369 SOMATERIA MOLLISSIMA
Common Eider

Classification   Order Anseriformes, Family Anatidae.
Characteristics   The male, some 62 cm. long (24.5″), has a black top of the head, sides, belly and tail, a pinkish breast, white areas on the sides of the rump, and greenish flashes on the sides of the head and nape of the neck. The postnuptial plumage of the male is blackish with white on the wings and sides. The female, 56 cm. long (22″), has brownish plumage, with blackish stripes and bars. Young birds resemble the female, but are darker uppermost.
Habitat   Coasts, beaches, cliffs, rivers and lakes near the sea.
Distribution   Europe, northern Asia and North America.
Life and habits   It nests on the ground in hollows often amid vegetation, laying a single clutch of 3–10 eggs (usually 4, 5 or 6), which are incubated by the female for 27 or 28 days. The nidifugous nestlings are reared by the female and are independent at 60–75 days. The Common Eider feeds on invertebrates (like mollusks and crustaceans) as well as vegetable matter.

---

370 SPEOTYTO CUNICULARIA
Burrowing Owl

Classification   Order Strigiformes, Family Strigidae.
Characteristics   About 25 cm. long (10″), this is a small, compact-looking bird. The upper parts are brown with white markings, the lower off-white with dark markings. Above the yellow eyes there are two white eyebrows. The legs are quite long.
Habitat   Prairie, desert and other open terrain.
Distribution   North and South America.
Life and habits   This is mainly a ground-dwelling bird, with diurnal habits; it nests in small colonies (maximum of 12 pairs). The nest is usually made in the abandoned dens of prairie dogs or other burrowing mammals. It lays 6–11 eggs (usually 7, 8 or 9), which are incubated by both adults for 3 or 4 weeks. We do not know the exact date at which the nestlings can fly. The diet consists mainly of large insects (orthopterans, coleopterans) and small mammals (mainly rodents) and birds. There is an interesting relationship between the Burrowing Owl and the prairie dog, which tolerates the former near its own den, even though the owl may sometimes catch the dog's pups.

371 SPHENISCUS HUMBOLDTI
Peruvian or Humboldt Penguin

Classification   Order Sphenisciformes, Family Spheniscidae.
Characteristics   About 65 cm. long (26″) and weighs 4.2 kg.
(9.25 lbs.). The length of the feathers reaches 2.1 cm.
(0.825″). The plumage is similar to that of all the other species
of *Spheniscus*: the upper parts are black, the lower are light
with a black stripe surrounding them, and the face is black and
white. Similar species are the Cape or Jackass Penguin (*S.
demersus*), the Magellanic Penguin (*S. magellanicus*) and the
Galapagos Penguin (*S. mendiculus*). The latter, about 53 cm.
long (21″), is found only on the islands of Fernandina and Isabela in the Galapagos Archipelago; there are only about 2,000
surviving individuals.
Habitat   Coasts and open sea.
Distribution   Along the western shores of South America
(Peru and Chile).

Life and habits   The four species of the genus *Spheniscus*
differ essentially in the pattern on the face and the throat striping; they all have the habit of frequently rubbing each other's
neck and beak. They are found in regions that are less cold
than those of other penguins, and they have very short feathers. Bernard Stonehouse points out that the Humboldt Penguin
has very short plumage compared with other penguins, such as
the Adelie Penguin, and a very small *panniculus adiposus*. It
nests almost exclusively on islands off the Peruvian coast.

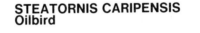

372 STEATORNIS CARIPENSIS
Oilbird

Classification   Order Caprimulgiformes, Family Steatornithidae.
Characteristics   The family Steatornithidae has just one very
distinctive species, the Guacharo, or Oilbird, which reaches a
length of about 45 cm. (18″), a wing span of 113 cm. (44.5″),
and a weight of 400 grams (14 oz.). The plumage is brown with
whitish markings, darker uppermost, paler lower down. The tail
is rounded with 10 rectrices; the beak is very strong with a
curved upper mandible, the tarsal bones are very short and
have no horny scales; the feet are weak, with the first toe facing forward but diagonally (in most other Caprimulgiformes the
toe faces rearward).
Habitat   Caves, from which it emerges at night to search for
food.
Distribution   Northern South America.

Life and habits   This strange bird was discovered in September 1799 by the explorer and naturalist Alexander von Humboldt in the Caripé caves in Venezuela. It feeds on fruit, which it
looks for at dusk and at night outside the caves in which it lives.
The young are fatty, and this fat is used by natives—hence the
scientific name *Steatornis* and its common English equivalent,
"Oilbird." The nest is made in rocks in the cave. It lays 2–4
eggs, which are incubated for 33–34 days. The nestlings fly
after 90–125 days. Ornithologist D. Griffin discovered in 1954
that the Oilbird guides itself in the dark by an echo-location
system.

373 STEGANURA PARADISEA
Paradise Whydah

Classification   Order Passeriformes, Family Ploceidae.
Characteristics   The male Paradise Whydah is a very beautiful bird in nuptial plumage. It is black uppermost, with two magnificent pairs of very long and wide central rectrices. The head is black, the nape and sides of the neck are yellowish, the breast is reddish and the lower parts are pale. The beak and legs are grayish. The female has a very modest coloration, tending to grayish brown, and darker uppermost. There are dark stripes on the sides of the head.
Habitat   Savanna, scrub and steppe.
Distribution   Africa south of the Sahara.
Life and habits   The whydahs are mainly granivorous birds, but when reared by adopted parents, being parasitic, they feed on invertebrates. The Paradise Whydah's nestling has down and violet blue markings on the palate identical to those of the nestling of the Melba Finch (*Pytilia melba*), a member of the Family Estrildidae used to rear the young of the Paradise Whydah. These imitate their hosts even in their behavioral patterns, and manage to copy the vocal expressions of the host species.

374 STEPHANOAETUS CORONATUS
African Crowned Eagle

Classification   Order Falconiformes, Family Accipitridae.
Characteristics   This eagle with short, rounded wings and a long tail, measures 80–90 cm. in length (31.5–35.5"). Its upper parts are brown, the lower being off-white with close black markings. On the head there is a double crest of dark feathers. In immature individuals the lower parts are almost entirely white. The iris is pale yellow. The female is slightly larger than the male.
Habitat   Forests and rocky hills.
Distribution   Tropical Africa.
Life and habits   It lives in all sorts of forest environment, and along rivers, sometimes at altitudes of more than 3,000 meters (10,000 ft.). The nest is built in trees with dry branches and green fronds; in it are laid 1 or 2 eggs, which are incubated by both adults, but mainly the female, for 49 days. The young fly at 110 days, but are fed outside the nest for a further 270–350 days, with the result that each pair reproduces only every two years. The prey are caught either by ambush from a branch on the edge of a clearing, or by flying low over the foliage of trees. 98 percent of the diet is made up of mammals, like small antelopes (*Nesotragus moschatus*), hyrax, Suni monkeys and other monkeys. The rest of the diet is accounted for by birds and reptiles such as monitor lizards.

375 STERCORARIUS PARASITICUS
Arctic Skua or Parasitic Jaeger

Classification   Order Charadriiformes, Family Stercorariidae.
Characteristics   About 46 cm. long (18")—including the tail
with the elongated central rectrices—it has, like the Pomarine
Skua (*S. pomarinus*), two color phases, one light, the other
dark. The plumage is usually quite uniformly brownish in the
dark phase, with lighter lower parts in the light phase. The legs
are blackish. In flight it shows its tail with the long central rectrices. A similar species is the Long-tailed Skua (*S. longi-
caudus*), about 53 cm. long (21"), with very long central rectrices.
Habitat   Tundra, open sea, coasts.
Distribution   Arctic Circle, moving south in winter.
Life and habits   It nests on the ground, in hollows, amid low
vegetation. It lays a single clutch, consisting usually of 2 eggs
(sometimes only 1), which are incubated by both adults for
about 24–28 days. The partly nidicolous nestlings are reared
by both parents; they stay in the nest for only a few days, but
remain nearby. They fly at about 30 days and are independent
at 7–8 weeks. The Arctic Skua feeds on small mammals, small
birds and their eggs, carrion, fish, invertebrates (mollusks and
crustaceans) and also some vegetable matter (berries, etc.).

376 STERCORARIUS SKUA
Great Skua

Classification   Order Charadriiformes, Family Stercorariidae.
Characteristics   About 57 cm. long (22.5") this is a stronger
and larger bird than the Herring Gull (*Larus argentatus*). The
plumage is almost uniformly dark with more reddish lower
parts. The tail is short; the beak is large, black and hooked; at
the base of the primary remiges is a clear white marking. The
legs are blackish, the wings broad and rounded. Young birds
have less white on the wings.
Habitat   Open sea, coastal regions, moors near the sea.
Distribution   Breeds on islands in the North Atlantic and winters in southern seas.
Life and habits   It nests on the ground in hollows amid vegetation, laying a single clutch of usually 2 eggs (rarely 1), which
are incubated by both adults for about 28–30 days. The partly
nidicolous nestlings are reared by both parents and become
independent at 6–7 weeks. Like the other skuas, the Great
Skua behaves piratically; it pursues other sea birds to make
them drop food they have already caught. The Great Skua
feeds on fish, crustaceans, mollusks, rubbish and carrion.

377 STERNA PARADISAEA
Arctic Tern

Classification   Order Charadriiformes, Family Laridae.
Characteristics   About 35.5 cm. long (14″), it is grayish in color, darker uppermost and pale lower down. Compared with the Common Tern (*S. hirundo*) it has a shorter beak (red in summer and blackish in winter), shorter legs and wings and a longer tail. The red summer legs also turn blackish in winter. The black cap is shaded in winter. Immature birds have white upper wing coverts (not gray as with immature Common Terns). The Common Tern has a red beak with a black tip and lighter lower parts.
Habitat   Coastal waters, lakes, marshlands.
Distribution   Northern parts of Europe, Asia and America, migrating to the Antarctic Ocean in winter.
Life and habits   It nests in colonies on the ground, on sandy expanses near water. It lays a single clutch of 1–3 eggs (but ordinarily 2), which are incubated by both sexes for about 20–22 days. The seminidifugous nestlings are reared by both parents, swim at 2 days and fly at about 20–22 days, but continue to be fed by the parents for a while. It feeds mainly on fish and invertebrates (mollusks and insects).

378 STERNA SANDVICENSIS
Sandwich Tern

Classification   Order Charadriiformes, Family Laridae.
Characteristics   About 40 cm. long (16″). The Sandwich Tern's plumage is grayish uppermost and light lower down. The beak is black with a yellow tip, and the top of the head has a black cap with feathers that can be erected like a crest when the bird is excited. The legs are black. In winter the forehead and the front of the upper head are white. Young birds resemble the adults in winter, but they have speckled upper parts. The tail is forked.
Habitat   Coasts, sandy islands, rocky or shingly shores, marshlands, et cetera.
Distribution   Europe, Black and Caspian seas, America, wintering south to the southern oceans.
Life and habits   It nests in colonies on the ground near water, laying a single clutch of usually 2 eggs (sometimes 1 and rarely 3) at intervals of a couple of days. These are incubated by both parents, once the second egg has been laid, for about 20–24 days. The seminidifugous nestlings are reared by both parents and fly at about 35 days. The Sandwich Tern feeds mainly on fish and invertebrates (mollusks and annelids).

379 STREPTOPELIA TURTUR
Common Turtle Dove

Classification   Order Columbiformes, Family Columbidae.
Characteristics   About 27 cm. long (10.5″). The plumage is brown with a brown back and rump; the head, neck and wing coverts are grayish. The lower parts are dark uppermost, the abdomen and undertail being white. There are small black markings on the sides of the neck. The scapulars and wing coverts are tawny, with the central part of the feathers black. In flight, it shows the white undertail and tail.
Habitat   Open woodland, parks, *maquis*, gardens.
Distribution   Europe, western Asia and Africa.
Life and habits   It breeds in trees in a nest like a platform or uses as a base old nests of other birds. It almost invariably lays two clutches, of usually 2 eggs (more rarely 1), which are incubated by both adults for 13 or 14 days. The nidicolous young stay in the nest for 19–21 days. The call is a distinctive and repetitive *rrurr-rrurr*. The Common Turtle Dove's diet consists largely of vegetable matter (grain, leaves and seeds) as well as an occasional invertebrate.

---

380 STRIGOPS HABROPTILUS
Kakapo or Owl Parrot

Classification   Order Psittaciformes, Family Psittacidae.
Characteristics   It has a strong body, short wings, fairly long tarsal bones and large toes, which end in tough, curved talons. It resembles a nocturnal bird of prey and has its eyes set less laterally than other parrots. The upper plumage is dark, greenish brown, and lighter with some yellowish lower down.
Habitat   Forest areas from sea level to 2,000 meters (6,500 ft.).
Distribution   Once common in the North and South islands of New Zealand and in the islands of Chatham and Stewart, it is now present only in a few western areas of the North Island.
Life and habits   Mainly ground-dwelling, it is rarely seen in flight. It digs out a nest in a rotten tree trunk, usually at the foot or among the roots. The female lays 2–4 eggs. The Kakapo usually nests every two years. It feeds on leaves, shoots, berries, fruit and other vegetable matter. It is in danger of extinction because of the progressive destruction of its habitat and by man's introduction of predatory or competitive animals. In 1960 there were two hundred individuals. At the present time their numbers have probably dropped to below a hundred.

383 STRUTHIO CAMELUS
Ostrich

Classification Order Struthioniformes, Family Struthionidae.
Characteristics The male Ostrich, with its distinctive black and white plumage, is up to 3 meters tall (10 feet) and weighs up to 150 kg. (330 lbs)—the largest living bird. The female is brownish. The foot has two toes. The Ostrich is one of the few birds with a retractile male sex organ. In the Ostrich—and this is unique among birds—the urine is concentrated in the cloaca and released separately from the excrement.
Habitat Savanna, open scrub, sandy expanses with sparse vegetation, also *maquis* and mountainous regions.
Distribution Parts of Africa, mainly eastern and southern.
Life and habits It feeds on vegetable matter plus invertebrates and a few small vertebrates. It lives in groups, nesting on the ground, where it digs a hollow in which it lays up to 20 eggs, each of which weighs 1–1.5 kg (2.2–3.3 lbs.). The two adults take turns incubating them. The young hatch after about 42 days, and the male rears them. The Ostrich can reach a top running speed of 70 kph. (44 mph.). Merciless hunting has drastically reduced this species and caused it to vanish from areas such as Arabia.

384 STURNELLA MAGNA
Eastern Meadowlark

Classification Order Passeriformes, Family Icteridae.
Characteristics It has a long, pointed beak and tough legs, with which it moves quickly on the ground. About 25 cm. long (10″), it is brown on the upper parts with black and ocher-colored barring. The lower parts are yellow, with a large black patch on the breast; the head, which is gray, has light and dark stripes. The sexes are similar, but the female is slightly smaller and has a less distinct coloration. A similar species is the Western Meadowlark (*Sturnella neglecta*), with a different song.
Habitat Cultivation, grassland.
Distribution North and Central America.
Life and habits In the northernmost zones it is migratory and winters farther south. The males establish themselves before the females in the breeding area and await their arrival. The nest is made in a hole in the ground among grasses and bushes. The clutch has 3–7 eggs (usually 5), which are incubated solely by the female for 13 or 14 days. The nestlings fly 11 or 12 days after hatching. There are usually two clutches a year. It feeds on insects and small ground-dwelling invertebrates; in winter it feeds mainly on seeds, grain and wild berries, but the young feed entirely on animal food.

385 STURNUS VULGARIS
Common Starling

Classification   Order Passeriformes, Family Sturnidae.
Characteristics   About 21.5 cm. long (8.5″). The adult plumage is blackish with metallic highlights; in winter it is densely speckled, whitish, particularly in the female. The beak is yellow in summer and grayish brown in winter. The shape of the body is compact with a short tail. The young are light brown and have a pale throat. The flight pattern is straight, with rapid wingbeats.
Habitat   Woods, parks and gardens.
Distribution   Europe, Asia, North Africa. Introduced to North America, southern Africa, Polynesia, Australia and New Zealand.
Life and habits   This is a gregarious species; during migration it gathers in huge flocks, which are often to be seen in cities, where it winters. It nests both in colonies and in isolated pairs, in holes in trees, walls, and cliffs and amid stubble. It often uses artificial nests. It lays 4–9 eggs (more often 5, 6 or 7), which are incubated by both sexes for 12–15 days. The nidicolous nestlings are fed by both parents and stay in the nest for 20–22 days. The Common Starling has a diet that is both animal and vegetable. It was the first bird to be ringed for the scientific study of migration in 1899.

386 SULA BASSANA
Northern Gannet

Classification   Order Pelecaniformes, Family Sulidae.
Characteristics   About 94 cm. long (37″). The plumage is white with black wing tips and a slightly brownish head. The young are dark, with white speckling; at the age of 2–3 years they are still dark uppermost and light lower down (this is the intermediate phase). The adult takes on its final coloring at age 5 or 6 years. In flight it has a distinctive shape, with long, narrow wings, pointed tail, and large pointed beak. It also makes characteristic plunges into the sea.
Habitat   Open sea, rocky coasts, cliffs.
Distribution   Europe and North America; during migrations and in winter it also reaches the west coast of Africa.
Life and habits   It nests in colonies on rocky coasts, sometimes with other species of seabirds. It lays just one egg (rarely 2), which is incubated by both adults for 43–45 days. The nestling is fed by both parents with regurgitated food and takes to the sea after 13 or 14 weeks. The Northern Gannet feeds on fish. In courtship the two mates face each other, fluttering their open wings with their tails tipped downward and shaking their heads.

387 SULA NEBOUXII
Blue-footed Booby

Classification   Order Pelecaniformes, Family Sulidae.
Characteristics   The Sulidae are seabirds that reach a length of 66–100 cm. (26–40″). They number nine species, all in the genus *Sula,* found along the coastal regions of all the continents except Antarctica. The Blue-footed Booby has dark brown coloration uppermost, a whitish and brown head, and white lower parts. The boobies have a large pointed beak, which is dark-colored, with no external nostrils. The legs are blue. Although there is a nostril groove, it is not open. For breathing, the air must be inhaled through the mouth.
Habitat   Sea, islands.
Distribution   Western coasts of South America.
Life and habits   The boobies and gannets have very interesting behavioral patterns. Ornithologist Brian Nelson in one of his studies shows that the smaller number of aggressive attitudes in the courtship ceremonies of the tropical boobies as compared with gannets is due to the lesser need in the tropical species to compete for a place in the colony or for food. The Blue-footed Booby nests in colonies; the nests are made on the ground among rocks in a hollow surrounded by plant matter. It lays 1 or 2 eggs.

---

388 SURNIA ULULA
Hawk Owl

Classification   Order Strigiformes, Family Strigidae.
Characteristics   About 35–40 cm. long (14–16″), the plumage is dark uppermost, with plenty of speckling and black and white bars; the lower parts are white with close black barring. The top of the head is almost black, the face is whitish with black edges. The tail is quite long.
Habitat   Coniferous forests, birch woods.
Distribution   Northern parts of Europe, Asia, America, moving southward in winter.
Life and habits   It nests in holes in trees or in old nests of other birds. It lays one clutch, two in good years, of 3–10 eggs (rarely 13), depending on the availability of food. It is mainly the female that incubates them, with the male taking some part, for about 25–30 days. The nidicolous nestlings are reared by both parents and leave the nest at about 23–27 days. The Hawk Owl's long slender tail likens it to a falcon, as does its call: *chi-chi-chi-chi.*

389 SYLVIA BORIN
Garden Warbler

Classification Order Passeriformes, Family Sylviidae.
Characteristics About 13.5 cm. long (5.5″). The upper parts are a uniform chestnut color, the lower pale tawny. The overall aspect of the coloration is rather dull. Among other species of the genus *Sylvia* are the Lesser Whitethroat (*S. corruca*), with grayish upper parts and light lower parts, and the Spectacled Warbler (*S. conspicillata*), with dark upper parts, pinkish lower parts chin and throat.
Habitat Woods and parks.
Distribution Europe, Asia and Africa.
Life and habits The Garden Warbler nests in low trees or bushes in a cup-shaped nest made by both partners. It usually lays 2 clutches, of 3–7 eggs each (normally 4 or 5), which are incubated by both sexes for 11 or 12 days. The nidicolous nestlings are reared by both adults and leave the nest at 9–10 days. It feeds mainly on invertebrates (insects and worms) and vegetable matter (fruit and berries) particularly in autumn and winter.

390 SYLVIA CANTILLANS
Subalpine Warbler

Classification Order Passeriformes, Family Sylviidae.
Characteristics About 12 cm. long (5″). The upper parts are ash gray, and the outer rectrices white. The male has at the start of the tail a white stripe that separates the grayish coloring of the head from the pinkish-chestnut color of the upper breast and throat. The abdomen and undertail are light colored. Young birds and females are lighter, tawny-pink lower down, with a less evident white stripe.
Habitat Woods, Mediterranean *maquis*, open clearings, bushy land.
Distribution Southern Europe, Asia Minor, northwestern Africa.
Life and habits It nests in bushes, where it makes a cup-shaped nest of vegetable matter. It probably lays two clutches, each one with usually 3 or 4 eggs (more rarely 5), which are incubated, mainly by the female, for 11 or 12 days. The nidicolous nestlings are fed by both parents and stay 11 or 12 days in the nest. It feeds mainly on invertebrates.

391 SYLVIA COMMUNIS
Greater Whitethroat

Classification   Order Passeriformes, Family Sylviidae.
Characteristics   About 13.5 cm. long (5.5″). The male has brownish upper parts, a gray head and a white throat; the pale tawny lower parts are shaded with pink. The outer rectrices are white, the coverts are reddish brown. The female has a darker coloration, with a browner head and a pinkish breast. Also worthy of mention is the Black Cap (*S. atricapilla*), the male of which has black on the top of the head, and the female reddish brown.
Habitat   Counryside with hedgerows, bushes, gardens, cultivated land.
Distribution   Europe, Asia and Africa.
Life and habits   It nests among bushes and low vegetation, rarely on the ground. The male makes several nests, and the female uses one or may build a new one. She generally lays two clutches of 3–7 eggs (most commonly 4 or 5), which are incubated by both adults for 11–13 days. The nidicolous nestlings are reared by both parents and leave the nest at 10–12 days. The Whitethroat's diet consists mainly of invertebrates (insects and spiders) and sometimes also plant matter (berries).

392 SYLVIA HORTENSIS
Orphean Warbler

Classification   Order Passeriformes, Family Sylviidae.
Characteristics   About 15 cm. long (6″). It has a dark top of the head which turns gray lower down. The throat and outer rectrices are white, the lower parts light. In the female the top of the head is lighter and the upper parts browner. The undertail is suffused with pink. A similar species is the Barred Warbler (*S. risoria*), with its grayish coloration and grayish-white lower parts markedly barred with dark gray.
Habitat   Cultivated land, woods.
Distribution   Southern Europe, North Africa, Asia.
Life and habits   It nests in the low branches of trees and among bushes. It usually lays two clutches, each with 4–6 eggs (usually 4 or 5), which are incubated by both sexes. The nidicolous nestlings are reared by both parents. The Orphean Warbler's diet consists of invertebrates (insects) and vegetable matter (fruit).

393 SYLVIA SARDA
Marmora's Warbler

Classification Order Passeriformes, Family Sylviidae.
Characteristics About 12 cm. long (5″). It has dark plumage with dark grayish upper parts, and darker head, wings and tail. The lower parts are whitish brown. The female is slightly browner; the young have a paler coloration. A similar species, the Dartford Warbler (*S. undata*), has dark reddish-brown lower parts.
Habitat Mediterranean *maquis*.
Distribution Islands in the western Mediterranean, and the east coast of Spain.
Life and habits It nests in bushes, building a cup-shaped nest made of vegetable matter. It lays one clutch, sometimes two, of 3–5 eggs (usually 3 or 4). There is no detailed data about the incubation (which in the Warbler is undertaken by the female for about 12 or 13 days) or the rearing of the young (the young of the Warbler staying in the nest for 11–13 days). Marmora's Warbler feeds on invertebrates and plant matter.

394 TADORNA FERRUGINEA
Ruddy Shelduck

Classification Order Anseriformes, Family Anatidae.
Characteristics About 63 cm. long (25″), for the male, and 61 cm. (24″) for the female. The plumage is orange-chestnut, with a paler head. The wing coverts are white (partly visible when the bird is resting, very visible when in flight). The tail and remiges are black. The male has a thin black collar and green wings. The young resemble the female, but have a darker brown back.
Habitat Lakes, lagoons, marshes, and rivers.
Distribution Southern Spain and southeast Europe, central Asia and northwestern Africa. It reaches other areas when migrating.
Life and habits It nests in holes in cliffs, sand dunes, banks, et cetera, laying 8–12 eggs (rarely 16), which are incubated by the female for 27–29 days. The nidifugous nestlings are reared by both parents. The Ruddy Shelduck feeds on plant matter (grass, grain, aquatic plants) and sometimes animals (small fish, toads and frogs, invertebrates). It makes a sound like a nasal and very loud *ah-onk*.

395   TADORNA TADORNA
Common Shelduck

Classification   Order Anseriformes, Family Anatidae.

Characteristics   The male is about 66 cm. long (26″), the female about 61.5 cm. (24.5″). It is a large, gooselike duck. Its plumage is unmistakable—the head and neck are greenish; a chestnut band runs across the front of the head; the scapular and primary feathers and tips of the rectrices are black; and the central part of the abdomen is dark colored. The wings are green with a chestnut edge, the lower tail coverts are chestnut, and the rest is white. The beak, which is red in spring, has at its base a large tubercle that is not present in the female. Young birds have brownish-gray upper parts, a white throat and face, and no chestnut stripe.

Habitat   Sandy coasts, estuaries, marshlands.

Distribution   Europe and Asia.

Life and habits   It nests in holes in the ground, often in old rabbit warrens. It lays one clutch, usually with 8–15 eggs (sometimes more), which are incubated by the female for about 28–30 days. The nidifugous nestlings follow their parents, who rear them, and they are independent at about 8 weeks. The Common Shelduck feeds mainly on invertebrates (mollusks, crustaceans, insects and worms) and small fish and plant matter (seeds, roots and aquatic plants).

396   TAENIOPYGIA GUTTATA
Zebra Finch

Classification   Order Passeriformes, Family Estrildidae.

Characteristics   About 10 cm. long (4″), this very well known bird is widely reared in captivity; there are many types with different colorations. As a rule the coloring of the male is gray-brown uppermost, with a reddish beak, brown markings beneath the eye bordered with black at the sides, black-striped throat and upper breast, brown sides speckled with white, and light yellowish lower parts. The female has a duller grayish coloring, darker uppermost. There are two known subspecies— *T.g. castanotis* and *T.g. guttata*.

Habitat   Open, grassy terrain with trees and bushes; fields, meadows and gardens.

Distribution   Australia.

Life and habits   The Zebra Finch is perfectly adapted to dry periods, which often occur in central Australia. Detailed studies by ornithologists Cade, Tobin and Gold have shown that this species can go without liquids for weeks and even months by drastically reducing the loss of water from its system: virtually all water is reabsorbed by the kidneys, and the excrement is dry. In addition the Zebra Finch can drink solutions of sodium chloride (common salt), which other birds cannot do.

397 TERATHOPIUS ECAUDATUS
Bataleur Eagle

Classification   Order Falconiformes, Family Accipitridae.
Characteristics   This bird of prey is about 60 cm. long (24″), with a very short tail. The upper parts are nut-brown, except for a black band on the rear edge of the wings. The lower parts are black, except for the wings, which have a brown band and another white band. The bare skin on the face and legs are red. Immature birds are brown all over, the parts that are red in adults becoming gray. The wing span is about 1.7 meters (67″) and the weight 1.9–2.9 kg. (4.2–6.4 lbs.).
Habitat   Savanna and lowlands with bushy vegetation.
Distribution   Southern and central Africa.
Life and habits   It nests from sea level to about 2,000 meters (6,500 ft.). The nest is built in a tree, usually an acacia, and is used for several years. A single egg is laid and incubated by the female for 42 or 43 days. The nestling makes its first flight at 90–125 days. One feature of the reproductive behavior of this bird of prey is its sociability: often a third adult tags on to a pair and helps to defend the nest. The diet consists of carrion, small mammals, birds and reptiles, including poisonous snakes.

398 TETRAO UROGALLUS
Capercaillie

Classification   Order Galliformes, Family Tetraonidae.
Characteristics   The male is bout 94 cm. long (37″) and the female is about 67 cm. (26″). The male's plumage is dark gray overall, the beak whitish, with a red area over the eyes; the wing coverts are dark brown, the breast greenish-blue speckled with white; the throat and sides of the head are black, the tail is also black, with a few white markings, and the legs are feathered. The female has brownish plumage, with grayish-black and white patches, a red area on the breast, and dark striping uppermost. The young resemble the female.
Habitat   Coniferous woods and forests in high, hilly regions, sometimes in lowland coniferous woods.
Distribution   Central and northern Europe, northern Asia.
Life and habits   Individuals have been observed up to 2,456 meters above sea level (8,058 ft.), as recorded by ornithologist U. Glutz von Blotzheim. It nests on the ground amid vegetation, laying a single clutch of usually 4–18 eggs (more commonly 5–8), which are incubated by the female for 26–29 days. The nidifugous nestlings are reared by the female and can fly after 2 or 3 weeks; they stay in a family group in the autumn. The Capercaillie feeds on shoots, buds of conifers, seeds, berries, fruit and invertebrates.

399 TETRASTES BONASIA
Hazel Grouse

Classification   Order Galliformes, Family Tetraonidae.
Characteristics   The male is about 36.5 cm. long (14.5″) and has mimetic gray and tawny plumage, with a series of chestnut, black and white stripes, markings and streaks. On the throat there is a black area, and a white band runs from beneath the eye to the top of the neck; the female is about 34 cm. long (13.5″) without the white band. On the head there is a crest, which is visible only when puffed up in the courtship period or when the bird is alarmed.
Habitat   Forests, especially coniferous (fir and larch) but also mixed forests with plenty of conifers in mountainous regions and lowlands.
Distribution   Central and northern Europe and northern Asia.
Life and habits   It nests in hollows in the ground among undergrowth in woods. It lays a single clutch of usually 6–10 eggs (sometimes up to 15), which are incubated by the female for about 20 days. The nidifugous nestlings develop their feathers at 10–20 days and are independent at about 8 weeks. The Hazel Grouse feeds on plant matter (berries and buds) and invertebrates.

400 THRESKIORNIS AETHIOPICA
Sacred Ibis

Classification   Order Ciconiiformes, Family Threskiornithidae.
Characteristics   A very distinctive bird, having white plumage with black on the head and wings. From the days of ancient Egypt this species was revered as the incarnation of Thoth, god of wisdom. The image of the Sacred Ibis is in fact present in a great many hieroglyphs.
Habitat   Banks of rivers and lake shores; near coasts, and marshlands.
Distribution   Africa.
Life and habits   It usually nests on the ground amid vegetation, in bushes or in trees, laying an average of 3 or 4 eggs per clutch. Incubation lasts for about 21 days, and the dark downcovered nestlings fly at about 5 or 6 weeks. The Sacred Ibis feeds mainly on invertebrates. In flight the flocks form a linear or V formation.

401 TICHODROMA MURARIA
Wallcreeper

Classification   Order Passeriformes, Family Sittidae.
Characteristics   About 16 cm. long (6.5″), this is an easily identifiable bird. The upper parts are gray, the tail is short, the beak is long and slender. The throat and breast are black in summer and whitish in winter. In flight the wings are black with red and white markings on the edges; they are broad and rounded. Young birds resemble the adults in winter, but are browner and have a straight beak.
Habitat   Rocky mountainous zones, crags and ruins; in winter it moves lower down to rocky valleys and the bottom of hills.
Distribution   Central and southern Europe, northern and southwestern Asia.
Life and habits   It makes sounds like *zee-zee-titi-zwee*. It nests in holes in rocks, where the female builds a cup-shaped nest of plant matter. She lays one clutch of 3–5 eggs (most often 4), which are incubated by the female for 18 or 19 days. The nidicolous nestlings are fed by both parents for about 21–26 days.

402 TOCKUS ERYTHRORHYNCHUS
Red-billed Hornbill

Classification   Order Coraciiformes, Family Bucerotidae.
Characteristics   This bird is about 50 cm. long (20″) and weighs about 180 grams (6.5 ounces). The plumage is whitish overall; the blackish wings and tail have white markings. The head is grayish, the beak strong and curved and reddish. Similar species are the Yellow-billed Hornbill (*T. flavirostris*), which is about 56 cm. long (22″), and Van der Decken's Hornbill (*T. deckeni*), which is about 50 cm. long (20″), with the female having a blackish bill. A strange species is the Helmeted Hornbill (*Rhinoplex vigil*), which has a huge casque (or helmet) and, cranium included, can weigh up to about 320 grams (11–12 ounces).
Habitat   Scrub and forests.
Distribution   Africa.
Life and habits   In holes the hornbills usually lay up to 5 eggs, which it incubates for about 30 days. The nidicolous nestlings stay in the nest for 30–45 days. As in other Bucerotidae, the female hornbill is walled into the nest, where, in addition to caring for the young, she molts. About 2 weeks before the nestlings take wing, she leaves them, whereupon they once more wall themselves inside the nest.

403 TRACHYPHONUS ERYTHROCEPHALUS
Red and Yellow Barbet

Classification Order Piciformes, Family Capitonidae.
Characteristics The barbets are found in open terrain and steppe, as well as in forest. They are about 20 cm. long (8"). The Red and Yellow Barbet is brightly colored, blackish with white markings uppermost, and whitish lower down. The two tail surfaces are reddish. The head is blackish on top in the male and reddish with small black spots in the female. The nape is yellowish with small black spots, and the eyes have a blackish ring; the upper breast is pinkish, and there is a blackish bar on the breast itself. The beak is strong with bristles at the base. The tail is quite long, and more reddish in the male.
Habitat Steppe, lowlands, open terrain.
Distribution From Ethiopia to Tanzania.
Life and habits The barbets feed mainly on invertebrates (particularly termites). They are very social birds, nesting in holes. The nidicolous nestlings stay in the nest for about 21 days. The Red and Yellow Barbet digs out a nest in steep slopes. Ornithologist A. H. Paget-Wilkes found a nest of this species with 2 eggs. The nest was about 30 cm. long (12") and about 7.5 cm. wide (3"), and ended with an incubation chamber.

404 TRICHOGLOSSUS HAEMATODUS
Rainbow Lory

Classification Order Psittaciformes, Family Psittacidae.
Characteristics The individual of Trichoglossinae ranges in length from 15 to 40 cm. (6–16"), has a narrow beak, and feeds on fruit, nectar and sap. In this subfamily there are 12 genera, among them *Trichoglossus*. The Rainbow Lory reaches a length of 28 cm. (11"), and has very bright plumage. The upper parts are green, the head bluish violet, the beak red, the neck yellow, green on the front, the breast yellowish pink, and the belly violet with greenish-yellow shading. The tail is green and wedge-shaped. Three subspecies are usually recognized—(*T.h. moluccanus*), (*T.h. rubritorquis*), (*T.h. haematodus*).
Habitat Scrub and light woodland.
Distribution Australia.
Life and habits The beak of the lories has no filelike "teeth," which are typical in granivorous species; they feed on fruit, sap and nectar. They usually lay 2 eggs, which are incubated for about 26 days. The nidicolous nestlings leave the nest after about 60–65 days.

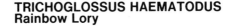

405 TRINGA ERYTHROPUS
Spotted Redshank

Classification Order Charadriiformes, Family Scolopacidae.
Characteristics About 30 cm. long (12″). The male's nuptial plumage is unmistakable: black with white speckling on the upper parts, a white rump and red legs (orange in winter). In its autumn-winter plumage the Spotted Redshank resembles the Common Redshank, but it has a more uniform gray plumage and a thin and longer beak; also, in flight no white is visible on the wings, and the longer legs jut out some way beyond the tail. Sometimes it will be seen perched on branches, bushes, or stakes and poles.
Habitat Open wetlands in northern coniferous forests; lakes, marshes, coastal wetlands.
Distribution Europe and Asia.
Life and habits It nests in hollows in the ground in moss, covering the nest with pine needles, grass and dry leaves. It usually lays 4 eggs (more rarely 3) and these are incubated, mainly by the male, or by the male alone. The nidifugous young are reared by both parents, even though the female soon leaves them. It makes a distinctive call like a *tchuit,* and feeds on insects, mollusks, crustaceans, et cetera.

406 TRINGA HYPOLEUCOS
Common Sandpiper

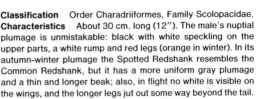

Classification Order Charadriiformes, Family Scolopacidae.
Characteristics About 19.5 cm. long (8″). The plumage is gray-brown uppermost and white lower down, with brown on the neck and on the sides of the neck. In winter the coloring is more uniform. It usually walks in a distinctive position, with the body bent forward and the head low; in flight it shows a white wing bar. Among the other sandpipers are the Wood Sandpiper (*T. glareola*) with greenish-yellow legs and whitish areas beneath the wings, and the Green Sandpiper (*T. ochropus*) with dark greenish legs and the lower part of the wings blackish.
Habitat Marshlands, hill streams, rivers and lakes.
Distribution Europe, Asia and Africa.
Life and habits It nests on the ground amid vegetation, laying one clutch of usually 4 eggs (sometimes 3, more rarely 5), which are incubated by both adults for 20–23 days. The nidifugous nestlings can start flying at 13–21 days and are independent by about 4 weeks. The Common Sandpiper feeds on invertebrates.

407 TRINGA TOTANUS
Common Redshank

Classification   Order Charadriiformes, Family Scolopacidae.
Characteristics   About 28 cm. long (11″), it has reddish-or-ange legs, a pale red beak with a black tip, brown upper parts with close blackish markings, and light lower parts with fine stripes and small speckling. The winter plumage is more gray-ish. The young have more tawny upper parts and yellow legs. In flight it shows dark wings with a broad white rear edge, barred tail and white rump. A similar species is the Greenshank (*T. nebularia*), about 31 cm. long (12.5″), with greenish legs; in flight the wings show no white, and the back, rump and tail are whiter.
Habitat   Expanses of marshland vegetation, moors, salt-works, lagoons, lakes and marshes.
Distribution   Europe, central Asia and northeastern Africa.
Life and habits   It nests in a hole in the ground amid grass, where it lays 3–5 eggs (most often 4), which are incubated by both adults for 23 or 24 days. The nidifugous nestlings are reared by both sexes and become independent at about 30 days. The Common Redshank makes a distinctive repeated call, sounding like a *tleu-hu-hu*. It feeds on invertebrates and some plant matter.

408 TROGLODYTES TROGLODYTES
Northern or Winter Wren

Classification   Order Passeriformes, Family Troglodytidae.
Characteristics   About 9 cm. long (3.5″), this is a very dis-tinctive bird. It has a compact little body, roundish in shape, with a tail held almost invariably upright. The plumage is brownish and lighter in the lower parts, with plenty of dark bar-ring on the wings, sides and tail. Young birds resemble the adults, but are less barred.
Habitat   Woods, hedgerows, canebrakes, cultivated areas.
Distribution   Europe, Asia, northwestern Africa, North America.
Life and habits   It nests in hedgerows, bushes, cracks or holes. The nest consists of plant matter and varies in shape from oval to almost spherical; it is built by the male. He builds more than one nest and the female then chooses which one to use. It lays a single clutch usually of 5–8 eggs (sometimes up to 16), which are incubated by the female for 14–17 days. The nidicolous nestlings are fed by both parents (the males may be polygamous) and leave the nest after 15–20 days. The nests may also be used as dormitories.

409 TURDUS ILIACUS
Redwing

Classification Order Passeriformes, Family Turdidae.
Characteristics About 20.5 cm. long (8″). The upper parts are dark brownish; the tail is dark brown with pale tawny-white at the tips of the feathers; the primary and secondary feathers are also dark brown. It has a broad whitish eyebrow. The sides are chestnut-colored, as are the axillary parts; the breast and sides are whitish, with tawny stripes. In flight it shows a distinctive chestnut-colored undertail and striping on the breast and sides. Another species, the Eye-browed Thrush (*T. obscurus*), found in Asia, has a fairly dark coloration in flight, gray underwing and head, an orange breast, and white belly and undertail.
Habitat Woods, parks, meadows.
Distribution Europe and Asia.
Life and habits It nests in trees, bushes, or in holes. The cup-shaped nest is made of plant matter and mud by the female. She usually lays two clutches, of 2–8 eggs (most often 4 or 5), which are incubated by the female for 11–15 days. The nidicolous nestlings are reared by both parents and stay in the nest for about 10–15 days. It feeds on invertebrates (worms, mollusks, insects) and plant matter (berries and fruit).

410 TURDUS MERULA
Blackbird

Classification Order Passeriformes, Family Turdidae.
Characteristics About 25 cm. long (10″). This is an unmistakable bird. The male is black with a yellow bill, while the female is dark brown uppermost, lighter in the lower parts, with a brown beak. The young are speckled and more reddish.
Habitat Woods, parks and gardens.
Distribution Europe, North Africa and central Asia.
Life and habits It builds a nest with plant matter, lining it with mud inside. It lays 2–3 clutches (sometimes even 4), each one consisting of 3–9 eggs (usually 4 or 5), which are incubated by the female for 11–17 days. The nidicolous young are reared by both parents and stay in the nest for 12–19 days. Once they have left the nest the young are fed by their parents for about another three weeks. For some decades now the Blackbird has become more and more frequent as a nonmigratory bird in the parks and gardens of European cities. It feeds on plant matter and berries, and is also insectivorous, particularly in the breeding season.

411 TURDUS MIGRATORIUS
American Robin

Classification   Order Passeriformes, Family Turdidae.
Characteristics   On average about 25 cm. long (10″), this is one of the commonest and most easily observable of birds. The plumage is brown uppermost and brick red lower down. The female and young have a duller coloring. The beak is yellow, long and thin.
Habitat   Wooded and cultivated land, gardens and city parks.
Distribution   North America.
Life and habits   The northernmost populations winter regularly in northern U.S. This is a very adaptable species and frequents any habitat that has a few trees and open terrain and is suitable for finding food. The nest is cup-shaped and is made with grass and roots, in trees, bushes and also rarely on the ground. It lays 3–6 eggs (most often 4), which are brooded for 12 or 13 days by the female. The nestlings fly at 14–16 days and follow their parents around for a while. There are usually 2 clutches each year. Food is sought on the ground, under leaves, in the earth, and in branches. It consists of insects, worms, larvae and other invertebrates in summer; fruit and berries in winter and during bad weather.

412 TURDUS PHILOMELOS
Song Thrush

Classification   Order Passeriformes, Family Turdidae.
Characteristics   About 23 cm. long (9″). The upper parts are brownish, the breast and sides tawny with close-set small black markings. The tail is reddish brown, the undertail white and cream-colored. The primary and secondary feathers are dark brown (almost black), and the wing coverts form two wing bars because the tips are tawny. In flight it shows a golden-brown color in the axillary areas and beneath the wings. Young birds have stripes on the upper parts.
Habitat   Woods, gardens and parks.
Distribution   Europe, Asia, North Africa. Introduced into New Zealand and New Hebrides.
Life and habits   It nests in trees or bushes, rarely on the ground. The nest is cup-shaped and is built by the female, of plant matter and mud. It usually lays 2 clutches (sometimes 3 or even 4) of 3–9 eggs (usually 4, 5 or 6), laid at daily intervals. The female incubates them, usually when laying has finished, for about 11–15 days. The nidicolous young are reared by both parents and stay in the nest 12–16 days. The Song Thrush feeds on invertebrates (worms, mollusks, insects and spiders) as well as plant matter (cherries, figs, strawberries, apples and pears).

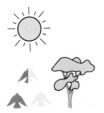

413 TURDUS PILARIS
Fieldfare

Classification   Order Passeriformes, Family Turdidae.
Characteristics   About 25 cm. long (10"). The nape and back are slate gray; the rump is chestnut-colored, the tail blackish. The top of the head is striped black, the throat and breast are brown, speckled with black. In flight it shows white axillary areas and undertail.
Habitat   Coniferous and mixed woods, parks, clearings in woodland.
Distribution   Europe and Asia.
Life and habits   It nests in pine, birch and alder woods (very rarely on the ground or in rocky parts), laying often two clutches of 3–8 eggs (usually 5 or 6), which are incubated by the female for 11–14 days. The nidicolous nestlings are reared by both sexes and stay in the nest for 12–16 days. The Fieldfare feeds on plant matter (seeds, fruit and berries) and invertebrates (insects, mollusks and worms). It utters a distinctive call that sounds like *tchak-tchak-tchak*.

414 TURDUS TORQUATUS
Ring Ouzel

Classification   Order Passeriformes, Family Turdidae.
Characteristics   About 24 cm. long (10"). The adult male has a distinctive plumage; the coloring is uniform dull black with a white pectoral band. The female is browner, with pale-edged feathers and a thinner collar, shaded with brown. After the autumn molt the male's plumage has feathers edged with white; there is a grayish marking on the remiges, visible when the bird is resting. Young birds do not have the collar and are grayish brownish, with lower parts speckled and striped with whitish and dark brown.
Habitat   Moorland, hills, rocky, mountainous regions, lowlands.
Distribution   Europe, central-western Asia, northwestern Africa.
Life and habits   It nests in trees and bushes, laying usually 2 clutches consisting of 3–6 eggs (usually 4 or 5), laid at daily intervals. Incubation is the task of both sexes and lasts about 13 or 14 days. The nidicolous young stay in the nest for about 13 or 14 days. The Ring Ouzel feeds mainly on invertebrates (worms, insects, mollusks) and plant matter (berries and fruit) in autumn and winter.

415 TURDUS VISCIVORUS
Mistle Thrush

Classification Order Passeriformes, Family Turdidae.
Characteristics About 26 cm. long (10.5″). The upper parts of the plumage are grayish brown, the lower parts are reddish white and densely speckled with large dark spots. The back feathers are edged with yellowish, those on the top of the tail with grayish white. The undertail is chestnut-colored, the axillary feathers and upper wing are white and the tail is grayish chestnut. Young birds are speckled with white on the upper parts. A similar species is the Fieldfare (*T. pilaris*), which is about 25 cm. long (10″) and has a dark nape and back.
Habitat Woods, gardens, parks, orchards, countryside, meadows, moorland.
Distribution Europe, Asia and North Africa.
Life and habits It nests in trees, in the forks of branches, or in bushes. The nest is a strong cup made of plant matter and built by the female. She lays two clutches of 3–6 eggs (ordinarily 4 or 5), which are incubated by the female, when laying is over, for 12–15 days. The nidicolous nestlings are reared by both parents and stay in the nest for 12–16 days. They fly at about 20 days and for a while are fed by the parents, even when they have left the nest. The Mistle Thrush feeds on plant matter (fruit, berries and seeds) as well as invertebrates (mollusks, worms and insects).

416 TURNIX SYLVATICA
Common Hemipode

Classification Order Gruiformes, Family Turnicidae.
Characteristics About 15 cm. long (6″). The male has a brownish plumage with some black and gray uppermost; the lower parts are white or cream-white; the sides of the breast have black markings, while the central part of the breast is yellowish brown. The legs have three toes. The female is usually larger and more colorful than the male.
Habitat Open terrain, zones with sparse, bushy vegetation.
Distribution Southern Spain, Africa and Asia.
Life and habits It nests on the ground amid vegetation in a hollow. It lays about 4 eggs (up to 8), which are incubated by the male, when laying is over, for 12–14 days. The nidifugous nestlings are reared by the male and are independent at 18 or 19 days; they reach complete development in about a month. The female plays the most active part during courtship, and the male builds the nest, broods and rears the young. Its diet consists mainly of plant matter (grass and seeds) and invertebrates (insects, etc.).

417 TYMPANUCHUS CUPIDO
Prairie Chicken

Classification   Order Galliformes, Family Tetraonidae.
Characteristics   Between 41 and 45 cm. long (16–18″). The upper parts are brown with dark stripes, except for the tail, which has white flashes. The lower parts are off-white with black barring. On the sides of the head the male has two tufts of feathers and two sacs of bare skin, which are yellow. The tail is very short and round. As in other members of the family, the legs are short and strong, designed for running over the ground.
Habitat   Prairies and woodland clearings.
Distribution   North America.
Life and habits   The males of this species, which once was more common, perform collective nuptial displays at daybreak in March. With their head feathers erect, their vocal sacs puffed out and their tails open, they vie for possession of the females by moving rhythmically. In the nest, made amid grass, the female lays 7–17 eggs (usually 10, 11 or 12), which she incubates for 23 or 24 days. The nidifugous nestlings, which are reared by their mother, fly after 1 or 2 weeks. The diet consists mainly of plant matter (seeds, buds, berries and leaves) and some insects (mainly grasshoppers). In winter the diet is mainly vegetarian, in summer animal, with the latter being the main diet of the young.

---

418 TYTO ALBA
Barn Owl

Classification   Order Strigiformes, Family Tytonidae.
Characteristics   About 34 cm. long (14″), it is a distinctive bird. The upper plumage is pale tawny golden brown; the lower parts are usually white (though some individuals have brown lower parts). The heart-shaped face is unmistakable.
Habitat   Feeds and nests in parks, woods, rocky areas, old buildings, towers, et cetera.
Distribution   Europe, Asia Minor, southern Asia, Africa, America and Australia.
Life and habits   It nests in ruins, hollows in trees, holes in rocks, towers, et cetera, laying one or often two clutches of 3–11 eggs (usually from 4 to 7), which are laid, as with all birds of prey, a few days apart. Incubation starts when the first egg is laid, with the female in charge, and lasts 32–34 days. The nidicolous young are fed by both parents, fly at about 60 days and are independent at about 10 weeks. The Barn Owl feeds mainly on small rodents and small birds.

419 UPUPA EPOPS
Hoopoe

Classification   Order Coraciiformes, Family Upupidae.
Characteristics   About 27 cm. long (11″). This unmistakable bird has brown plumage suffused with pink, a long, curved beak, an erectile crest with a black edge, and white wings and tail with large black bands. In flight the large, rounded wings, which are black and white, are extremely distinctive. The crest is erected when the bird is excited.
Habitat   Woods, parks, areas with bushes.
Distribution   Europe, central and southern Asia, Africa.
Life and habits   It can often be seen on the ground, looking for invertebrates. It generally lives alone or in pairs, with small groups forming during migration. It makes a distinctive call like *pu-pu-pu*. It nests in holes in trees and walls, laying a single clutch (sometimes two) of usually 5–8 eggs (up to 12 in exceptional cases). The female incubates them for 16–19 days. The droppings of the young are not removed from the nest, and these have a musklike odor, which comes from the fluid secreted by the uropygial gland of the brooding female and the nestlings. The latter are nidicolous and leave the nest at 20–27 days.

420 URIA AALGE
Thin-billed Murre

Classification   Order Charadriiformes, Family Alcidae.
Characteristics   About 43 cm. long (17″), it is dark brown on the head, nape and upper parts (in winter the throat and front of the neck are white). The lower parts are white, the beak slender and pointed, the legs are of various colors. A specific variety is the Thick-billed Murre (*U. lomvia*), which has a white ring round the eyes, the ring extending into the stripe behind the eyes.
Habitat   Coasts, cliffs, and islands.
Distribution   Northern Europe, North America, eastern Asia; sometimes found farther south.
Life and habits   It nests in colonies on rocky prominences on coasts and cliffs, laying a single clutch of usually just one egg. Both parents incubate it for about 28–35 days. The nestling is reared by its parents and takes to the sea at 18–25 days; it flies after about 3 weeks. Thin-billed Murres feed on fish and marine invertebrates (crustaceans, annelids and mollusks).

421 VANELLUS VANELLUS
Northern Lapwing

Classification   Order Charadriiformes, Family Charadriidae.
Characteristics   About 30 cm. long (12″), it has a distinctive coloration, iridescent blackish green on the upper parts, with a black breast and white lower down. It has a long black crest. The undertail is chestnut-colored. The young bird has an embryonic crest and is lighter in color. In flight it shows broad, rounded wings; the tail is white with a large black band at the tip.
Habitat   Cultivated land, marshlands.
Distribution   Europe, central and eastern Asia, northwestern Africa.
Life and habits   It nests on the ground, laying in a hollow a single clutch of 2–5 eggs (usually 4). Both parents incubate them, but mainly the female, for 24–29 days after all the eggs have been laid. The nidifugous young are reared by their parents and become independent at about 36 days. The Northern Lapwing makes distinctive calls sounding like a loud, nasal *peese-weet* and a longer *pee-r-weet*. This pretty bird is gregarious and feeds on insects, mollusks, worms and plant matter.

---

422 VIDUA FISCHERI
Straw-tailed Whydah

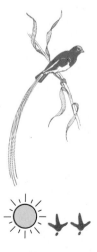

Classification   Order Passeriformes, Family Ploceidae.
Characteristics   The whydahs (or widowbirds) form the subfamily Viduinae. They have a dull plumage in autumn and winter, but the male has a bright one in breeding season. The Straw-tailed Whydah is black uppermost and at the base of the head and throat; the beak is red, the lower parts and top of the head are light pinkish-yellow with two very long pairs of central rectrices. The female is duller.
Habitat   Savannah, scrub.
Distribution   Africa south of the Sahara.
Life and habits   The whydahs are parasitic: they do not build their own nests but lay their eggs in the nests of the species of four genera belonging to the family Estrildidae (*Estrilda, Lagonosticta, Uraeginthus* and *Pytilia*). They are extraordinarily adapted to this specific reproductive behavior; in fact, the young of the whydah have a palate coloration, down and other particular features that are akin to those of the host's nestlings. The offspring of the Straw-tailed Whydah has, at the corners of its mouth, the same small blue ''warts,'' and on the palate the same orange design with three spots, as those of the young of the Purple Grenadier (*Uraeginthus ianthinogaster*).

423 VULTUR GRYPHUS
Andean Condor

Classification Order Falconiformes, Family Cathartidae.
Characteristics This vulture, the largest of all in an absolute sense, reaches a length of 101–116 cm. (40–46″). The adult's plumage is dark gray on the upper parts and lower down, except for a large white marking on the wings. The bare skin of the neck and head (topped by a caruncle) is pinkish, surrounded by a small collar of white feathers. The young are a uniform brown. The male, which is larger than the female, reaches and exceeds a wing span of 3 meters (10 ft.). The weight of the male is about 12 kg. (26.5 lbs.) and of the female 9–10 kg. (20–22 lbs.).
Habitat Mountains and coastal cliffs.
Distribution South America, mainly in the Andes.

Life and habits It lives in the highest and most inaccessible parts, flying to an altitude of 7,000 meters (21,000 ft.); the nest is made in crags, often in a spot exposed to wind and bad weather. A single egg is laid and incubated for 54–58 days by both sexes, who together take care of the nestling, which flies at 6 months, when it has almost reached adult size and weight. The Andean Condor feeds on carrion (especially guanacos) and will sometimes kill dying or wounded animals. Couples nesting in coastal areas go on periodic raids to colonies of sea birds, in search of eggs and chicks.

---

424 ZOSTEROPS PALPEBROSA
Oriental White-eye

Classification Order Passeriformes, Family Zosteropidae.
Characteristics The Zosteropidae (white-eyes) are small birds ranging in length from 10 to 14 cm. (4–6″). They are called white-eyes because they have a ring of white feathers around the eyes—yellow in Wallace's White-eye (*Z. wallacei*), which is found in the Lesser Sunda Islands—in nearly every species. The plumage is usually rather dull. The tongue is protractile, with a brush-shaped tip designed for collecting the nectar from flowers. The Oriental White-eye is greenish yellow, grayish and whitish, with distinctive white rings round the eyes.
Habitat Forests.
Distribution Southeast Asia, China.

Life and habits The white-eyes are found in Africa, southeast Asia, Australia, and the western portions of the South Pacific. In-depth studies of them have been made by the ornithologists R. F. Moreau, G. F. Mees and C. van Someren. Apart from the breeding season, these birds usually live in groups of 3 to 20. They nest in the forks of branches, laying 2–5 eggs which are incubated by both parents for about 11–13 days. The young stay in the nest for about 10–12 days. These birds feed on invertebrates, nectar and berries.

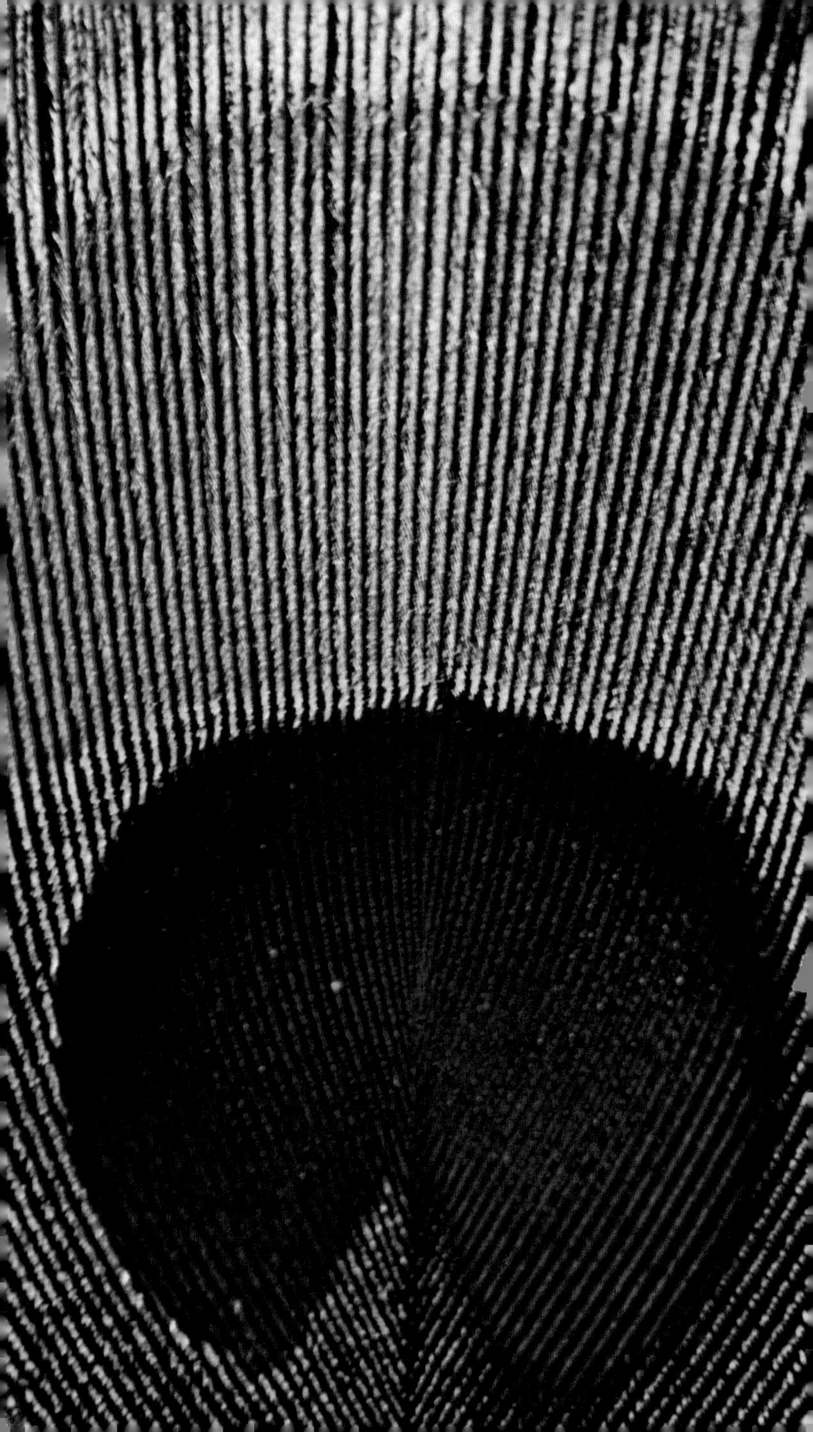

GLOSSARY

adaptive radiation   Evolutionary diversification of different species with a common ancestor into various ecological roles.

air sac   In birds, one of the nine membranous sacs connected with the lungs and the pneumatized bones.

androgen   Hormone that gives rise to the appearance of special features in males. Testosterone is an androgenous hormone produced by the interstitial cells of the testes.

anthophilous   Having a fondness for flowers; characterizing birds that feed on nectar, pollen or insects attracted by the flowers.

apterium   Featherless area of skin.

apterous   Without wings, or with very rudimentary wings that do not enable the bird to fly.

aspergillosis   Disease caused by a microscopic fungus belonging to the genus *Aspergillus;* in birds, it attacks the respiratory apparatus or other organs.

autotrophous   Literally, self-nourishing; characterizing plants that, through photosynthesis, convert inorganic compounds into food.

axillary   Characterizing the feathers at the base of the lower part of the wing.

barb   Part of the feather situated on the central axis, known as the rachis.

biocoenosis   Community of living beings that live in the same habitat (biotope).

biomass   Amount of living matter, partial or total, of a community, population or organism.

biome   Community of living beings present in a biogeographical area such as tundra, desert, virgin forest, et cetera.

biotope Area or habitat in which a species lives, or a biocoenosis.

botulism Poisoning, usually fatal, caused by the ingestion of a substance in which the bacterium *Clostridium botulinum* has developed.

bursa fabricii Organ situated in the wall of the cloaca (very developed in young individuals but atrophied in most adults).

calamus Hollow quill of a feather implanted in the skin.

carina Bony elongation in the middle of the sternum which supports the pectoral muscles.

carotins Pigments soluble in fats and responsible for the yellow, red, orange, and violet feather colors.

cere In certain groups of birds (diurnal raptors, parrots, pigeons and certain curassows), the naked skin at the base of the beak, where the nostrils are situated.

chalaza At each end of the yolk sac, a dense mass of albumen that keeps it in place even when the egg itself is moved.

choana Aperture that connects the palate with the nasal cavities.

chromatophore Cell with pigment granules.

cline Variation, generally linked with corresponding environmental variations, in the characteristics of a population in a geographical area.

cloaca Outlet at the end of the large intestine in birds. The intestine, urino-genital ducts (ureters) and sex glands (vas deferens in males and oviducts in females) open into it.

coccidiosis Morbid condition caused by infestation by certain protozoans of the order Coccidia in the intestine of birds.

community Populations that interact with one another in a given area; a community that, via a series of environmental conditions, has achieved stability is called a *climax.*

corpuscles of Grandry Tactile organs on the tongue and in the mouth of certain birds.

corpuscles of Herbst Small tactile organs on the tongue of woodpeckers, in the mouth of geese and ducks and on the edges of the beaks of nestlings.

crop In some birds, an extension of the esophagus wherein partly masticated food is stored before it can reach the stomach.

crop milk Term used to denote the mass of cells which are released from the crop of pigeons when these are rearing their young. This secretion, which contains fats and proteins and looks like a white cheese, is essential for feeding the nestlings of pigeons in the earliest stages.

down Product of the skin that covers the body of birds.

duodenal loop Loop in the small intestine which surrounds the pancreas.

ecosystem Complex of living beings and environmental factors which interact in a given area with clearly defined characteristics.

ectoparasites Parasites, such as fleas, lice, and ticks, that live on the surface of the body of birds. See also ENDOPARASITES.

electrophoresis Method of analyzing organic liquids, based on the movement of particles in suspension in liquid due to the difference of electro-motive force.

endoparasites Parasites (worms, etc.) that live inside the host's body.

enzyme Substance which accelerates the chemical reactions in a living organism.

erythrocyte Blood cell also known as red corpuscle.

estrogen Female sex hormone produced by the ovary and acting on the secondary sexual features and the bird's behavior.

eumelanin Pigment responsible for black and gray colors.

feathers Largest plumes on the body of birds (remiges and rectrices).

feeding ground Place where birds go to feed.

fitness Genetic contribution of descendants of an individual to the successive generations of a population.

fovea Also known as the *macula lutea*, being the depression of the retina in which the maximum sharpsightedness is achieved because of the presence of a great density of sensitive cells.

furcula Bony formation resulting from the fusion of the two clavicles at their lower ends caused by a cartilaginous part.

genetic pool Complete genetic set of a given population existing at a given time.

genotype All the genetic characteristics that determine the structure and functioning of an organism.

gonadotrophic hormones Produced by the anterior lobe of the pituitary body that stimulates the functioning of the sex glands.

heterotrophy Use as food of organic matter (as is the case with herbivores, predators, decomposers, etc.).

homochromatic Striking similarity of the coloring of an animal with the environment in which it lives. Mimetism (or mimicry), on the other hand, is the imitation of the general appearance of an animal by another (as for protection).

homoiothermia Capacity of maintaining the body temperature constant despite fluctuations in the outside temperature.

incubation Warming of an egg or eggs by the brooding bird or by some other major source of heat so that the embryo can develop into the nestling.

leg Lower limb, the skeleton of which consists of the femur, tibia and fibula (or *perone*), the tarso-metatarsus and toes. Depending on the arrangement of the toes, we can tell whether birds are anisodactylous (with three toes in front and one behind); pamprodactylous (with all four toes in front like swifts and mousebirds); heterodactylous (with two toes in front and two behind); or zygodactylous (with the first and fourth behind and the second and third in front). A typical heterodactylous type of bird is the quetzal, in which the third and fourth toes are directed forward and the first and second rearward.

migration Seasonal movements made regularly between breeding grounds and wintering areas.

BIBLIOGRAPHY

ENCYCLOPEDIAS AND GENERAL ORNITHOLOGY

AA.VV. *The Mitchell Beazley World Atlas of Birds*. London: Mitchell Beazley, 1974.

Amadon, D. *Dove vivono gli uccelli* (*Where Birds Live*). Bologna: Zanichelli, 1974.

Bologna, G. *Il mondo degli uccelli* (*The World of Birds*). Milan: Mondadori, 1976.

Bologna, G., and Frugis, S. *Voci relative agli uccelli in dizionario della natura* (4 vol.) (*Entries Related to Birds in Dictionary of Nature*).

Cockrum, L., and McCauley, W. *Zoologia* (*Zoology*). Padua: Piccini, 1970.

Curry, Lindahl K. *Gli uccelli attraverso il mare e la terra* (*Birds Across the Sea and the Earth*). Milan: Rizzoli, 1976.

Dorst, J. *La migrazione degli ucceli* (*The Migration of Birds*). Florence: Editoriale Olimpia, 1970.

Dorst, J. *La vita degli uccelli* (2 vol.) (*The Life of Birds*). Milan: Garzanti, 1973.

Farner, D.S., and King, J.R. (ed.). *Avian Biology*. New York: Academic Press, 1971.

Fisher, J., and Peterson, R. T. *The World of Birds*. London: MacDonald, 1964.

Frugis, S. *Uccelli* (*Birds*). Novara: De Agonstini, 1977.

Gilliard, E.T. *Il libro degli uccelli* (*The Book of Birds*). Milan: Mondadori, 1974.

Grasse, P.P. (ed.). *Traités de zoologie xv: oiseaux* (*Treatises on Zoology XV: Birds*). Paris: Masson, 1950.

Griffin, D.R. *Le migrazioni degli uccelli* (*The Migration of Birds*). Bologna: Zanichelli, 1965.

Grzimek, B. (ed.). *Vita degli animali, uccelli* (volumi 7, 8, 9) (*The Life of Animals, Birds* (volumes 7, 8, 9,)). Milan: Bramante, 1969.

Lanyon, W.E. *Biologia degli uccelli* (*Biology of Birds*). Bologna: Zanichelli, 1973.

Marshall, A.J. (ed.). *Biology and Comparative Physiology of Birds* (2 vol.). New York: Academic Press, 1960–61.

Matthews, G.V.T. *Bird Navigation*, 3rd edition. New York: Cambridge University Press, 1968.

Peterson, R.T. *Gli uccelli* (*Birds*). Milan: Mondadori, 1965.

Pettingil, Olin S., Jr. *Ornithology in Laboratory and Field*. Minneapolis: Burgess, 1970.

Rodriguez, De La Fuente F. (ed.). *Gli animali e la loro vita* (11 vol.) (*The Animals and Their Life*). Novara: De Agostini, 1973.

Thomson, A.L. (ed.). *A New Dictionary of Birds*. London: Nelson, 1964.

Van Tyne, J., and Berger, A.J. *Fundamentals of Ornithology*. New York: Wiley & Sons, 1965.

Welty, Joel C. *The Life of Birds*, 2nd edition. Philadelphia: W.B. Saunders, 1965.

Yapp, W.B. *The Life and Organization of Birds*. Baltimore: University Park Press, 1970.

EVOLUTION AND ECOLOGY

Cody, M.L. *Competition and Structure of Bird Communities*. Princeton, New Jersey: Princeton University Press, 1970.

Dajoz, R. *Manuale d'ecologia* (*Manual of Ecology*). Milan: Isedi, 1972.

Dorst, J. *Les oiseaux dans leur milieu* (*Birds and Their Environment*). Montreal, Paris: Borda, 1971.

Lack, D. *Ecological Adaption in Breeding for Birds*. London: Chapman & Hall, 1968.

Lehman, J.P. *Le prove paleontalogiche dell'evoluzione* (*Paleontological Proofs of Evolution*). Milan: Newton Compton, 1977.

Maynard, Smith J. *L'ecologia e i suoi modelli* (*Ecology and Its Models*). Milan: Mondadori, 1975.

Mayr, E. *L'evoluzione nelle specie animali* (2 vol.) (*The Evolution in the Species*). Turin: Einaudi, 1970.

Odum, E.P. *Ecologia* (*Ecology*). Bologna: Zanichelli, 1963.

Odum, E.P. *Principi di ecologi* (*Principles of Ecology*). Padua: Piccin, 1973.

Ricklefs, R.E. *Ecologia* (*Ecology*). Bologna: Zanichelli, 1976.

Snow, D.W. *The Web of Adaption*. New york: Demeter Press, a division of Times Books, 1976.

Wilson, E.O., and Bossert, W.H. *Introduzione alla biologia delle popolazioni* (*Introduction to the Biology of Populations*). Padua: Piccin, 1974.

ANIMAL BEHAVIOR

Armstrong, E.A. *Bird Display and Behavior*. New York: Dover, 1965.

Barnett, A. *Istinto ed intelligenza* (*Instinct and Intelligence*). Turin: Boringhieri, 1972.

Carthy, J.D., and Ebling, E.J. (ed.). *Storia naturale dell'aggressività* (*The Natural History of Aggressiveness*). Bologna: Zanichelli, 1973.

Frings, H., and M. *La communicazione animale* (*Animal Communication*) Torino: Boringhieri, 1971.

Lorenz, Konrad. *Evolution and Modification of Behavior*. Chicago: University of Chicago Press, 1967.

Sparks, J. *Il comportamento degli uccelli* (*The Behavior of Birds*). Milan: Mondadori, 1970.

THE PROTECTION OF NATURE AND BIRDLIFE

Commoner, Barry. *The Closing Circle*. New York: Bantam Books, 1972.

Curry and Lindahl, K. *Conserve per sopravvivere* (*Conserve to Survive*). Milan: Rizzoli, 1974.

Dorst, J. *Prima che la natura muoia* (*Before Nature Dies*). Milan: Labor, 1969.

Fisher, J., Simon, J., and Vincent, J. *The Red Book, Wildlife in Danger*. London: Collins, 1969.

BIRDS FROM SPECIFIC REGIONS OR GROUPS OF BIRDS

Blake, E.R. *Manual of Neotropical Birds*. Chicago: University of Chicago Press, 1977.

Bond, James. *Birds of the West Indies*, 2nd edition. Boston: Houghton Mifflin, 1971.

Brown, L., and Amadon, D. *Eagles, Hawks, and Falcons of the World* (2 vol.). New York: McGraw-Hill, 1968.

Brunn, B., and Singer, A. *Uccelli d'europa* (*Birds of Europe*). Milan: Mondadori, 1975.

Cramp, Stanley, Bourne, W.R.P., and Saunders, D. *The Seabirds of Great Britain and Ireland*. New York: Taplinger Co., Inc., 1974.

Cramp, Stanley, and Simmons, K.E.L. (ed.). *Handbook of the Birds of the Western Paearctic* (7 vol.). Oxford: Oxford University Press, 1977.

Etchecopar, R.D., and Hué, F. *Les oiseaux du nord de l'afrique* (*The Birds of North Africa*). Boubée, 1964.

Frugis, S. (ed.). *Enciclopedia degli uccelli d'europa* (3 vol.) (*Encyclope-dia of Birds of Europe*). Milan: Rizzoli, 1971–72.

Geroudet, P. *La vie des oiseaux* (6 vol.) (*The Life of Birds*). Neuchâtel: Delachaux et Niestle, 1965.

Glutz von Blotzhein, U.N., Bauer, K.M., and Bezzel, E. (ed.). *Handbuch der Vögel Mitteleuropas* (*Handbook of Birds of Central Europe*). Wiesbaden: Akademische Verlaggellschaft, 1969.

Gruson, Edward. *Checklist of Birds of the World*. New York: Times Books, 1976.

Harrison, C. *A Field Guide to Nests, Eggs and Nestlings of British and European Birds*. New York: Demeter Press, a division of Times Books, 1976.

Hayman, P., and Burton, P. *The Birdlife of Europe*. London: Mitchell Beazley, 1976.

Heinzel, H., Fitter, R.S.R., and Parslow, J. *The Birds of Britain and Europe with North Africa and Middle East*. London: Collins, 1972.

Hoeher, S. *Nids et oeufs des oiseaux d'europe centrale et occidentale* (*The Nests and Eggs of Birds of Central and Western Europe*). Neuchâtel: Delachaux et Niestle, 1973.

Hué, F., and Etchecopar, R.D. *Les oiseaux du proche et du moyen orient* (*The Birds of the Near and Far East*). Boubée, 1970.

King, B., Woodcock, M., and Dickinson, E.C. *A Field Guide to the Birds of Southeast Asia*. London: Collins, 1975.

Mayer de Schauensee, R. *A Guide to the Birds of South America*. Wynnewood, Pa.: Livingstone, 1970.

Palmer, R.S. (ed.). *Handbook of North American Birds*. New Haven: Yale University Press, 1962.

Peterson, Roger T. *A Field Guide to the Birds*. Boston: Houghton Mifflin, 1947.

Peterson, Roger T. *A Field Guide to Western Birds*. Boston: Houghton Mifflin, 1961.

Peterson, Roger T., Moutfort, G., and Hollom, P.A.D. *Guida degli uccelli d'europa* (*Guide to the Birds of Europe*). Milan: Labor, 1967.

Prozesky, O.P.M. *A Field Guide to the Birds of Southern Africa*. London: Collins, 1970.

Reade, W., and Hosking, E. *Uccelli nidificatori, uova e prole* (*Nesting Birds, Eggs and Offspring*). Turin: Saie, 1969.

Reilly, M.E. *The Audubon Illustrated Handbook of American Birds*. New York: McGraw-Hill, 1968.

Scott, Peter. *A Coloured Key to the Wildfowl of the World*, revised edition (illus.). New York: International Publications Services, 1972.

Searle, W., Morel, J.G., and Hartwig, W. *A Field Guide to the Birds of West Africa*. London: Collins, 1977.

Sharrock, J.T.R. *The Atlas of Breeding Birds in Britain and Ireland* (illus.). New York: Buteo Books, 1977.

Williams, J.G. *A Field Guide to the Birds of East and Central Africa*. London: Collins, 1963.

INDEX OF ENTRIES

Photographic Credits